14–18
UNDERSTANDING
THE GREAT WAR

Stéphane Audoin-Rouzeau
and Annette Becker

14–18
UNDERSTANDING
THE GREAT WAR

Translated from the French by Catherine Temerson

HILL AND WANG
A division of Farrar, Straus and Giroux
New York

Hill and Wang
A division of Farrar, Straus and Giroux
18 West 18th Street, New York 10011

Copyright © 2000 by Éditions Gallimard
Translation copyright © 2002 by Farrar, Straus and Giroux, LLC
All rights reserved
Distributed in Canada by Douglas & McIntyre Ltd.
Printed in the United States of America
Originally published in 2000 by Éditions Gallimard, France, as
14–18, retrouver la Guerre
English translation originally published in 2002 by Profile Books, Great Britain,
as *1914–1918: Understanding the Great War*
Published in 2002 in the United States by Hill and Wang
First American paperback edition, 2003

Library of Congress Control Number: 2002111422
Paperback ISBN-13: 978-0-8090-4643-0
Paperback ISBN-10: 0-8090-4643-1

www.fsgbooks.com

11   13   14   12   10

Contents

Contents

14–18
UNDERSTANDING
THE GREAT WAR

Introduction

Understanding the Great War

The Great War, because it was both European and international in scope, because of its long duration, because of its enormous and long underestimated effect on the century that followed, has become a paradigm case for thinking about what is the very essence of history: the weight of the dead on the living.

In November 1998, eighty years after the signing of the armistice, West European countries saw a marked increase in the number of commemorations of the Great War in which various approaches were superimposed – historical, memory-related, political, journalistic and audiovisual, sometimes contradicting, sometimes substantiating one another. Invoking the 'duty to remember' and often forgetting the obligation to history, people experienced a spectacular return of the Great War to the collective consciousness. In some ways, this reawakening helped in the re-evaluation of the great conflict's place in the twentieth century. But the mania to be 'historically correct' unfortunately clouded the issue at a time that might have been an important moment in public history, a moment for historical reflection and civic pedagogy.[1]

The commemorative writers and speakers caused great

intellectual confusion by going to extraordinary lengths to stress the victimisation of the soldiers: not only were the combatants depicted as mere non-consenting victims, but mutineers and rebels were called the only true heroes. Hadn't the mutineers of 1917 been, in a sense, the precursors of the European Union? And hadn't the Nivelle offensive been the first 'crime against humanity'?[2] We could give many examples. The failure to treat history as History reached new heights. In a century of total war everyone is so afraid of not having suffered enough that 'competition among victims'[3] becomes urgent and the vocabulary becomes inflated. There are people who believe that thinking like this shows their humanism.

Obviously we should move towards a history of the war that shows greater empathy for all the actors involved and that comprehends their suffering (that of women, men and children, Europeans and non-Europeans), but fine sentiments must not be confused with intellectual analysis. We agree with Henry Rousso's disillusioned remark: 'Since being able to pass judgement has become one of the terms of our relationship to the past, and the memory of the Genocide the yardstick for measuring any approach to history, we now expect real or imaginary guilty parties to be clearly designated for all the tragedies of the century that our age has not yet assimilated.'[4]

Actually the intellectual confusion of the Great War commemorations was superimposed on a long tradition. A peace-loving, indeed pacifist, ideology about the war to end all wars had prevailed for a long time. More was written (and fantasised) about the Christmas truces and the fraternising among enemies than about their hatred of each other. And it is easier, however painful, to accept the idea that one's grandfather or father was killed in combat than that he might have killed others. In the context of personal or family memory, it is better to be a victim than an agent of suffering and death. Death is always inflicted, always anonymous, never dispensed: one is always a victim of it. Or a victim of one's leaders, who are then promoted to being organisers of a massacre. By transforming combatants into sacrifi-

cial lambs offered to the military butchers, the process of victimisation has long impeded thought, if not prevented it, and much
of what was said in November 1998 is the consequence of this.
Hence the essential question of why and how millions of Europeans and Westerners acquiesced in the war of 1914–18 has remained buried. Why we accept the violence of warfare has
remained a taboo subject.

The 1998 commemoration resulted in another, more positive, 'achievement', however. It seemed that the pain of bereavement, the pain of lost love experienced by families, which had
been so difficult to express right after the war and which historians had considered so difficult to apprehend, suddenly resur-
faced during those anniversary weeks. Of course, the mourning
process during the 1920s and 1930s had not failed completely to
do its work: the sacral quality of local commemorative ceremonies around monuments to the dead, or of national rites concerning the French, British, Italian and American Unknown
Soldiers, had an undeniable spiritual content. Everyone was able
to come away bearing a sacred flame for his or her personal bereavement. And yet historians could not but realise how much
they still had to understand about the mourning process. It has
often been described in terms used to assess the glaring demographic factor of mass death, but it has not really been analysed
using the yardstick of deep pain.

Retrospectively, therefore, we can see the commemoration of
the eightieth anniversary of the 1918 armistice as the symptom
of a growing 'presence' of the Great War. Indeed, everything suggests that '1914–18' has been given a new lease of life. And although France is the country where this phenomenon is most
clearly apparent, it is also manifest elsewhere. In England, in the
summer of 1998, the Minister of Defence expressed his 'regret'
that 306 British soldiers had been executed for not facing the
enemy, though he did not accord them 'a posthumous pardon'.
On 7 November of the same year, six of the executed soldiers'
families placed a wreath in their memory at the Whitehall cenotaph in London: this was the first public homage paid to these

soldiers in England. In Italy, on 8 November, the Minister of Defence stated that 'honour should be returned' to the 750 soldiers who had been executed by firing squad. Germany's Chancellor, however, wishing to shift the focus from the First World War on to the Second, refused to take part in joint commemorations with France. (The date also commemorates Kristallnacht, 8–9 November, 1938.)

An opinion poll assessing respondents' spontaneous views of the history of the twentieth century, conducted in France on 6 and 7 November, 1998,[5] gives an interesting hint as to how the major events of the past century, including the Great War, were rated. As might be expected, the Second World War was ranked first in importance, followed by the student movement of 1968, and then the collapse of the Soviet Union; fourth was the Great War.[*] Among the men polled, however, it ranked third alongside the events of May 1968. It ranked third among the women, too, but alongside the collapse of the Soviet Union rather than May 1968.[†] The ranking of the Great War is striking, for on a scale comparing the 'most significant periods in the twentieth century' it outranked, in descending order, the creation of a united Europe, decolonisation, the oil crisis of the 1970s, the 1929 stock market crash, the Russian Revolution of 1917 and the Islamic Revolution in Iran. (The survey distinguishes the Russian Revolution from the Great War, which is understandable but in our view confusing, since the two are essentially inseparable.)

---

[*]The figures are as follows: Second World War, 62%; May 1968 student movement, 43%; collapse of the Soviet Union, 38%; First World War, 35% (the percentages total over 100 because of multiple answers).
[†]It is because of this ranking discrepancy between men and women that the First World War comes in fourth, by a very tight margin, among the 'most important events in the twentieth century'. Among the men, the Second World War received 64 per cent of the votes; the collapse of the Soviet Union, 44 per cent; May 1968 and the First World War, 37 per cent. Among the women, the Second World War received 61 per cent of the votes; May 1968, 48 per cent; the collapse of the Soviet Union and the First World War, 33 per cent.

The rankings are even more significant when the results of the poll are grouped according to the respondents' ages. Then we have quite a surprise: people over 50 ranked the Great War lowest, followed by people aged 35–50, and finally by people under 35; better still, the youngest group polled, 15–19-year-olds, ranked it second. Thus the younger the group, the more they saw the war of 1914–18 as an important event in the twentieth century; the fourth generation, whose great-grandparents lived through the Great War, had selected it by an overwhelming majority. In other words, it is as though the time that has passed since the war were irrelevant; the Great War tends to be ever more present in the minds of successive generations.

For any historian of the First World War, however, this result is more of a confirmation than a surprise. It is one more indication among many that, since the early 1990s, and in France particularly, the Great War has been increasingly important; the 1998 commemoration only confirmed this. The Great War's continued presence is the driving force behind a wide spectrum of associations that are not perhaps well known but are very active – groups that look after battlefield sites, associations that collect original texts and documents, editors of small magazines who write their own history of the war, free of the 'accepted' or 'official' historiography. Museums also have a part to play. The Historial de la Grande Guerre in Péronne, which paved the way in 1992, is a key institution. There are other places that people can visit, and new ones are being set up: at Ypres, the Caverne du Dragon on the Chemin des Dames; the underground passages in the city of Arras; and then of course Verdun, where there are big museum projects for the 1916 battlefield. One temporary site was the excavated grave of Alain-Fournier, the author of *Le Grand Meaulnes*, who, with twenty comrades from the 288th infantry regiment, was buried by the Germans after the battle of 22 September 1914, at Saint-Rémy-la-Calonne. This grave site provoked such fetishist fervour that the area had to be guarded day and night. Indeed, the very fact that an archaeology of the battlefields of 1914–18 – starting with an archaeology of burial places – can now be considered[6] is a good demonstration of the presence of an essential aspect of the Great War – death and mourning.

The eightieth anniversary of the armistice in 1998 marked countless initiatives on the part of local communities, town halls and schools: never had the desire to know about the 'public history' of the war been greater, and never before did it have such success. The historian Henry Rousso has written about what he calls the '*trop-plein du passé*', a paralysing obsession with the past.[7] But professional historians specialising in the Great War have been for many years seeking new approaches to the study of the conflict, using anthropological and cultural insights,[8] which is another sign of how present the matrix event of the twentieth century still is. Since historians of the 1914–18 period are actively involved in this phenomenon, they may not be in the best position to give an account of it or to suggest explanations for it. Yet let us offer several hypotheses for discussion.

First, we should remember the surprising re-shuffling of the international cards, since this was the context in which the war was recollected in the 1990s. The fall of the Soviet Union and attendant events opened new distancing possibilities, of which the historians involved in the creation of the Historial de Péronne were fully aware at the time. As one of them, Jay Winter, liked to say, 'The war of 1914 is over.' The statement must be given the same meaning it had for François Furet when he said of another matrix event, 'The French Revolution is over.'[9] Indeed, 'the end of the Great War' was becoming an evidence in the early 1990s with the death of the last veterans, whose stories had allowed the experience to be handed down through families but simultaneously kept it from being historicised.[10] Most important was the collapse of communism in Eastern Europe, which meant that one of the last and most dramatic political, ideological and geopolitical consequences of the First World War seemed to be fading as well. Meanwhile, with the final stages in the building of a united Europe virtually complete, the way appeared to be open for a form of integration that would bring about the 'end of nation states', at least as they were understood in the nineteenth and early twentieth centuries. And hadn't the Great War been primarily a war of clashing nations and national sentiments? The hour was ripe in the 1990s for a partial weakening of national sentiments. What better opportunity could there be for historicising 1914–18 and seeing it from a new, unprecedented analytic distance? The Historial de Péronne, with its silent, detached and rather cold museography and its rigorously fair comparative treatment of France, the United Kingdom and Germany, may be considered one of the best expressions of this new approach.*

But this was a fleeting time – an illusion. Very soon, in the vacuum left by the decline of Soviet communism, Europe began to see a return to various aggressive forms of nationalism. This was mostly the case in Eastern Europe, although Western Europe did not remain unscathed. In 1992, for the second time since the summer of 1914, Sarajevo was in the news. When war broke out in the former Yugoslavia, a link was re-established with the Balkan conflicts of 1912–13 and, of course, with the European crisis of July 1914. From then on, war throughout Europe, though never a direct threat, seemed again within the realm of the possible. An enduring historical link was re-established with the Great War and its Balkan epicentre, the very scene where the logic of war had been set in motion in the summer of 1914. The roots of the century were re-emerging – and now could be better understood. The forms and practices of the Great War, violent in the extreme, helped to reinforce the initial impression that the past was being revisited. It was a tragic

---

*The Historial de Péronne consists of five rooms, leading the visitor successively from the pre-war to the post-war periods. The Western Front is displayed in the centre of the rooms in open boxed pits on the ground. The home fronts are showcased along the walls, interacting with the world of the front lines. The visitor can re-create the flow of the war by walking back and forth from the front lines to the home front. The museography focuses on the Western Front and presents a detailed comparative study of the three powers, France, Germany and the United Kingdom.

update; the assumption that the Great War was 'over' was replaced by one about the Great War 'beginning again'. No doubt these events made people think afresh, and differently, about 1914–18. It was as though the Great War had been simultaneously placed at a distance and brought closer, the two perspectives in no way affecting each other but instead becoming combined, generating many new opportunities for historical study, as well as, perhaps, further expression of an unfinished mourning process.

Paradoxically, the Great War had for a long time brought with it a kind of oblivion about one of the essential features of wartime, the weight, as we have said, of the dead on the living. It might at first seem shocking to say this, given the huge amount of commemorative activity that went on in the period following 1918 and still vigorously continues to this day. But wasn't the primary goal of these commemorations to exorcise death and help the survivors overcome the grief of bereavement? In this sense, with their emphasis on death in combat, the commemorations in fact partially repressed one of its main consequences – the pain of bereavement.

It is striking that until very recently, mourning was scarcely an object of study among the historians issued from the nations that had experienced the war and mass death.[11] No one has calculated the extent of what one might call 'the circles of mourning' that the deaths in combat created within the belligerent societies. But even very tentative estimates show that mourning occurred on an immense scale. For example, in France, if we apply the concept of 'entourage' that modern demographers use, we can estimate that two-thirds or even three-quarters of the population were affected, directly or indirectly, by bereavement or, more accurately, *bereavements*, the intensity of which was much greater than that experienced in peace time. Young people had died violent deaths, having suffered unprecedented mutilations of the body. Their families often did not even have the corpses of their loved ones to honour. So the mourning process was complicated, sometimes impossible, always protracted. Moreover, the survivors were by and large not allowed genuinely to mourn; it was one of the hidden objectives of the post-war commemorations to forbid protracted mourning, which was seen as a betrayal of the men who had sacrificed themselves on the battlefields. These were impossible bereavements to come to terms with, and all the more complicated because there was no agreement as to the meaning of the war. Whereas in the years 1914–18 the war had created a deep consensus – built on millenarianist hopes for a new mankind, hopes that can be likened to a veritable 'crusade myth'[12] – the effects of the war later, particularly during the 1930s, provoked a rejection as profound as the initial eschatological expectation had been powerful. Never, in contemporary times, had European societies been so massively in mourning. Yet between the two wars, this post-1918 mass mourning gradually opened on to a void.

It is not clear that the former belligerent nations have completely recovered from this mourning or from the distress that its lack of meaning engendered. The concepts of infinite mourning, or interminable mourning, borrowed from psychiatry, are perhaps relevant in describing the particular relationship French society, for example, still has with the Great War, given its immense emotional investment in the conflict and the equally huge sacrifices it agreed to. The commemoration of 1998, and the polemics surrounding it, can be seen as related to France's unfinished mourning process. In the 1990s we witnessed 'a return of the repressed', a return whose effects are now shifting from the second to the third generation. Similarly, specialists think they now detect traces of 'survivor's syndrome' among the grandchildren of Holocaust victims – what they call the third-generation phenomenon,[13] – which one can also perceive among the third-generation descendants of the survivors of the 1915 Armenian genocide, with their vivid 'memories'. Perhaps it is in the third generation that we should look for the existing scars of the great mass massacre of 1914–18.

However, this hypothesis seems to contradict another phenomenon which the 1998 commemoration showed most eloquently, namely, the breach in understanding. The system of representations which characterized First World War contemporaries – soldiers and civilians, men, women and children – is now almost impossible to accept. The sense of obligation, of unquestioned sacrifice, which held most people in its tenacious, cruel clutches for so long and so profoundly, and without which the war could never have lasted as long as it did, is no longer acceptable. The foundation on which the immense collective consensus of 1914–18 was based, particularly in France, has vanished into thin air. War left its mark on all successive generations of French society in the twentieth century until the end of the Algerian War, but it is now completely alien to it, as the elimination of the draft and the conversion of the French armed forces into an external deployment force make clear.

Disengagement from war was certainly a slow process. For instance, at Dien Bien Phu, the battle in Indochina which, in 1953, General de Castries called 'Verdun minus the Sacred Way', the Great War remained an operative and effective reference, contemporary covers of *Paris-Match* and letters of the Dien Bien Phu soldiers show.[14] Today, it has become all but incomprehensible, insofar as nothing experienced by people then – their patriotism, the significance of the war to them and the meaning of their deaths in battle – can be understood or even apprehended. This is why there is a great need for historical explanations, even when they are sometimes rejected because the perceptions of the men of 1914, when disclosed, clash so greatly with the sensibilities of most people today.

We are therefore confronted with a strange paradox. The presence of the Great War in our lives is due to two developments: on the one hand, a feeling of proximity because of its re-emergence on the international political scene and the reappearance of mourning; on the other, a feeling of estrangement, due to the more distanced historiography and a lack of references that might help us understand it, though it is now a subject of permanent questioning for which there are no satisfying answers. It is as though we wished to understand the Great War more than ever before without being sure of ever having the means to do so. Therefore, it seems all the more essential that we take a fresh look at it.

Perhaps it is not irrelevant briefly to clarify our personal backgrounds. We were both born at the end of the French war in Indochina, and our first 'war memories' were of the Algerian War, which came to us as scattered, mostly unintelligible images. We belong to a generation that has no immediate connection with the activity of war – possibly the first generation of this kind in Europe since the eighteenth century – unlike our contemporaries in the United States, who have had direct knowledge of the Vietnam War. War was within the realm of expectations, or in the memory, of our great-grandparents, grandparents and even parents, when they were children or adolescents. But we are the children of the West's disengagement from war. Does this mean that we have a cold, disembodied view of our object of study? Certainly not. The Great War is still a source of powerful emotions, but our feelings can't be of the same kind as those that gripped the witnesses or the sons and daughters of witnesses. We could feel this tension in our early childhood as we stood before monuments to the dead, when a great-uncle or grandfather 'who had done Verdun' recounted the horror, the terror and the patriotic feelings. Then the 1970s and 1980s swept away that version of the war for good. Like it or not, the umbilical cord was severed.

Our way of writing about the Great War is closely linked to our museum experience at the Historial de la Grande Guerre in Péronne. This project brought together an international team of specialists, made up of both former allies and former enemies, who met in the mid-1980s and created a centre for international research in 1989.[15] The museum opened its doors three years later. Thanks to the very generous support of the *Conseil général de la Somme*, fifteen years of team work – museographic work, research and publications – were undertaken in an atmosphere of complete friendship and intellectual enthusiasm. This should be apparent in our bibliographical references: most of the works cited are scarcely a decade old and many are still in manuscript at the time of writing. We have set out to examine the Great War in a way that can be considered new – but it is for others to assess the value of our work in revitalising the war's historiography.[16]

The *raison d'être* of this book is to offer a way to understand the Great War. The reader will have guessed from our introduction that we intend to explore the three pathways that we feel are most likely to lead to the heart of 1914–18 – violence, crusade and mourning – and that this study is the synthesis, indeed the outgrowth, of collaborative historical efforts. We should like to thank those friends, far more experienced than us, from whose immense knowledge we have benefited for so many years. We are fully aware of our debt to them.

I
VIOLENCE

Everyone knows war is violence, and though many readily acknowledge this, they refuse to draw the inevitable consequences. The history of warfare – particularly academic and scholarly history, but also traditional military history – is all too often disembodied. Why such a shortcoming is especially serious when it comes to the First World War is something we shall try to explain. But it might first be useful to consider briefly the reasons for so much reticence and to try to get to the root of this unacceptable way of sanitising war. Alain Corbin has said about the history of sexuality, 'An obvious puritanism has, until very recently, weighed heavily on university research.'[1] This harsh but we think justified statement can just as well be applied to the historiography of warfare, especially that of the Great War.

1

Battle, combat, violence: a necessary history

The violence of war inevitably takes us back to a history of the body. In war, bodies strike each other, suffer and inflict suffering. So the reticence of historians over the violence of warfare is connected to the reticence that has long attended a genuine history of medicine (military medicine even more so). Here again Corbin is right when he notes that any history of bodily suffering engages historians. They *expose* themselves not only to their readers – far more, certainly, than is the case with other kinds of history (with the possible exception of the history of sexuality) – but also to the specific pain associated with the subject matter. Propriety, together with an understandable need for personal security (not to mention academic security), are at the root of the widespread, long-standing reticence of many French historians who have chosen to study the violence of warfare.

'*Annales* historians' in the narrow sense of that term tended to discredit the study of actual warfare, of battle, and caused damage with their hostility to '*histoire-bataille*', or battle history. Actually, the battle history that the *Annales* founders decried was anything but an actual history of what went on in battles. And Marc Bloch himself, one of the founders of the *Annales*, was a marvellous historian of combat in both world wars.[1] But in any case, the violence of warfare belongs only outwardly to what Fernand Braudel somewhat condescendingly described as 'history that is restless' for it touches on the essential in the history of mankind. If the aim of historians is to start with people, and to undertake a 'history from the bottom up', as the *Annales* school believed, who can deny that for the men who have lived through wars and survived them, wars and their violence have been the most important experiences of their entire lives? One should note the immense need for self-expression that warfare has always aroused, from the Napoleonic wars to more recent conflicts. It was in order to recount their experiences of war, describe its violence, or at least try to say something about it (the great majority never succeeded in verbalising it) – or just to leave behind a humble trace of it, if only for their descendants – that, from the late eighteenth century on, so many warriors took up the pen, sometimes for the first and last time in their lives. And to neglect the violence of war is to neglect all those men who in growing numbers in the nineteenth and twentieth centuries endured that immense ordeal.

Of course, military history has always existed, in every country. But all too often military historians consider it indecent to deal with the problem of violence in combat or to study it as such. Battles and warfare are discussed only from the tactical or strategic angle; military events are viewed only from a social or political standpoint. On the whole, the reality of war is kept at bay. As a rule, French historiography of warfare has been unconcerned with the violence of the battlefield, the men in the arena, the suffering they endure, the perceptions of the men who try to survive and, in a nutshell, the immense stakes that are crystallised in the combat zone.

Avoiding these issues is an error. The violence specific to warfare is a prism that refracts many otherwise invisible aspects of the world. Entire societies can be seen anew, but one must be willing to *look* closely. In paroxysms of violence everything is stripped naked – starting with men, their bodies, their fantasies and desires, their fears, passions, beliefs and hatreds. The meaning they attribute to the violence of warfare and the result they hope it will bring, the motivations that allow them to kill their fellow men and endure the terror of confrontation – these pertain to something essential – something we shall call their 'representations', though the term is too vague. In the end, what happens in combat is inseparable from these representations, for soldiers always fight with their whole selves.

It is not just combatants who can be seen with uncommon clarity through the violent practices of warfare; entire societies emerge in the background, with all their technical, demographic, economic possibilities and, sometimes, their 'desire to live together'. We also see political power anew, the legitimacy of which is often rooted in the actions of its representatives on the battlefield. For war is a staging of the political, it renders visible things that are ordinarily hidden from view – the power of some men over others, their power to make men kill one another in a combat fury of extreme brutality. This brutality – and here is the whole problem – is usually widely accepted and borne by all the ordinary combatants charged with implementing it.

In short, by paying too little attention to the violence of war, an essential vector of historical understanding is overlooked and we deny ourselves access to many phenomena of memory-building and recollection, and to the profusion and variety of literary and artistic creation that has accompanied warfare. The history of combat violence is therefore a necessary history.

In countries other than France, schools of history with different traditions of national historiography have less false modesty. American and British historians developed an often remarkable military history as early as the 1920s and 1930s, and they have none of the mental blocks that hamper many of their colleagues elsewhere. A certain pragmatism in the study of history, combined with a kind of instinctive suspicion of abstractions and grand systems of thought, allows them to broach the violence of warfare without inhibition. John Keegan, for example, is still not well known to historians on the French side of the Channel. Yet he is among those who has delved deeply into the wide-ranging problem of warfare. Plainly challenging Clausewitz and his overrated dictum that war is 'the continuation of policy by other means', he states a deep truth: war is first and foremost a cultural act.[2]

In his major work, *The Face of Battle*,[3] Keegan daringly focussed *exclusively* on violence, in defiance of the discipline's most established rules of caution; he aimed for a diachronic comparison among the battles of Agincourt, Waterloo and the Somme, investigating the attitudes, behaviour and systems of representations prevailing in each. Not only his approach but the content was original, for what interested Keegan was precisely what no one had usually been interested in: behind the words used in the conventional accounts, he asked, behind the meaningless expressions everyone used, what *exactly* is happening on the battlefield, in the opaque sphere of interpersonal violence? Indeed, he tried to focus, to use one of his other expressions, on a 'history of flesh'.[4] He therefore did not hesitate to borrow, for instance, from zoology (and its notions of 'flight distance' and 'critical distance') to explain human behaviour in attack and retreat during combat: the oft-recounted behaviour of Napoleon's Imperial Guard at Waterloo, in its last charge against the unflinching British squares, is reinterpreted in this light. This is audacious. No need to add, of course, that Keegan never 'recounts' a battle. He dissects it and pries open its mystery, meticulously describing different types of confrontation, as determined by the combatants' weaponry. As a result, our vision of armed confrontation and its violence is radically altered. In fact, his isn't a history of battle in the usual sense but an anthropology of combat.

Equally revealing of the great gulf that still exists between different approaches to history is the intellectual shock provoked by another study, the American classicist Victor Davis Hanson's attempt to understand the violence peculiar to the clash of phalanxes in ancient Greece.[5] To gain an understanding of classical infantry warfare, he didn't hesitate to burn grain, vines and olive trees in order to see in fact what the destruction of the territory of one Greek city state by another might mean, and to show its true significance in political, not just economic terms. Nor did he hesitate to make his students bear replicas of Greek weapons and armour in order to understand better the range of possibilities at the moment of a charge, to define some of the technical and physical predicaments more clearly. Then the ancient texts could be re-read in the harsh, if not cruel light of this experimentation.

It is striking how much historians, though they profess to be discussing war, are cut off from areas of relevant knowledge. Weapons, for example – how they are used, how they work, and what effect they have – are outside the competence of most of them, while military historians who may be learned about weaponry don't know how to apply their knowledge. So one cannot exaggerate the value of having at least some concrete knowledge of the instruments of violence; tactile contact with them is not a superfluous historical experience. Objects lead to objections, as the etymology hints; they stand in the way of the most established historical certitudes.

Taking the First World War as an example, we can see that familiarity with the infantrymen's guns, with the truncheons and daggers used in the trenches that were manufactured according to the needs and requirements of combat, even touching and handling pieces of shrapnel, is just as essential as a close acquaintance with the terrain and a more than passing knowledge of battleground topography. Modern historians should not cut themselves off from the expertise of archaeologists, whose discoveries (salvaged in digs done during highway construction for example) can contribute greatly to the knowledge of certain battle practices.[6] A vast store of empirical knowledge is available for study and often within immediate grasp.

For instance, there is a highly specialised expertise (which would merit historical studies of its own) among military collectors and battlefield enthusiasts. But this generally reliable erudition, which has spawned journals, specialised books, meetings of devotees and networks of buyers and sellers – a very useful body of knowledge for professional historians, which they would be hard put to find elsewhere – is almost completely cut off from academic scholarship. This reaction on the part of 'scholarly' historians stems from distrust, indeed denial, mixed with a touch of arrogance. With chilling humour, Keegan recounts how he once offended the curator of a war museum:

> I constantly recall the look of disgust that passed over the face of a highly distinguished curator of one of the greatest collections of arms and armour in the world when I casually remarked to him that a common type of debris removed from the flesh of wounded men by surgeons in the gunpowder age was broken bone and teeth from neighbours in the ranks. He had simply never considered what was the effect of the weapons about which he knew so much, as artefacts, on the bodies of the soldiers who used them.[7]

But historians of war may be no more aware of these things than the curators of military museums.

Thresholds of violence in the Great War

Reticence in discussing violence is particularly unfortunate in the case of the Great War, for one important characteristic of this four-and-a-half-year conflict is its unprecedented levels of violence – among combatants, against prisoners and, last but not least, against civilians. To grasp these many-sided forms of violence is an indispensable prerequisite to any basic understanding of the 1914–18 conflict, and to any interpretation of the mark it left on the Western world. To understand the Great War is to try to understand that. We have to start with the fighting.

We shall not try here to describe this in detail, if indeed such an endeavour is possible, but simply to point out the salient factors.[8] The Great War brought into being a new kind of armed confrontation and thus became a historical watershed, representing a complex rupture with the circumstances and conditions of

warfare as they had been known before that had huge consequences for the rest of the century.

Already in 1914, at the beginning of war, battle was much
more violent than it had ever been before. And then military and
civilian suffering gradually intensified the violence over the duration of the conflict. This progressive intensification lent its own
dynamic to the conflict; in the very first days and weeks of the
war the practices of war took a brutal turn, not only on the battlefields but also for prisoners and civilians. Even for the ordinary
soldier, the enormous explosion of violence that occurred in the
summer of 1914 immediately and scathingly refuted all the pre-
dictions that had been made in the years prior.

The death toll of the Great War is well known: around 9–10
million, nearly all soldiers. Looking at the total mobilisation
figures, we find that the smaller nations were proportionally
most affected, given the techniques of warfare used in the
Balkans already in 1912–13; the treatment of the wounded and of
prisoners, as well as the inadequacies of medical procedures,
greatly contributed to the losses. (Serbia lost 37 per cent of its
soldiers, Turkey close to 27 per cent, Romania 25 per cent, Bulgaria 22 per cent.) Among the great powers in the war, France
holds the worst record in proportional losses: 16 per cent of its
mobilised men were killed (against 15.4 per cent for Germany).
But late in the war not all the men who were mobilised actually
fought. If we count only the French troops who were engaged
in fighting, the proportionate losses are much greater: 22 per
cent of the officers died and 18 per cent of the soldiers. In the infantry itself, the most exposed branch, one out of three officers
was killed and one out of four privates.

Perhaps because they are of too great an order of magnitude,
or because they have been cited so often, or perhaps because
when we are confronted with such statistics of war, powerful reflexes kick in to make them seem unreal, these numbers, oddly,
are a weak evocation of the horror. This changes if we adopt a
different, less frequently used scale and count the number of
dead in relation to the days of war. Taking just the two powers

most affected, we can say that on average almost 900 Frenchmen and 1,300 Germans died *every day* between the outbreak of war in August 1914 and the armistice in November 1918. Of course, these are averages, and they don't show the considerable disparities from year to year, or the differences between periods of calm and periods of offensive operations. But these numbers were far from abstract for those living at the time of the conflict. In the British press, for example, the big battles immediately drew the attention of the men, women and children of the 'domestic front' because of the sudden, spectacular increase in the number of dead listed in *The Times* (not to mention the transport of the wounded through train stations and large cities).

Surprising as it may seem, when we compare the average number of daily casualties in 1914–18 to the average number in the First and Second World Wars, we find that the mortality rate is almost always higher for the First. True, total military losses in the Western zone were twice as high in 1939–45 as in 1914–18 (about 8.5 million killed in combat in Europe in 1914–18 as opposed to 16–17 million in 1939–45), but these comprehensive figures give a misleading impression of the actual intensity of the combat violence. In fact, only the USSR recorded much heavier losses between 1941 and 1945 than between 1914 and 1917. Whereas Russia lost 1,459 men a day (killed or missing) during the First World War, it lost nearly four times that many (5,635 a day) during the Second, thanks mostly to Stalin, and this does not include those who died in German prisoner-of-war camps.[9] The figures for Germany are 1,083 fighting men lost per day in 1939–45,* and 1,303 in 1914–18. And for the United States, the totals are 123 men per day lost in 1941–45 and 195 during the earlier conflict (820 a day when the nation became fully engaged on the battlefield, beginning in the summer of 1918). And finally

---

*Again the figure does not include German soldiers who died in prisoner-of-war camps in Russia; if it did it would increase the number to 1,564 deaths a day. In the Russian case, the inclusion of deaths in the German camps would increase the average number of dead to 8,000 a day.

Great Britain, which lost 147 men per day in 1939–45, lost 457 men a day, three times as many, a quarter of a century before.[10]

Some of the peaks of violence are especially revealing: on the first day of the British offensive on the Somme, 1 July 1916, 20,000 men from Britain and the Dominions were killed, and 40,000 men were wounded. *No* day in the Second World War was so deadly, even on the Eastern Front. For today's Western societies, which are relatively unfamiliar with death, and even with the idea of death in war, it is extremely difficult to begin even to imagine the meaning of such numbers.

True, mass carnage in war was nothing new. In fact, total war losses in Europe during 1792–1815 were comparable, proportionately, to those of 1914–18, though of course spread out over more than twenty years. Furthermore – and this is probably the most significant difference – the cause of death changed in the span of a century. In the early nineteenth century, disease killed more men in wartime than combat did. The numbers were about equal fifty years later, for the first time, in the Italian war of 1859. A half-century later, in 1914, the situation had reversed: deaths in battle were almost exclusively violent ones, even though the number of sick soldiers remained very high.* Disease was responsible for the deaths of one-sixth of the fighting men who were swallowed up by the Great War.

Not only did the nature of death during combat change in 1914–18, but so did the nature of the injuries. In the French army, 3,594,000 injuries were counted and 2,800,000 wounded.†

---

*According to the records of the French army, 5 million soldiers were reported ill in the four years of war, but the number includes soldiers who were ill several times. In the military operations on the Eastern Fronts (the Dardanelles, for example), lack of preparation on the part of the health services caused health disasters among the Western armies, particularly due to malaria, fevers and dysentery.[11] See Alon Rachamimov, *POWs and the Great War: Captivity on the Eastern Front*, Oxford, New York, Berg Publishers, 2002.

†It is extremely difficult to arrive at the real figures because, in all the countries, wounds were counted but not the wounded, which means that a soldier wounded several times was counted several times over.

Half the men were wounded twice and more than 100,000 three or four times. The ratio of wounded to mobilised men is thus around 40 per cent, a proportion that was typical for all the large armies engaged in the conflict. This change in the violence of warfare involved first the bodily flesh of the fighting men, both victims and witnesses; combatants in earlier times had never seen injuries of that kind and on such a scale, either on themselves or on the bodies of their comrades.

Indeed, the gravity and type of wounds inflicted in 1914–18 had no precedent. Direct hits from large-calibre shells can literally pulverise the body, leaving no identifiable remains. Very large pieces of shrapnel can actually slice a man in half. Ignoring this, failing to mention it or recall it, not thinking about what it means, is tantamount to consenting to a historiographical denial. It is a denial that inspired a flash of black humour from Paul Fussell, a pioneer in the study of First World War literature[12] and a veteran of the Second World War, in which he was seriously injured: 'In war, as in air accidents, "insides" are much more visible than it is normally well to imagine.'[13]

The history of violence in the 1914–18 war thus cannot be separated from a history of the body, for bodies had never previously suffered so much and on such a scale. The fate of those who were wounded was by and large atrocious, and a history of military medicine is indispensable to understand the war. 'Medicine intersects with everything,' wrote Jacques Léonard. Of course, military medicine in 1914–18 benefited from the medical advances of the nineteenth century, as well as from the genuine therapeutic breakthroughs that occurred as a direct consequence of the need to deal with the new injuries of 1914. Better evacuation systems and medical infrastructures; the possibility of having antiseptic surgery using anaesthetics on the battlefield; the removal of damaged tissues when treating fractures, limiting the risk of gangrene and reducing the number of amputations; the X-ray detection of projectiles embedded in the flesh; facial plastic surgery; vaccination against typhus and tetanus; and blood transfusions – all these were therapeutic capabilities that had no equivalent in earlier conflicts. Entirely new specialties were created during the war.[14] But these health-care advances were counterbalanced by the greater gravity of the wounds inflicted. The latest artillery and the new intensity of fire power caused unprecedented physiological damage, so much so that the rate of survival from injury in combat was probably higher in the early nineteenth century than at the beginning of the twentieth, or so John Keegan has suggested.

Lastly, combat violence, suffered but also inflicted, caused irreparable psychological damage. Psychiatry at that time had at best only primitive explanations of the stresses and traumas of the battlefield. Germans had a quite sophisticated concept of *Kriegsneurose*, or war neurosis, but the principal interpretative tools among the British and Americans was the simplistic notion of 'shell shock', and, among the French, *commotion* and *obusite* ('shellitis'), in a context where exacerbated patriotism caused physicians invariably to suspect soldiers of simulating insanity, or at least of engaging in an unconscious psychological and bodily ruse in order to escape duty.[15] It is now known that soldiers on a battlefield can hope to preserve their psychological equilibrium for only several months at best; the strict selection process notwithstanding, one-tenth of mobilised American men were hospitalised for mental disturbances between 1942 and 1945, and after thirty-five days of uninterrupted combat, 98 per cent of them manifested psychiatric disturbances in varying degrees.[16] As it happens, the combatants of 1914–18, when they were lucky enough to survive, were constantly sent back to the trenches, often in the same areas, even after they had already been wounded several times. This prolonged immersion, unprecedented in duration, constitutes another specific aspect of their experience of violence.

More than half of the 70 million soldiers engaged in the Great War suffered physically from its violence, whether it killed them or 'only' wounded them. And, if we are to trust present-day epidemiological studies on the invisible consequences of combat, we should not rule out the possibility that almost half of the survivors sustained more or less serious psychological disturbances. All these factors, as Keegan emphasised, show the extent to which, starting in 1914, the battlefield had become the site of a much more extreme terror than ever before. The greater range of weapons changed the very conception of 'battlefield'; the Somme in 1916 – the site of one of the most costly battles of the century* – was ten times more spread out than Waterloo.

The circumstances and conditions of combat were thus completely transformed. In the big battles of the early twentieth century, commanders could no longer grasp in its entirety the scene of the conflict. A hundred years earlier, soldiers stood shoulder to shoulder, but now they were dispersed over the terrain, isolated, and almost entirely lost when the confusion of battle set in. Sometimes, when the tactical links were broken, they were completely on their own, as in Verdun, where infantrymen were scattered haphazardly wherever there were shell-craters. True, battlefields of the past were always scenes of horrendous terror for the combatants, as shown by the panic that so often gripped the contending parties. And there have also always been sites of massacres, including 'pointless' ones perpetrated by victors when, at the sight of their enemies surrendering or turning their backs, they lost control. Yet before the battles of the Great War, the confrontations had never been so totally dehumanised. A combatant's skill and training, his courage and prudence, played no small part in his ability to survive a raging battle. But given the immense increase in fire-power in the late nineteenth and early twentieth centuries, this individual know-how counted for very little. It was not entirely useless, however, as the high death toll of novice soldiers in the trenches shows. In

---

*In less than six months 1.2 million men were counted wounded, dead or missing (counting all sides), of which one-third were killed – in other words it was a slaughter even greater than Verdun, and with weightier consequences. The German decision to wage unrestricted submarine warfare, which led to the United States' entry into the war, was directly linked to their recognising the Allies' superiority in this 'war of equipment' during the second half of 1916.[17]

1914–18, the disparity between the methods of killing and methods of self-protection became overwhelmingly disproportionate. Given the fire-power's new intensity and the width of the terrain swept by bullets, shells and gas, escaping the onslaught becomes a mere matter of chance. Even buried in the ground, men had fewer defences than ever before.

Moreover, the periods of extreme violence lengthened spectacularly, going from a few hours to several weeks or months. The first confrontations of 1914 put an end to the brief, brutal clashes that were characteristic of what Hanson calls the 'Western way of war'. The Battle of the Somme lasted for more than five months; Gallipoli, more than eight; Verdun, around ten; and the third Battle of Ypres, in 1917, four months. Paradoxically, what this adds up to is the death of battle in the traditional meaning of the term. Battles were transformed into a series of sieges in open countryside, during which the besieged could re-supply freely, receive transport reinforcements and build new lines of defence (as the French did at Verdun in 1916, and the Germans on the Somme in the same year). The depth of the rear, some ten kilometres wide, permitted an efficient resistance to almost any enemy attack. On the Somme, in July–November 1916, an enormous force of 4 million men could thereby take turns, on both sides, in supplying a front line some forty kilometres wide. More than a quarter of them were killed, taken prisoner, or listed as missing.

These 'sieges' left the areas of confrontation completely devastated and devoid of life over thousands of square kilometres. It could be said that battle in the traditional sense died of its own violence, since the intensity of the bombardments, drastically changing the terrain as it did, forbade or made extremely difficult any forward movement by the artillery, in spite of the fact that artillery support is indispensable to any infantry advance. Movement was now not possible. Even the German offensive of March 1918 in Picardy, with its spectacular initial results, progressively lost momentum before finally being halted by the entry of Allied reserves on the front lines. Until the combined intervention of tanks, aircraft and American forces in the summer of 1918, which enabled the Allies to drive back an adversary weakened by the last-ditch efforts of the preceding months, no genuine return to movement had been possible on the Western Front since the autumn of 1914.

Was a new type of battle born in the Great War? We lack an adequate vocabulary to talk about the change that took place. Field-Marshal Hindenburg and General Ludendorff, astounded by their visit to the Somme in September 1916 – for until then they had known only the Eastern Front – coined the expression 'battle of equipment' (*Materialschlacht*) to try to define the great break. Does the term adequately express what really happened from 1916 on? The soldiers spoke spontaneously of '*Verwüstungschlacht*', a difficult word to translate, which combines the ideas of ruin, devastation and butchery and that emphasises the human slaughter involved. We could also suggest the term 'total battle'. We lack the words to explain that a form of warfare which since antiquity had seen battle as a climactic moment, condensed in time, was now called into question. The violence of the 1914–18 confrontation was magnified tenfold as a result of this change, for the demise of the old types of battle, far from reducing the suffering and casualties, multiplied them in unprecedented proportions. The Western world's entire relationship to war was permanently and drastically altered.

Thus a certain kind of war died with the twentieth century, at least in that part of Western Europe that had already produced so many atrocious innovations in warfare and where, since the late eighteenth century, more than 150 conflicts and about 600 battles had taken place. It died as a result of its own violence, of its own paroxysms. In spite of the extraordinary brutality of the Napoleonic battles, the soldiers of the Empire could still spontaneously use the term 'field of glory' to designate the place where they had fought, been wounded, or lost their comrades. Could the term 'field of glory' be applied after Verdun or the Somme? An aesthetic and ethical code of heroism, courage and battle violence vanished in the immense cataclysm of 1914–18.

The successive stages leading to such a change are worth considering. The Revolutionary and Imperial wars in France certainly constituted a significant break with earlier military practices for reasons that were not so much technical (there were no innovations in armament) as ideological, strategic and tactical. From the first, the battles of the French Revolution stressed the role of mass and impact – in other words, the bayonet charge – the two elements being combined with a new determination on the part of the conscripted combatants. We know that Clausewitz's concept of 'absolute war' came directly from this great transformation in troop movements and from the soldiers' new motivation. The development continued throughout the Napoleonic period, particularly during the last Imperial campaigns. Starting with the Battle of Wagram in 1809, the primacy of frontal impact over manoeuvre in Napoleon's tactics gave rise to the highest death tolls of nineteenth-century Europe; later battles in the century, when armament had completely changed (rifled cannons rather than cannon balls shot over great distances, and long-range artillery), did not cause such heavy proportionate losses as those sustained by the Grande Armée during the last battles of the Napoleonic Empire.

A second stage was reached with the American Civil War and the Franco-Prussian War of 1870–71. In both these conflicts – more clearly in the first than in the second – several signs of total war appeared, both in the circumstances and conditions under which the combatants engaged and in the treatment of the civilian populations, who for the first time became a major strategic stake.[18] Nevertheless, the old tradition of 'regulated warfare' was still very much alive during the Franco-Prussian War, and, similarly, several checks on violence were still in effect during the Civil War, even during the final phase with General Sherman's famous 'march to the sea', the aim of which was to terrorise the Confederacy and to seal the defeat of the South.

It was precisely this tradition of the 'self-containment' of combat violence that suddenly and permanently crumbled in 1914–18. Whereas sieges of cities had once followed a precise

ritual, up to and including the circumstances and conditions of
surrender, metropolitan areas were now bombarded until they
were destroyed. Whereas officer prisoners had once been treated
with genuine consideration (even made prisoners on parole, like
the defeated French officers at Sedan in 1870, and allowed to
return home for the duration of the campaign), they now
endured the common lot of internment camps. That a threshold
had been crossed was even clearer in the treatment of the
wounded: gone was the traditional truce for stretcher-bearers to
do their work and for the retrieval of survivors after the battle. In
1914–18, except for some rare exceptions – in the Dardanelles in
1915, for instance, or on the Somme in a very brief and localised
way, on 1 July 1916 – soldiers who fell wounded between the
lines were found and rescued only very late. From then on,
except during local truces tacitly observed by the soldiers themselves (without commanders being involved), the wounded and,
of course, potential rescuers too were fired upon, while prisoners, wounded or not, were sometimes simply finished off. It is a
striking paradox: this intensification of violence against the very
people that international agreements had been expected to
protect occurred precisely when the International Committee
of the Red Cross came into existence and when all the belligerents adhered to its provisions and to the 1899 and 1907 Hague
agreements.

The very high mortality rate of 1914–18 had not just 'material' causes, linked to important innovations in weaponry and armament, but other causes, too, starting with reciprocal hatreds,
often brought to a climax by the tension of combat, and without
which many soldiers might have survived, with rapid evacuation
and timely medical assistance. The fact that the removal of
wounded soldiers was often so difficult, belated and incomplete
was not only due to purely 'technical' problems: without a truce
for stretcher-bearers, or because the short, spontaneous, unoffi-
cial and unilateral truces were too precarious, soldiers who fell
wounded between the lines lay dying for hours, sometimes days,
with only makeshift bandages. It is estimated that one-third of

the 20,000 men who died on the Somme on 1 July 1916 might have been saved had the wounded men been aided as they would have been a half century earlier.

Did all the restraints that were still in effect in nineteenth-century warfare disappear? Examined more closely, things are more complex, of course. Even in this greatly dehumanised war, some areas managed precariously to escape the intensification of combat. The tacit truces clearly indicated the soldiers' determination to limit the level of reciprocal violence: this is the real meaning of the usually badly understood or over-interpreted 'fraternisations'.[19] Moreover, combat takes various shapes. A high level of violence was not necessarily permanent; moments of extreme tension were broken up by long periods during which the ever-present front-line risks became more diffuse and sometimes even rather low. In fact, the dangers were varied. Mines, bombardments, gases, assaults made for a range of very different perils, fears and practices. And the fronts did not all experience the same forms of violence. For example, until 1918, raids by small groups were an important feature of battle on the Eastern Front, which was more fluid than on the Western Front, where such practices vanished quite rapidly. And on the Western Front, starting in the summer of 1918, air power and tanks were decisive, whereas in the East a classic cavalry offensive broke the German-Bulgarian front in September and led to the first armistice. It is not wrong to assert that there were as many experiences of combat as there were combatants.

That said, it is also right to state that the very old system that had kept war violence in check suddenly collapsed. The collapse is all the more spectacular given that important measures had been taken internationally to buttress the old system. The sudden intensification of warfare was provoked by new technical conditions of combat, but not solely by them. It is impossible to account for the degree of truly unprecedented brutality reached in the confrontations of 1914–18 if we fail to consider the new behaviour of the combatants.

'Civilising process' or 'brutalisation'?

War violence on such a scale, and perpetrated by such large sections of European society for the first time during 1914–18, should contradict the attractive idea that social violence in Western civilisation since the early modern era slowly ebbed away – an idea for which we are indebted to the German sociologist Norbert Elias. Historians studying the nineteenth century have also stressed the spectacular decline of violent practices in the social body as a whole, emphasising the progress of the 'long and difficult work of in-depth self-containment achieved by human beings'[20] – as revealed, for instance, in the growing rejection of all spectacles of massacre, in the progress of analgesic techniques and anaesthetics, and in the individual and collective participation in the cult of the dead.

The argument that violence gradually decreased meets with one main objection, however: the phenomenon of war. Indeed, war is not really included in Elias's scheme, or only in a cursory way, as for example, in his depiction of medieval warfare, the accuracy of which has now been shown to be uncertain. As for the First World War, which took place twenty years before his major work was published, he seems not to consider it a serious obstacle to his thesis about a 'civilising process' except in one respect: it does not escape him that the increasing refinement of table manners since the beginning of modern times suffered a sudden setback on the battlefields of 1914–18; the men swiftly and easily reverted to practices that had vanished from the Western world centuries before. Elias explains:

Retroactive movements are certainly not inconceivable. It is sufficiently known that the conditions of life in the World War I automatically enforced a breakdown of some of the taboos of peacetime civilization. In the trenches, officers and soldiers again ate when necessary with knives and hands. The threshold of delicacy shrank rather rapidly under the pressure of the inescapable situation.

But for him this was only an 'incident' that could not invalidate the general 'line of development'.[21]

In fact, Elias preferred mostly to disregard the Great War and failed to give it its proper place. Yet one cannot deny that it left visible scars, particularly in his native Germany, where one could not avoid the sight of mass mourning and of mutilated veterans and men with facial wounds – like the ones painted by George Grosz and Otto Dix. But for Elias, while the 'civilising process does not follow a straight line' and 'on a smaller scale there are the most diverse crisscrossing movements', nevertheless, 'if we consider the movement over long periods of time, we see clearly how the compulsions arising directly from the threat of weapons and physical force gradually diminish, and how those forms of dependency which lead to the regulation of the affects in the form of self-control, gradually increase'[22]. However, the violence of the First World War and of subsequent twentieth-century wars cannot be regarded as small-scale minor accidents.

Yet war as waged in the Western world in the twentieth century has rarely been acknowledged to contradict the presumption that there has been an 'advance in the threshold of repugnance'[23] in the modern period, an advance that might seem at first to have reached its peak in the nineteenth century. For after all, the experience of the violence in the 1914–18 war gave contemporaries the impression that, throughout Europe and in all nations, the apparent 'dynamic of the West' had been snuffed out. And this radical and radically new violence was not only massively *accepted* by the belligerent societies but also *implemented* by millions of men over four and a half years. Even more troubling, the about turn – from a social state where violence had become very controlled, repressed and unreal to a state of war where extreme violence had free rein – occurred in an extremely brief span of time. In a matter of days and with hardly any transition between the two, Europeans who had benefited from the 'civilising process' left their work, their families and their often sophisticated, cultivated social life to accept extreme violence.

Consider reservists, for example; they went to the front lines not from barracks, like regular troops, but from their homes, with virtually no period of adaptation, and their immersion in violence was immediate. Someone like Marc Bloch returned to Paris from holiday on 1 August 1914, and received his baptism of fire on the Belgian frontier just three weeks later.[24] Moreover, this extremely sudden change occurred as an equally rapid crumbling of the barriers customarily thrown up against certain war excesses took place. In Europe, many of the worst war 'atrocities' committed against the enemy – including wounded soldiers, prisoners and also civilians – happened in the first days or weeks of battle. No invading army was exempt from it: neither the Germans in Belgium, France or the Russian part of Poland; nor the Austro-Hungarians in Serbia; nor the Russians in East Prussia. The French committed astonishing acts of brutality on soil that was supposedly 'theirs', the section of Alsace which they re-conquered at the beginning of the war.[25]

The sustained violence of the Great War, particularly in its first weeks, the fact that it was widely approved and accepted by millions of people in every part of the European continent and every social group, is certainly a major rebuttal to the thesis of 'civilising progress' in modern history. Unprecedented violence became integrated with disconcerting ease into the daily life of every civilian and every soldier to the point where it became commonplace, and in the end it was accepted for more than four years, albeit with significant variations. An in-depth study still remains to be done of these 'short-term' years of 1914–18, which get overlooked by historians, who consider the evolution of sensibilities exclusively over the long term – or who may not be skilled at handling the prism of war.

Seen through that prism's extraordinary power of refraction, the 'civilising process' appears under a quite different light, almost like a veneer that can be easily stripped away from entire societies. The specific, momentary 'decline of civilisation' that Elias later thought he perceived in National Socialist totalitarianism[26] actually took place in 1914–18; to a large extent, the totalitarian regimes of the twentieth century, including Nazism's, were but an aftershock of the first upheaval.[27] The work of this German sociologist is perhaps one of the most attractive intellectual attempts made during the twentieth century to defend the old idea of the West's civilising progress. But a construction of this kind necessarily involved a denial of the 1914–18 war – a denial formulated, ironically, on the eve of a second world conflict that was to visit even more violence against unarmed populations than the first had; and this greater violence descended directly and in every respect from the Great War.

It is appropriate here to contrast the ideas of 'civilising process' and 'dynamic of the West' with an opposite concept, also inspired by Germany's war and inter-war experience: the concept of 'brutalisation'. It was formulated by George Mosse, a German Jew who escaped Nazi Germany in 1933 and later became an American authority on the history of fascism and nationalism. This great pioneer's very original work is noteworthy especially for its ability to discuss the cultures of both the First and Second World Wars *together*. Mosse sees brutalisation as the real change brought about by the world's first global conflict in 1914–18. He uses this term primarily to describe the post-1918 political landscape, made enduringly brutal by the practices and representations of war, notably in Germany, where the effect of the defeat was to turn politics into war pursued by other means. It could equally describe the Soviet Union, given the part played by former soldiers in the 'violence from below' that helped to set the revolutionary process in motion in 1917.[28]

We shall return to the connection between the experience of total war and the phenomenon of totalitarianism, a theme without which any analysis of Soviet Communism and German National Socialism remains inadequate. Suffice it to say here that the concept of brutalisation gains in first being applied in the sustained violence of war itself. And indeed, compared to nineteenth-century conflicts, war was much more brutal after 1914. The concept is much less abstract and theoretical than it may seem at first glance. The new brutality of the war left enduring marks on the bodies and souls of the participants. Yet this new brutality of combat – more precisely the new brutalisation of men through combat – nonetheless raises complex issues that historians find very difficult to resolve, regarding the way millions of human beings inflicted, endured and finally accepted this violence, and also the way they helped to make it commonplace. The combatants' systems of representation thus remain the central issue.

We do not mean to suggest that the violence of the 1914–18 war should be mistaken for a situation of complete anomie. The armed confrontation never permanently destroyed systems of norms, or at least not entirely. Most troubling, in this respect, was the persistence, on the front, of a rather impressive cult of the dead, something that had been more or less absent from battlefields a century earlier. Combatant communities, for whom death had become completely banal, and who were obliged to face it in emergency conditions of great danger, expended a great deal of energy in giving their dead decent burials, in organising funeral ceremonies, in seeing to the upkeep of sepulchres, in sending families information, sketches to show where tombs were located, and letters of condolence. An archaeology of the battlefield would help us sort out the different gradations and nuances in these activities – depending on whether the people involved were friends, allies or enemies, whether they were located on the front lines or in less exposed areas, in calm sectors or in combat areas.[29]

On other levels, too, extreme violence and mass death never led to the complete disappearance of all norms. The maintenance on the front of a cultural life – indeed of an artistic and literary life – the enthusiasm with which peacetime social practices were transferred and sustained there by the combatants (for instance, the British soldiers' soccer games and music hall entertainment[30]), the preservation of close bonds with the home front so that combatants could manage their professional and family affairs from a distance[31] – all this shows the extent to which the old systems of norms coexisted, apparently smoothly, with the anomie of the battlefields.

Battlefield violence and things left unsaid in the history books

We have stressed that the violence of combat must be fully disclosed because historians have for too long sanitised this aspect of the Great War, to the point of making it all but incomprehensible. In addition to the general reasons for this sanitisation, which would be applicable to other conflicts as well as this one, there is, in the case of the 1914–18 war, the ambiguous service rendered by the unprecedented and huge number of first-person accounts by the combatants themselves. The appearance of these accounts began during the conflict itself, reached its peak between the two wars, and they are still appearing, thanks to the publishing dynamism of so many descendants of the generation that knew front-line combat. This testimony from combatants, a nearly inexhaustible documentary fund reservoir, has made historians of the First World War feel guilty and inadequate. 'I told the truth. Let them contradict me if they dare!' exclaimed one witness in the inter-war period.[32] And indeed, who would dare to? How could an historian question the narratives recited by men who lived through such trials, when he himself had no comparable experience? What made things even more difficult was that already, during the war, the soldiers set themselves up as historians of their own experience, reacting against and wanting to correct the distortions and misperceptions in the home front's view of them.

Let us briefly consider one of them, Paul Tuffrau, forgotten today but very well-known during the war years.[33] A graduate of the École Normale Supérieure with a degree in literature, he went to war in 1914 at the age of thirty, with the rank of sublieutenant in an infantry regiment; he fought the entire war on the front lines, was wounded several times but survived, and was given the Legion of Honour and the rank of major. His career as a French officer was like that of thousands of others between 1914 and 1918, thousands of others often cut down by death or mutilation. But what was special about him was that between

1916 and 1918 he managed to publish, in an important newspaper of the time, many pseudonymous articles under the heading 'Carnet d'un combattant'. His exceptional venture was emblematic, for many soldiers wanted to write their own accounts of the war for the sake of their comrades and for the sake of the civilian population – or one might say, *against* them.

In the early 1930s this was how Tuffrau explained his motives:

> At the end of 1915, disgusted like many others by the absurdity of the military accounts in the newspapers, I took advantage of a leave to offer the *Journal* some accounts of the war, under a pseudonym ('Lieutenant E. R.'), that would be accurate without being defeatist. I wanted to give the soldiers, whose angers I witnessed every day, the satisfaction of seeing that the home front was no longer ignorant about their real life – and I wanted to give the home front a more accurate picture of the miseries and greatness on the front lines.[34]

Henri Barbusse, who was in the same brigade as Tuffrau and who wrote his *Feu, journal d'une escouade* (Under Fire: The Story of a Squad) as a serial during the same year, 1916, shared the same basic impulse.

What complicated matters was that the veterans, who obviously had the incontestable status of witnesses to the war experience, also gave themselves the status of historians with the exclusive right to talk about the experience. Until the 1980s in France, the major accounts available on the 1914–18 battle experience were written by veterans. Jean-Norton Cru's book *Témoins* (Testimonies), published in the late 1920s and constantly cited as a model even today, is typical. Though he claims he carefully sifted through the testimonies of his fellow veterans to separate the wheat from the chaff (i.e. reliable testimonies from untrustworthy reconstructions), Cru actually imposed a rigid, selective standard on the combatant's narrative. Another example is provided by the 1931 film *Les Croix de bois*, one of the first great manifesto films based on personal experience of the war, for which the director, Raymond Bernard, turned down professional actors and used only former infantrymen, or *poilus*, and, in a quasi-fetishist way, arranged to have scorched trees and earth from the very sites of the former battlegrounds delivered to the studio. [35]

Eyewitness accounts are the source of both invaluable information and major inhibitions; in fact, it is probably from the period of the Great War that a kind of 'tyranny of the witness' established itself.[36] We must free ourselves from this tyranny. Refraining from discussing the combatants' experience under the pretext that only the men who have lived through the war can analyse it is tantamount to abandoning the elementary rules of historical study.

This is all the more true when you consider that the combatants chose to remain silent on many essential points about the subject of war violence. True, all their stories emphasise the extreme horror of the battlefield, but the brutality described is always anonymous and blind. In other words, it is a violence the responsibility for which is unidentified and hence from which they are themselves exonerated. Interpersonal violence of the kind that fosters lasting feelings of guilt is barely mentioned, if at all. As anthropologists have noted (they may be less embarrassed on this point than historians), 'people are killed' in war, but people do not kill.[37]

Of course it is true that the front was primarily the site of usually anonymous mass death, where you didn't know who killed you or whom you killed. The combatants were correct, both then and later, to emphasise this anonymity, a salient characteristic of the violence of the Great War. But did they understate the instances when they themselves had killed? Direct confrontations did occur. The best marksmen, for instance, waited for hours for opportunities to shoot at targets in the opposite trench; grenade 'duels' took place between assault troops; night patrols conducted surprise raids; trenches were captured before their denizens could escape; and it was impossible to take on the burden of prisoners without endangering one's own life.

In the violence of hand-to-hand combat, regulation weapons were replaced by spade-shovels, truncheons and knives, usually manufactured by the men themselves (as can be seen in the museum collections dedicated to the Great War).[38] One consequence of the extreme brutality of this kind of confrontation was that it was all the riskier to surrender; on-the-spot slaughter of men who surrendered, wounded or not, by 'trench cleaners' (often volunteers) was a widespread practice on all fronts. Prisoners of war in the camps were often survivors of this type of violence.

But very few combatants spoke of such matters. It took someone like the poet Blaise Cendrars, expressing himself with great candour – mixed, perhaps, with unconfessed guilt – to broach this aspect of the war experience in a text written in early 1918:

> And now, today, I'm holding the knife in my hand ... I've faced the torpedo, the cannon, the mines, the fire, the gases, the machine guns, the whole anonymous, fiendish, systematic, blind machinery. I'll face man. My fellow creature. A monkey. An eye for an eye, a tooth for a tooth. Now it's just you and me. With fists and knives. Mercilessly. I jump on my antagonist. I deal him a dreadful blow. His head is almost unstuck. I've killed the Kraut. I was more alert and rapid than he. More direct. I struck first. I have a sense of reality, me, a poet. I acted. I killed. Like someone who wants to live.[39]

Similarly, it took a nearly cynical fascination for the battle-field of Verdun and the cruel practices that occurred there for the Cubist painter and stretcher-bearer Fernand Léger to recount his November 1916 conversation with a trench cleaner in a letter to a friend:

> He hadn't asked to do this. He'd been picked. This is what he said to me: 'I go with the assault waves and I stop at the first German trench, and my friends and I do the work.' It was precisely that work which I was interested in ... Also, I wanted to know what

he did specifically. So he said to me, 'Oh, well, it doesn't just depend on me, it also depends on the buddies. Certainly, it's a pain to take them back with us because you get bumped off on the way back.' I understood that he preferred to kill them but had to discuss it first with his buddies.[40]

In such moments of direct, close and personal violence, a fundamental taboo was transgressed, the taboo not to kill. There is a specific hypnotic state that can occur, it seems, when death is dispensed to someone from close quarters, and it is sometimes experienced by individuals who are normally very hostile to any idea of physical violence, but only a minute number of people dare to mention the kind of pleasure involved. The case of the German writer Ernst Jünger is still a rare one; he described his experience explicitly, not so much in *The Storm of Steel* published in 1920, but in his later writings – and the timing is not irrelevant – such as *Feuer und Blut* (Fire and Blood), which was published in 1925.[41] This is a complete retelling, in minute detail, of his first narrative account of the big offensive of March 1918, in which he was the leader of an attacking company of storm troopers. His long description of killing at very close range includes no apparent feelings of guilt.

Yet guilt was expressed on occasion. In a course he taught at the Institut d'études politiques in Paris in the early 1970s, Antoine Prost used to cite an extraordinary text, which follows here, to help his auditors understand the pacifism of combatants in the 1930s. It is tempting to interpret it instead as one of the very rare confessions we have of how the violence of war – here so guilt-inducing – left its mark on combatants in the Great War:

> Not only did the war make us dead, impotent or blind. In the midst of beautiful actions, of sacrifice and self-abnegation, it also awoke within us, sometimes to the point of paroxysm, ancient instincts of cruelty and barbarity. At times, I ... who have never punched anyone, who loathes disorder and brutality, took pleasure in killing. When we crawled towards the enemy during a raid, a

grenade in our hand and a knife in our teeth, like cut-throats, we felt fear in our gut, and yet an ineluctable force urged us on. Taking the enemy by surprise in his trench, jumping on him, enjoying the terror of a man who doesn't believe in the devil yet suddenly sees him dive down to the ground! That barbarous, horrendous moment had a unique flavour for us, a morbid appeal; we were like those unfortunate drug addicts who know the magnitude of the risk but can't keep themselves from taking more poison.[42]

The writer of this passage, incredibly bold for the period, goes on to describe how war and the habit of combat distorted the way he looked upon even the most peaceful landscapes. Robert Graves described exactly the same experience in Wales:

When I was strong enough to climb the hill behind Harlech and revisit my favourite country, I found that I could only see it as a prospective battlefield, I would find myself working out tactical problems, planning how I would hold the northern Artro valley against an attack from the sea, or where I would put a Lewis-gun if I were trying to rush Dolwreiddiog Farm from the brow of the hill, and what would be the best position for the rifle-grenade section.[43]

This kind of acknowledgement of the traces left by violent warfare is rare. Similarly, the terrible psychological damage caused by modern combat, damage that is inevitable when one is immersed in extreme violence for a protracted period, was usually hushed up. Hence the silence that also weighs on the subject of soldiers' suicides. Otto Dix, in the series of lithographs entitled *Der Krieg*, made in 1924,[44] depicted the corpse of a German soldier sitting in a trench, his flesh decomposed, his skeleton visible. Two details capture one's attention: the butt of the gun is set on the ground with the barrel aimed at the soldier's face, and one of his feet is shoeless, naked and raised. Indeed, this is the way suicides were committed on the front lines: the barrel of the gun was too long for a soldier to reach the trigger and take aim at himself, so a stick had to be used or he had to take off his shoe and push the trigger with his toe. Dix's work is a revelation, the transgression of a rarely transgressed taboo in the combatant's memory – but only a partial one, since the acknowledgement is simultaneously concealed: the title of the work, *German Sentinel in a Trench* doesn't allude to suicide.

This is an instance of the 'silence of painters' about the violence of war, a silence that the French critic Philippe Dagen has well diagnosed, though he failed to point out that the silence also applied to painters' support of the war.[45] At least Dix lifted part of the veil; Fernand Léger made no drawings of the corpses he saw at Verdun, though he noticed that some had stumpy fingers because extreme suffering had led the dying to eat their own hands.[46]

The silence of writers matches that of painters, which is why fear is evoked so incompletely in their works. The inability to control basic bodily functions in moments of greatest terror, a fact that is rather extensively described in ancient sources, among the soldiers in Napoleon's army, and among American servicemen in the Pacific during the Second World War,[47] is virtually absent from the testimony of combatants in 1914–18 and in following years. A whole facet of the humiliation inflicted on soldiers by the violence of war is thus concealed, which obscures the issue of how combat undermined self-esteem and the definition of personal identities.[48]

The violence that took place during the Great War gave rise to very specific taboos. One of them concerns sexuality: it can reasonably be assumed that the moral norms that were common in peacetime were weakened among soldiers cut off from the home front and exposed to front-line dangers. And yet, aside from some very rare allusions in the combatants' accounts of their wartime experiences, masturbation, prostitution and homosexuality are shrouded in the deepest silence.[49]

This silence has spread to historians. It is plausible that the participant-witnesses nearly all wanted to exorcise the actual war and reconstruct a different one that would make the trauma of their experience easier to endure. Memories – particularly traumatic memories – are always reconstructions and reworkings, and, depending on the period and expectations, the testimonies of different belligerents at different times vary greatly. Historians, trusting 'testimonies' too readily, have forgotten that, by their very nature, accounts of extreme violence are set apart, that they don't fit into the same analytical and interpretive categories as accounts of ordinary temporal events. We should give greater thought to the dreadful conditions of terror and guilt caused by violence, whether inflicted or endured, and to the ensuing consequences on the way things are recounted. As Pierre Chaunu, whose vision of the Great War is so perceptive, put it: 'Memory serves to forget.'

To forget violence, especially. Yet that is precisely what professional historians must avoid doing; they must overcome the guilt that scholars are prone to, face the testimony of combatants. This hidden aspect of the Great War should be brought to light as fully as possible and as much as it deserves to be.

2

Civilians: atrocities and occupation

Memory of the Great War has focused almost exclusively on the combatants as victims of violence and has ignored the violence suffered by the unarmed civilian population. By and large, the opposite occurred with the Second World War. Such imbalances – often magnified by historians – can easily be understood: they reflect the differences between the conflicts. To understand the Great War properly, where it fits in relation to the violence that took place in the century, the balance should be redressed. Unarmed civilians (invaded, occupied, deported) and people who laid down their weapons (prisoners of war) experienced a specific kind of torment, and to examine it will allow us better to understand the singular scar that violence leaves. It is high time that their story be told.

Let us first describe the practices and experiences to which civilian populations were subjected. From the first days of the war, horrendous acts of violence were committed against civilian populations found along the invasion routes on all fronts –Western, Eastern and Balkan – and particularly against women. Many rapes were documented in confirmed eyewitness accounts published at the time.[1] The beginnings of all wars are marked by such occurrences, and all troops have behaved in a similar fashion in enemy territory – the Russians in East Prussia and Galicia, the Germans in Belgium and northern France, the Austro-Hungarians in Serbia. But the best-known atrocities – those of the Western Front – have usually been called, with quotation marks, the 'German atrocities'.

There are two reasons for this. On the one hand, specific allegations of atrocities committed by German troops were so exploited for propaganda purposes that later, real atrocities were largely passed over in silence, and the victims themselves found it hard to speak out, or when they did, they were not heeded. On the other hand, various myths that developed during the war managed to replace the real atrocities. First, the shifting of atrocities from their reality to their mythicised unreality froze our way of seeing things, and then the misperception was subsequently reinforced by historical research and commentary. The paradox of the post-war amnesia is that the tragic experience of these atrocities, relatively well known during the conflict and used by all the belligerents to denounce the barbarity of their enemies, was buried and repressed once the war was over, both by those who had had indirect knowledge of the atrocities and by the victims themselves. As one historian has written, 'Circumstantial silences are not just the result of taboos imposed from above, they can also be the consequence of internalised feelings of inferiority, shame and anticipated discriminations.'[2]

The Balkan Front is particularly relevant since the civilian populations there were exposed to very specific forms of violence before anyone else. Some excerpts from the *Report upon the atrocities committed by the Austro-Hungarian army during the first invasion of Serbia*, by R.A. Reiss, professor of criminology at the University of Lausanne, suggest the tenor of numerous texts published during the war. Reports on the 1914 invasions and on the Armenian massacre of 1915 were, of course, among the writings used by the respective enemies for their war propaganda,[3] but that does not mean that the information they contain is erroneous or invented. The case of the Reiss report is evidence to the contrary. His study, published in English in 1916, was based on investigations conducted on the ground in September and November 1914. He interviewed Serbian witnesses and Austro-Hungarian prisoners (principally Austrians, whose testimony about their fellow soldiers he trusted, though one might suspect that some Austrian soldiers blamed Hungarian ones, since they considered them inferior, hence capable of barbarity); he examined the war equipment used, particularly the explosive or dum-dum bullets, and he photographed and published pictures of mutilated bodies. His cross-checking of the various facts makes the report virtually irrefutable, and they are unbearable in their veracity:

> Breziak consists of three villages. In this district the Austrians killed 54 persons in various ways. Most of them were disembowelled with the large sabres that were carried by four prisoners ... A.J., aged 32, eyes put out, nose and ears cut off. S.J., aged 14, nose and ears cut off ... K.K., aged 56, eyes put out, nose and ears cut off ... M.V., aged 21, violated by about 40 soldiers, genital organs cut off, her hair pushed down the vagina. She was finally disembowelled, but only died immediately after. L.P., aged 46, one hand cut off and eyes put out. One family: M.P., aged 45, breasts cut off; D.P., 18, eyes put out; S.P., aged 14, eyes put out, nose cut off; A.P., aged 7, ears cut off. They were found in a ditch, with their dog, pinioned and all tied together, including the dog.[4]

Reiss listed dozens of cases like these. We might note that facial mutilations, particularly of the eyes, were the most frequent, and done to men and women, though women were also the victims of sexual violence and mutilations of the genital organs. Anthropologists of violence have long recorded that such attacks aim at people's most human features, the face and reproductive organs. Women are victimised twice over, as human beings and as future child-bearers, and they are the first whom invaders want to humiliate. Their tortured, raped bodies become proof of the conqueror's power. Dr Reiss himself wrote:

The evidence submitted to me also proves that the manner in which the soldiers of the enemy set about killing and massacring was governed by a system. It was ... the system of extermination ... It is impossible to look upon the atrocities that have been committed as the acts of a few apaches, such as certainly may be found in every army. This might have been believed if the number of victims ran into several dozens, but when they have to be counted by the thousand, the excuse of misbehaviour on the part of isolated blackguard elements is no longer admissible ... The Austro-Hungarian soldiers, finding themselves on Serbian territory and face to face with people who had always been represented to them as barbarians, were frightened. It is from fear, lest they should be massacred themselves, that they probably perpetrated their first cruelties. But at the sight of blood, the phenomenon took place which I have often had occasion to observe: man was transformed into a bloodthirsty brute ... A true attack of collective sadism took possession of these troops ... The work of destruction was duly carried out by men who are fathers and probably kindly in private life.[5]

In incriminating 'the instincts of the wild beast, which slumber in every human being',[6] Reiss offered his version of the etiology of violence, based on man's animal instincts. But while acts of violence committed by soldiers against civilians are a perennial fact of warfare, the acts committed in the summer of 1914 greatly exceeded 'classic' rampages or what we might be tempted to describe as such. To take only European examples, when the Palatine was ravaged by Louis XIV's troops, or Spain by those of Napoleon, there were rapes, disembowelments, burned houses, and executed hostages. But in his report, Reiss mentions the desire to *exterminate*, and indeed never before had civilians been treated like this on such a scale. Admittedly, there was the desire to conquer quickly, in order to end the war in a few weeks. There was also the fear of potential snipers, particularly 'tramps, gypsies, assassins and bandits'[7]. But above all, there was the desire to enforce the law of the conqueror, a law that was not merely military or political, but stemmed from the over-whelming conviction of belonging to a superior civilisation. The Russian poet Mayakovsky expressed it in verse:

> *Near Warsaw and Grodno we flattened them,*
> *Yes we flattened and crushed the Germans,*
> *Even our women can easily kill the Prussians.*[*8]

Russian women were superior to Prussian cockroaches just as German women could more easily be raped by the invaders from the East. Russian propaganda twisted to its own advantage the terror that so-called Cossack troops had inspired in Germans for centuries.

German reactions to those same Russian atrocities, termed 'Cossack atrocities', are symptomatic of the mixed-up political and mental attitudes of the time. Even the left in Germany, which rallied to the war with some difficulty, reinforced its ad-herence to the *Burgfrieden*: the unnatural alliance of Britain and France with the Tsarist regime must be broken, and this obliga-tion justified the war against them. On all sides, nineteenth-century Social Darwinism was at work: racism, ethnic and social contempt, hygienics were activated, and then poisoned, con-sciously or unconsciously, people's ways of representing the con-flict. Once war was declared, especially during that period of anomie which is typical of invasions, acts of violence against civilians helped to free the invaders from their own fears.

Though the reality of German atrocities in Belgium can't be challenged,[†] it remains to be understood how they evolved during the conflict. Here we can turn to Marc Bloch, historian

---

[*]Mayakovsky was making a pun: the Russian word for 'cockroach' is *prusak*.
[†]John Horne, a specialist on German atrocities in Belgium and northern France, cites the facts: apart from the damage of the war itself, 5,500 Belgian civilians were executed in two months, collective executions of hostages took place, and there was arson and the deliberate destruction of buildings.[9]

of the war he himself participated in. But first he explains the technical problems for an historian:

> Unquestionably ... the historian is mortified by comparing his position with that of a reliable witness of a present event. He is as if at the rear of a column in which the news travels from the head back through the ranks. It is not a good vantage point from which to gather correct information. Not so very long ago, during a relief march at night, I saw the word passed down the length of a column in this manner: 'Look out! Shell holes to the left!' The last man received it in the form 'To the left!', took a step in that direction, and fell in.[10]

Though Bloch knew well from his own eyewitness experience how difficult it was to make sense of wartime accounts and testimonies, he wanted to make 'incorrect news' and rumours a valid object of historical study. And the stories that interested him most were the ones concerning the German atrocities in Belgium, though he hadn't personally witnessed such atrocities – whereas at the front he had either been told about atrocities by the soldiers or else had witnessed them himself. After reading his few pages of analysis, one can only regret that he didn't pursue his investigations of the subject beyond his famous blueprint article of 1921.[11]

Bloch points to two stages. First German soldiers felt terror – a terror fed by the myths they had been told, which drove them to retaliate against civilians. This was the aspect that most interested Bloch the medievalist. Then these atrocities were transformed into new myths, this time about the Germans.

> Initially, we are dealing with a collective state of mind. The German soldier who ... marches into Belgium has just been brusquely removed from his fields, his workshop, his family ... From this sudden dislocation, this unexpected severing of essential social ties, there arises a great moral confusion. The marching, the uncomfortable quarters, the sleepless nights completely exhaust

the body ... Add to this that the mind is filled with a host of old literary motifs that come in the form of unconscious memories – all those themes that the basically quite impoverished human imagination keeps trotting out, as it has done since the beginnings of time: tales of betrayals, poisonings, mutilations and women gouging the eyes of wounded warriors.[12]

Since the Other is the eternal spy, the eternal sniper, for ever ready to torture the wounded, the only protection is preventive attack. Hence the atrocities. And, Bloch concludes, 'Once error had caused blood to flow, it became established in perpetuity ... Even today most people in Germany are probably convinced that many of its soldiers fell victim to Belgian ambushes ... People readily believe what they need to believe. A story that inspired memorable acts and, especially, cruel actions is just about indestructible.'[13]

Unfortunately Bloch didn't study the other aspect of rumour and 'false news' about the atrocities: the creation of the double myth about Germans cutting off hands and crucifying their enemies. But the method he pointed to is worth pursuing: 'Incorrect news items always stem from collective representations that predate them; they merely appear to be fortuitous ... Incorrect news items are a mirror in which the "collective consciousness" contemplates its own features.'[14] Indeed, the atrocity myths were conveyed through a very lively oral tradition prior to being represented in images because people believed that censorship – whether enforced by the enemy, along the invasion and occupation routes, or enforced by one's own side, for security reasons that people accepted but also tried to subvert – had to be circumvented by eyewitness accounts.

An endless chain of rumour was set up, from those who had seen with their own eyes to those who told with their own mouths. The Belgians and French, stunned by their defeat and by the German invasion, had now to lodge and feed people whom they were determined to see only as barbarians. The destruction of churches and the execution of priests proved that the

Germans were attacking God directly. Soon stories of Belgians and Frenchmen being crucified by mirthful roughnecks proliferated, and these were accepted by public opinion as a whole. They were repeated by the writer Léon Bloy:

> You must be just as upset as I am by the clearly diabolical nature of this war. One fact out of ten thousand. On entering a cemetery in Flanders our soldiers saw a large cross. Instead of the Christ figure, a man had been crucified by the Germans … Something like this can only be explained by the entire German army being collectively possessed … It is the Lutheran abscess, coming to a head after four centuries and finally bursting.[15]

Many witnesses claimed to have met families in flight with children whose forearms were wrapped in bandages because their hands had been cut off.[16]

Later, in 1916, the kidnapping of women in the region around Lille brought the return of this fantasising yet genuinely terrorised climate. The most horrible rumours sprang up again, and drawings of women with their breasts cut off, sometimes crucified sometimes not, were legion outside the occupied zone. In Lille, word went out that women were being 'summoned to the *Kommandanture* [sic] so their breasts could be cut off'.[17] Once the war is viewed as a religious war, a crusade, it is logical enough to believe that God's innocent children and defenceless women are being specifically singled out (by real criminals) and used (in the opposing propaganda). The French and Belgians were easily convinced that the Germans, in conducting such a war, were completely devoid of moral conscience.

And these were the notions that French intellectuals set to music – sometimes in the literal sense, as in the case of Debussy, who wrote himself the lyrics for this hate-filled carol, typical of the period:

> *We no longer have a house,*
> *The enemies took everything, everything, down to our little bed,*

They burned the school and Monsieur Jesus-Christ
And the poor old man who couldn't get away ...
Of course, daddy is at war, poor mother is dead, and they didn't have to
*   see all this ...*
Santa Claus! Little Santa! Don't visit them, don't ever visit them again,
Punish them! Avenge the children of France! the little Belgians, the little
*   Serbs, and the Poles too ...*
Try to give us again our daily bread ...
Santa, listen to us, we don't have any socks,
But give victory to the children of France.[18]

For the writers, musicians and painters who composed many representations of these alleged atrocities, the Germans truly incarnated a complete rejection of morality and civilisation, a rejection that reached a demented level with the crucifixion of an enemy or the mutilation of children. Yet this wasn't orchestrated 'war propaganda' meant to persuade the French to fight against an enemy devoid of conscience and soul. These were convictions born of great suffering: seeing France 'raped' by an enemy who was believed capable of committing all manner of barbarity in order to win.

Faith in the veracity of these sordid stories remained strong among most of the French population for the entire duration of the war. It was even reinforced and given new impetus in 1918, when the Germans hit the Paris church of Saint-Gervais during the Good Friday service with 'Big Bertha', their long-range cannon. The protests about this made by the Chief Rabbi, Israël Levi, show that the sense of a shared, sacred and spiritual bond was a fundamental cement that held together the French at war.[19] Accounts of true and false atrocities aimed at France's spiritual structures 'proved' to everyone that civilisation itself was at stake, the world of God struggling against the world of the devil. France's culture of war was rooted in Judeo-Christian convictions about a world that would know how to find its redemption. Real atrocities, as well as atrocity myths, played an essential part in the implementation of this scheme.

What still needs to be understood is the complete post-war reversal of this situation. After 1918 the refusal to believe in atrocities was to become as strong as the readiness to believe in them had been in wartime. This had dramatic consequences – especially by the middle of the Second World War.

Occupation, bombardment, blockade

People living under the exceptional circumstances of military occupation went through especially violent experiences, for they lived through two wars simultaneously: that of those directly involved in the conflict, like all the soldiers, and that of a civilian population which, while protected from military operations, was not protected from the hardships of death, additional labour, and ideological pressure. Though occupied civilians under occupation experienced many tragedies, their situation was scarcely studied after the war, however much it had been exploited politically during it. They shared more or less the same fate in the history books as the invasion-period atrocities, and for the same reasons since they were, of course, on the front lines.[20]

Since the occupied zones in Eastern Europe have hardly been studied, let us take better-known examples from the *départements* in northern and north-eastern France. There we get an inside view from the personal diaries and letters of people who were trapped in the occupied zones: men who were too old or too sick to be mobilised, women and children.

The double label 'occupied/invaded' was very important throughout the war, all the more so since international law, and human rights law, had not given sufficient thought to this category of people prior to 1914. The relatively fuzzy concept of 'human rights' served as a reference, but a variable reference depending on the viewpoint – that of the victims, the jurists interested in their fate or the humanitarian and charitable organisations trying to help them. Indeed, because circumstances were new and complex, problems with terminology added to the victims' plight. This was a stumbling block that the French Minister of the Interior Louis Malvy had perceived in 1916, when he wrote to the prefects of the *départements* that had become battlefields:

> Difficulties have arisen on the subject of defining *refugees* and, consequently, their eligibility for assistance. Of course, there is no uncertainty concerning the inhabitants of localities in regions *occupied* by the enemy (who have either *moved away*, or *been repatriated from Germany*) or those in townships which, though part of the *non-invaded* or *recovered* zone, have been *evacuated* by decision of the [French] military or administrative authorities. The same is not true for inhabitants whose townships are *not occupied* by the enemy and *not evacuated* and who are in a zone that is affected in varying degrees by the bombardments ...
>
> Individual cases may have to be assessed; in other words, it must be determined if the inhabitants *who have left their homes* were in a situation that justified their departure and therefore makes them eligible for a subsidy ... These are in fact individual cases that cannot be determined *a priori* and that should be referred for assessment to the prefects in the zone of military operations; for prefects have always brought to questions of this kind the most sound and equitable solutions. In the case where there would be doubt concerning the circumstances of the interested party, it would be proper to make the most generous and humane decision.[21] [italics ours]

One notes that Malvy had to use ten different terms or circumlocutions to describe the fate of 'occupied' or 'non-occupied' people, all of whom had been forced to leave their homes. It was very clear that in the invaded battlefield territories, the front line and the home front were one and the same, all the more so when they were occupied by the enemy: every civilian then became a potential hostage risking imprisonment, deportation or forced labour. From the point of view of the occupied civilians, their situation was unambiguous: they saw themselves

as being on the front, as French citizens who had been cut off
from France – worse, cut off from France at war, a France attacked and defending itself. Day after day they encountered a
fate in which war's inherent harshness was compounded by acts
of moral and physical brutality committed by the occupying
German forces. For them, the atrocities (no quotation marks
here) were the terrible miseries, misfortunes and deaths caused
by the occupation; the war for them may have been mostly
devoid of blood and mud, but it was fraught with suffering.

The first three months of the German invasion in 1914 have
for a long time been considered the most terrible: it was then
that people experienced the abrupt transition from peace to
tragedy, from normal life to disruption and change; and this was
also the time when the atrocities took place. Then came the
static period, when French soil was occupied by the Germans,
and this lasted of course four years. And though it was much
longer, this period has been and remains less well known and less
studied than the three months of invasion in 1914. It is less
studied, first, because there was an initial refusal to consider that
the German occupation had settled in: by continuing to talk
about *invasion* the inhabitants could continue to see themselves
as an integral part of the war; for the French, English and Belgian
soldiers, it was a way of emphasising that they were still fighting
for the entire invaded territory, for the entire war zone. This is
why throughout the Great War, these territories were rarely
called 'occupied' (which they were) but 'invaded' (a temporary
condition that would vanish thanks to the Allies' victorious
advance). When Maxence van der Meersch used the word 'invasion' to describe the sufferings of the population of Lille in his
1935 novel *Invasion 14*, this was a militant, anti-German act, a way
of perpetuating in literature the wartime representations,
whereby people expressed whose side they were on through
their choice of vocabulary.

We must try to gain as clear an understanding as possible of
the suffering, trepidation, acceptance, compromises and non-
compliance of these occupied populations, who were directly

subjected to the most dreadful aspects of total war. The systematic use of the words *barbares* and *sauvages* beginning in late 1914 shows that, in the occupied zone, the concept of barbarian arose spontaneously from French contact with the Germans and owed nothing, in this particular case, to Allied propaganda or brainwashing.

If the people themselves were convinced, out of patriotism, that they were on the 'front line', it must also be said that they were treated as if this were the case. Added to the psychological trauma of the defeat, and the unbearable feeling that they were no longer among the combatants fighting for their country, people living in the occupied zones suffered real financial and economic hardship. Life was lived 'on German time', with a one- or two-hour time difference, depending on the season, from the rest of France. (The symbolism of time is very strong during the war: can a soldier's hour of death be changed? This led to an important debate in the Chamber of Deputies when clocks changed over to winter time in 1915.) The days were punctuated by the German forces' various requisitions and demands. Every move required a pass; meetings were prohibited. Armed German soldiers even stood guard during burials in cemeteries. Between the higher price of bread (and of food in general) and its poorer quality, people survived on the verge of famine. Living conditions were worse in the city than in the country, since it was virtually impossible to work there – the main businesses were closed – and it was difficult to find food. The textile and sugar industries, very productive in the north of France before 1914, suffered terribly from deliberate destruction or requisitions.

In addition to the constant decline in their material living conditions, the people experienced collective atrocities when German demands were not willingly met: forced labour for the German war effort, the taking of hostages, forced deportations and evacuations. A genuine reign of terror was instituted as of 1914 and maintained throughout the four years of conflict. This was undoubtedly a paradigm of enforced brutality, of terrorism in the primary sense, intended to instil fear in the civilian population.

The idea was to keep people in a state of shock with the systematic use of exceptional, violent measures, based on a desire to humiliate. We can trace the peaks of this violence: in their chronology they match the progress of the war itself. And this supports our hypothesis: the war against civilians, the civilians' war, was in itself a genuine war, with objectives no different from those of the war waged on the battlefield. We might even say that the civilians in the occupied regions endured a kind of siege during which military and administrative terror alternated in maintaining their subjection to the enemy.

In the regions of northern France that became battlefields in late August 1914, the inhabitants lived through the usual devastation of armed confrontations. Communication with the rest of the country immediately became almost impossible. Eventually the Belgians and the people of northern and eastern France were able to get news of military operations from German newspapers or from newspapers like the *Gazette des Ardennes* or the *Bulletin de Lille*, written in French but published by the German occupation authority. They were read primarily for their lists of prisoners; when there was no direct news of a soldier who had left in August 1914, one could hope that he would be found, captive but alive, in the published lists of prisoners. Occasionally, a plane succeeded in dropping newspapers or pamphlets over the region. This modern form of wartime communication was also used to reach soldiers. The Alsatian artist Hansi, for example, who was working for the French, made drawings for a number of pamphlets written in German urging the Alsatians in the German army to go over to the French side.

News about the progress of the war came mainly via the grapevine, prefaced by 'they say' and 'they think', and confirmed rumours, among which was information about troop movements. The news coming from Germany – particularly military communiqués – was stripped as much as possible of its propaganda content and turned inside out, before being presented as bulletins about the positions of the Allies, invariably referred to as 'we'. Catastrophes were first perceived from their sounds: the noise of cannon, particularly, was heard almost constantly. Bombs and shells fell, and planes crashed right in the middle of cities and towns, killing civilians.

In France, people believed the war required sacrifice. Hope that the war would be short was maintained for a relatively long time, at least until the summer of 1916, at which point the brutal stalemate on the Somme severely damaged morale. Statements made by civilians in the war zones, which quite accurately mirrored the general state of home-front morale during the war, show, however, that morale in the occupied zones began to flag much earlier, not in 1916 but as early as June 1915, which is not surprising given the hardship of the occupation, the food shortages and the reprisals against the population whenever there were military setbacks for the Germans. Morale continued to worsen through 1916, until the summer of 1917, when a new sense of resolve and a new spirit of victory developed.

But it was a weak, drained and devastated region that rejoined France. Most of the people still living in northern and north-eastern France in 1918 had been evacuated by force to Belgium or Germany under terrible conditions. Industries, roads and rail lines had been methodically destroyed, either during the years of occupation or during the German retreat. Industries and people had been requisitioned, either for Germany's economic benefit – machinery was crated and moved across the Rhine – or simply as a way to terrorise the population. War became total war by means of economic coercion, requisitions in money or in kind and forced labour: modernity and primitive archaism coexisted in the Great War.

Forced labour is a good illustration of this. During the first weeks of the German occupation in 1914, men, women and adolescents old enough to work were conscripted by the Germans to repair railway lines, roads and sometimes even fortifications that had been damaged in the fighting. This was contrary to the Hague Convention: no civilian is supposed to be forced to work in the war effort against his or her own country. Because of their lack of manpower, the Germans also called on volunteers to work in the fields and to revitalise certain businesses. There was a *Kommandantur* in every large town who was primarily responsible for military affairs and an *Inspecteur des Étapes* who dealt with economic affairs, but the use of military force to compel the residents to serve German interests added to the confusion. This military-administrative complication, often incomprehensible at the time, is still very difficult to unravel today: by using a double terminology like requisitioned/volunteer and military/economic, the German occupying forces intended to assert one of their war rights, since the Hague Convention entitles victorious invading forces to requisition assistance in fulfilling their occupation tasks. But the defeated, humiliated and terrified French inhabitants saw everything from the militarised angle, and their concerted mass refusal to volunteer was to confirm them in their view of the occupation: the German army soon used coercion to put insubordinates to work, first in the occupied areas and then in forced labour camps.

The crisis occurred when French civilians in June 1915 refused to work for the German war effort, specifically to make the bags that would be filled with sand and used to protect German trenches. Not surprisingly, women textile workers led the fight, refusing to 'manufacture shrouds for their children'. The mayor of the town of Halluin led the resistance movement: 'I can't forget that there are 2,500 Halluinois under the flag, including my five sons; I wouldn't want them to blame me one day for having helped make arms against them, in defiance of all patriotism or the imperatives of natural law.'[22] As in all cases of non-compliance, the occupying forces imposed sanctions: fines, hostage-taking, threats. The retaliatory measures became harsher as the German need for manpower increased. It is no coincidence that a compulsory work order to all unemployed or non-compliant workers was handed down by German headquarters on 3 October 1916, just after the battles of Verdun and the Somme.

The occupation also sheds light on the international dimension of the war. Consider the following document:

> In a complete denial of human rights, on 13 and 31 May 1915,
> French war vessels destroyed the German consulates in the
> Turkish open cities of Alexandrette and Haïfa. As reprisals against
> these attacks and in order to cover the damages to Turkish and
> German properties, a fine of 150,000 francs is levied by the
> *Kommandantur* on the cities of Roubaix and Vale.[23]

Reprisals of this sort affected civilian populations throughout the war; they were hostages to the enemy just like prisoners of war. None of the belligerent parties had any qualms about using every possible weapon to achieve their ends.

The battlefields were only one aspect – central, of course, but not unique – of the violence of this world war. For the globalisation of war signified both its spatial expansion and the spreading of its violence, indeed cruelty, to all the different places affected. The logic of the total mobilisation of states and societies meant that retaliations of the sort mentioned above would be made against civilians located thousands of miles away. The only worldwide coherence was that of violence, which swept everything along in its wake. Still, civilians were not merely unarmed victims of aggression by states and occupation armies, and they should not be viewed as such. For, having demonised the enemy, they rallied and resisted, which only worsened the cycle of repression.

Still other forms of modern brutality in warfare involving civilians directly added to the cumulative violence that so accurately defines the Great War: the bombardment of cities and economic blockade. Deliberately or accidentally, artillery barrages hit large French cities like Rheims that were close to the front. Though some of the inhabitants behind the front lines were evacuated, others continued to live in these cities, in more or less precarious conditions, sometimes scarcely able to leave their basements, for months or even years. Later on, technical advances made it possible to bomb and terrorise the people in large cities far from the front: London, where air raids began in 1915; Paris, which was hit in 1918 by the 'Kaiser Wilhelm' cannon located almost 100 kilometres away in the Saint-Gobain forest; and Cologne, bombed by English planes in 1918.

This technical turning point, which enabled belligerents to take action against civilian populations in the hope that they would rise up against their own country at war, was in some ways similar to the blockade enforced by the Allies against the Central Powers. Excessive violence was exercised on the one hand (bringing with it the shock of destruction and death far from the front), while deprivation was used on the other (there was lack of food and essential products), in the hope of provoking the same panic. The German population considered the blockade a war crime, and German propaganda denounced the intrinsic inhumanity of the French and British. This view can be substantiated: historians estimate that the blockade caused the death of a million people in Germany during the war. [24] And in some cases, there was a process of interaction between occupation, resistance and blockade: for instance, we find a shopkeeper in Roubaix, a city cut off from France, wanting to believe that he is participating in the French war effort from his little store: 'We close on Sunday afternoon. It is mostly the Germans who buy on Sunday. That way we contribute to the effects of the blockade in our small way.'[25]

Much more dramatic were the deportations of women from French territory occupied by the Germans to other *départements* or to Belgium or Germany. This took place at Easter in 1916, in the midst of the Verdun offensive, when the Germans undoubtedly found it harder and harder to obtain food supplies; these deportations were actually like forced evacuations. Why they chose to evacuate women and young girls at just that point is something that is still not understood. Was it because they were considered useless mouths to feed? Was it a way of humiliating the enemy by violating the 'honour' of their women? Witnesses emphasised the sexual role reversals and the levelling of social class distinctions suggested by these deportations: women were made to work like men; middle-class women were treated like prostitutes; girls were treated like mature women. The trauma was complete. This new threshold of terrorism probably brought with it the realisation for the French that the German occupation would not be short-lived, that the Germans were in complete control and, as conquerors, entitled to arbitrary rule. Women became choice weapons in the total war.

There was also a uniquely German aspect to these deportations of women. In early 1915, women in Berlin and other large German cities, tired of the endless food lines and rations, began demonstrations; riots broke out over butter and, later, potatoes. In most belligerent countries, women were struggling with a very high cost of living, and now they spoke a language of social justice inflected with their own conception of patriotism. Because of the effects of the blockade, German women were the first to stage such violent demonstrations.[26] Did the German authorities want to forestall similar rebellious action in the occupied territories by deporting the enemy's women? The warring German state, losing some of its legitimacy at home because of its inability to feed its own population, may perhaps have wanted not to let itself be exposed to any difficulty in the territories it was occupying. The issue of civilian food supplies was taking on a moral cast: what if the residents of Berlin – suffering from malnutrition and holding the imperial state responsible for this catastrophe as much as it was responsible for the war – should learn that the residents of Lille, under German rule, were being fed as a result of the same military bureaucracy that was so inefficient at home? The great majority of consumers in the occupied territories were women, since women were responsible for the family food supplies in France as in all of Europe at the time, and primarily because they vastly outnumbered men: no mobilised men from the area had returned to their jobs, as some workers in other parts of France had (and the north was the biggest industrial region in France after Paris).

This context provides an explanation for a measure meant specifically to terrorise women. By demonstrating to them that they would not be spared just because they were women, the Germans made it clear that the war was a total war, an all-out war, and that the occupied territories could be used as a weapon. And by deporting women from the large occupied cities to the countryside, they were also telling the women of Berlin and other German cities that the enormous effort demanded of them was not wasted. The women of Lille could be seen to be paying with their own persons for the German home front's (particularly Berlin's) restored – if limited – confidence. But it was at just this point that the Battle of Verdun, which was supposed to defeat France once and for all, became a huge nightmare stalemate, in which the German army was just as frustrated as its opponent.

Deportations and mass slaughter: the Ottoman Empire and the Armenians

The massacre of the Armenians, which, using a significant anachronism retrospectively, has been termed a genocide,* was the greatest of all war crimes committed during the Great War. Needless to say, the decision to deport more than a million men, women and children and leave them to die of hunger and exhaustion on the roads of Anatolia can't be understood without reference to the long history of violence among different ethnic groups within the Ottoman Empire and the effects of the Empire's disintegration. One must be careful to assess the distinctive nature of this most important mass slaughter of the Great War, but one must also include it in the general picture of war violence against civilians.

While massacres of this kind had occurred in the 1890s, this one took place during a world war that provided the Young Turks with the chance to exploit the national trauma that Turkey had

---

*The word *genocide* was coined in 1944 from a bizarre Greco-Latin root by the American lawyer Raphael Lemkin as a way of describing the extermination of European Jewry, for which – wanting to preserve its uniqueness – Anglo-Saxon historians now use the term Holocaust and the French, Shoah.

endured in the Balkan wars in order to settle the national question and establish frontiers that would contain, to the north, what they saw as the threat from Russia. The Allied landing at the Dardanelles intensified this feeling, and there was a fear that the enemies from abroad, the English and the French, who were allies of Russia, would side with the enemy at home, the Armenians. The first arrests and the assassination of prominent Armenians took place on the night of 25 April 1915, the night of the Gallipoli landing. The effort on the part of the Allies – it was Winston Churchill's idea – to break the stalemate on the Western Front by means of an indirect offensive in Turkey turned into a military disaster in the Dardanelles and a horrendous tragedy for the Armenians. Seen as potential traitors because they were 'allied' with Armenians living in the hated Russian Empire, the Armenians in the Ottoman Empire had to be isolated; paradoxically, the Turkish authorities – or at least some of them – claimed that the aim of the measure was to ensure the safety of the Armenian community, as is suggested, for example, by a strange public notice posted in Trebizond at the time of the deportations:

> Our fellow citizens, the Armenians, who make up one of the races of the Ottoman Empire, have for years adopted, at the instigation of foreigners, many perfidious ideas that are upsetting public order; they have provoked bloody conflicts … Moreover, since they have dared to join their 'long-time enemy' [Russia] and the enemies presently at war with our empire, our government has no choice but to take extraordinary measures and make sacrifices, for the maintenance of order and the security of the country, as well as for the well-being and preservation of the Armenian community. Consequently, as a measure that will be enforced for the duration of the war, the Armenians will be sent to destinations prepared to that effect within the *vilayets*, and all Ottomans are strictly enjoined to obey the following orders:
>
> 1 All Armenians, with the exception of the sick, are obliged to leave within five days of this proclamation, by villages or quarters, and under the escort of the gendarmerie.

2 Though they are free to carry with them on their journey
the transportable items of property that they wish to have, they
are forbidden to sell their lands and their other effects, or to leave
the latter here and there with other people, because their exile is
only temporary. [27]

The exile was not temporary. Death awaited most of the deported Armenians. No food supplies for their exodus had been
planned along the way, and those who could not keep moving
were systematically killed. One Armenian soldier, disarmed like
many of his compatriots in 1915 and employed in the Engineers,
recounted a massacre he witnessed before escaping to Russia.
His testimony was published in anti-Ottoman documents, of
course, but the precise details, checked against German and
American sources, leave no doubt as to the horrifying truth of
his account. Moreover, as it was published in 1917, it can't have
been influenced by later descriptions of massacres and graves
filled with civilian corpses:

In the month of July 1915, one day we saw a long convoy of our
Armenian compatriots led by policemen. They numbered at least
5,000, mostly women, the elderly and children ... The following
day our company was ordered to cross the mountain, and we
were instructed not to forget our shovels and pickaxes ... As soon
as we were near the procession, we saw a dense crowd; it was the
deported Armenians whom we had seen the day before, but now
they were surrounded by Turkish and Kurdish 'brigands' ... I
haven't got the patience or the strength to describe that orgy of
blood, for what went on before our eyes was horrible. There was
carnage everywhere, dreadful pursuit, blood everywhere ...
Several young and pretty Armenian girls, bound together, whom
the leaders had chosen for their harem, watched the carnage like
us, petrified and wild-eyed. We were ordered to bury the corpses
immediately and to eliminate the traces of blood ... We dug large
graves, but only a metre deep, and laid down the corpses of
Armenian soldiers dressed like us. These unfortunate men had

dug graves for other victims a few days earlier and they were massacred in turn.[28]

There was no concentration camp at the end of the journey for those who were strong enough to walk for days on end and who survived the deportation. The barren, desert land closed in on them like a death sentence. Women, children, old people, so-called subversive elements opposed to the victory of Turkey in the all-out war, had to perish. As for their land and their homes, they would be used by the Turks and the Kurds who were re-warded for their loyal services to the nation.

How did the various belligerent parties react to this un-precedented aggression aimed at an entire people? After all, it was the war that had triggered this mass slaughter; the Ottoman Empire's allies and enemies were defined in relation to the war. Germany had difficulty accepting the accounts of events that had been witnessed by its observers along the deportation roads, but it could not repudiate an ally it truly needed, as was clear from the statement made by its Under-Secretary of State for Foreign Affairs, Alfred Zimmermann (he of the famous telegram instructing his ambassador in Mexico to work for an alliance with Mexico and Japan against the United States): 'A break with Turkey over the Armenian question is not deemed opportune. Admittedly, it is regrettable that these innocent people should suffer from the Turkish measures. But the Armenians, after all, are not so close to us as our own sons and brothers, whose bloody struggle and sacrifice in France and Russia are indirectly assisted by the military support of the Turks.'[29] In fact, the Germans were convinced that Russian atrocities in the German part of Poland and in Galicia, where Jews had been deported to Russia, were just as dreadful if not worse. Did this not prove that the Russians – the Armenians' 'protectors' – were encouraging them in be-trayal and rebellion, and did this not suggest that to deport them far from the armed operations was a justified punishment?

From the point of view of the Alliance, things were identical but reversed. On 24 May, a telegram was sent by the British,

French and Russian Ministers of Foreign Affairs to Constantinople: 'Faced with Turkey's new crimes against humanity and civilisation, the Allied governments wish to make it known publicly to the Sublime Porte that they will hold the members of the Ottoman government personally responsible, as well as those among its agents who might be implicated in such massacres.' They were, after all, at war with the Ottoman Empire, and they wanted it known that once again the enemy was conducting the war in defiance of all the rules of 'humanity and civilisation'. Also, it was tempting to use the massacres to show the need for a strong British and French presence in the Near East, though the two allied and friendly powers were in fierce competition in colonial matters there. 'Protecting' Armenians and denouncing the crimes perpetrated against them served a dual purpose: it permitted the planning for and justification of strategic Allied objectives in the region; and it allowed them to condemn the barbarity of the Germans and their allies. The previous massacres in the Ottoman Empire (in 1894-6, for example), the German atrocities in Belgium and northern France in 1914, the deportations of 1915 were all part of the same fabric:

> The Turks are clearly worthy allies of the slaughterers in Belgium. The Germans' methods against the unfortunate population in the Liège region in August 1914 were the same as the Muslim methods against the Armenians. And understandably, the Allied victories awakened the same hopes in both East and West: hope of deliverance, hope that the martyred people would escape the horrors of this dreadful barbarity.[30]

In 1916, Allied newspapers commonly linked the deportations of the women of Lille and of Armenia. For example, caricatures showed Teutonic brutes dragging women and children away or taking aim at them; in one drawing, we see a soldier with a spiked helmet saying of their French captives: 'They're complaining. But what would they say if they were in Armenia?'[31]

Yet as soon as aid had to be extended to the victims, world public opinion, with very few exceptions, lost interest in the issue. From 1915 and through the 1920s, secrecy, denial and failure to prosecute the guilty were at the heart of the extermination enterprise. This is what can be called the internal dynamic of impunity: denial of the truth is believed, and efforts to fight against amnesia are unavailing. (There existed an entire 'literature on the catastrophe' in Armenian in the 1920s and 1930s, but who bothered to read it?) Paradoxically, it was in Germany, partly because of its military alliance with Turkey, that most questions were raised about what had happened to the Armenians. Missionaries – notably Johannes Lepsius – recounted what they had witnessed. Yet when the novelist Franz Werfel wrote his *Forty Days of Musa Dagh* in the 1930s, he was attacked in a Nazi periodical as a propagandist 'of the so-called Turkish horrors perpetrated against the Armenians'.[32]

Hitler, as early as 1931, linked his desire for a new order and for living space, to which he believed the Germans were entitled, to the deportation of whole populations: 'Everywhere, people await a new world order. We intend to introduce a major repopulation policy ... Think of the biblical deportations and the massacres in the Middle Ages ... and remember the extermination of the Armenians.'[33] And by 1939, the Führer could legitimately mock the Europeans' failing memory of the massacre of 1915: "After all, who still talks about the annihilation of the Armenians today?'[34] But as for the other consequences of the 1914–18 experience of total war – the fate of the once occupied territories and of the former prisoners – even Hitler no longer remembered anything about them. The 1920s and 1930s witnessed a calamitous failure of humanitarian policies towards all the new civilian victims of 'peace' – the Greek and Turkish refugees, the Armenians and Russians, the Germans and Austrians.[35] The increasing banality of the brutality that the Great War had induced, the internalising of violence which had enabled people to accept even its most cataclysmic consequences and accept them permanently, played no small part in this failure.

3

The camp phenomenon: the internment of civilians and military prisoners

The various internment systems used during the Great War are a key to understanding what was new about the conflict. Knocking men out of combat in order to weaken the adversary is the aim of all wars, and there was nothing new about taking prisoners. But from the late nineteenth century, war increasingly involved civilians in its violence, and internment camps were part of this development.

It is worth noting that particularly violent and cruel atrocities were committed during the colonial wars of nineteenth century. Was it simply that the Great War perpetuated them in Europe?[1] It was probably the Spanish General Weyler who 'invented' internment camps during the all-out war he waged against the Cubans in 1896–7. He combined pillage and the systematic destruction of property and cultures with what he called the 're-concentration' of civilians, and he caused thousands of deaths. Later the British used the same measures against the

Boers in South Africa.[2] The camps of the Great War took up where the two colonial episodes left off. People were 'concentrated', assembled and crowded together, preferably behind a barbed-wire fence or stockade, so they could be supervised and punished. In these 'concentrations', soon called 'concentration camps', men, women, children and old people were trapped by the war, imprisoned and mixed with common-law criminals.

But the concentration-camp-like phenomenon is not the same as a concentration-camp system.[3] In the former case the camps were usually improvised, the haphazard consequence of totalized war, which led to the imprisonment of all enemies, whether captured on the battlefield or in areas the troops travelled through or occupied. And though the end of the war should logically have brought about the end of internment and the release of these civilian or military prisoners, this didn't actually happen, or at least not for all of them. The Russian *bolsheviki*, who were taken to East Prussia by the German conquerors after the Treaty of Brest-Litovsk in early 1918, were a typical example of such methods. As for military prisoners, who were used as bargaining chips during different phases of the war, they were still prisoners after the armistice on 11 November 1918, at least those who had been on the defeated side. After the Peace of Versailles, the German war prisoners served as a guarantee that their country would ratify its own punishment as meted out at Versailles.

Once we recognise that most of the soldiers in the Great War were really civilians in uniform – the great majority of them, in any case, except for career officers – we can also see that the world of the camps was primarily a world of civilians, whom one can divide into two categories. One, the military prisoners, or civilian-military so to speak, kept their strong ties to the home front, where their real lives were. When soldiers became prisoners, their military status was transformed as evidenced both physically and symbolically by their ever more tattered uniforms. For many of these men, their exposure to army life had been very brief; this was especially true of the soldiers captured *en masse* in 1914 during the very first weeks or months of the war. But no matter how they showed loyalty once they were imprisoned, whether through vehement recriminations or painful apathy, they remained determined and wholehearted members of a fighting nation.

The other category was that of civilians caught up in the war simply because of their geographical location. They were on the path of the conflict and swept into it; their imprisonment was deemed necessary as part of their captors' war effort. Such civilians were divided in the internment camps into various groups, either mixed with or separate from the military prisoners. No international convention had foreseen the problem of civilian prisoners, not to mention that of civilian prisoners on occupied territory or that of those who were deported and sent to forced labour. These civilian prisoners actually formed two very distinct entities.

The first group consisted of civilians interned in enemy country, whether or not they were eligible for the draft (men between the ages of eighteen and forty-five). Such people could be found worldwide: civilians from enemy countries were interned not only in the belligerent countries but in their colonies. Geographically, the most extreme cases were, for example, Germans interned in Australia or Belgians in German Africa.[4] Paradoxically, detention in internment or 'concentration' camps saved male prisoners from being killed at the front. A German interned as an enemy alien in the Vendée or a Frenchman interned in Saxony did not have to fear dying at Verdun. Similarly, draft-eligible civilian prisoners were, like military prisoners, protected from death in combat by having been captured.

The second category of civilian prisoners, and by far the largest, included all those who were captured by invading or occupying armies, who in different ways were subjected to internment and stripped of their rights – whether by being isolated from their compatriots or deported to concentration camps or forced to do labour. Depending on the country, anywhere from hundreds to hundreds of thousands of Belgians, French, Russians, Serbs, Romanians, Italians and Germans suffered this fate in Europe and in its colonies. According to the International Committee of the Red Cross, about 100,000 Belgians and French were deported to Germany and about the same number of Germans were deported to Russia. The number of Serbs deported to Austria, Hungary and Bulgaria may have been even greater.

A sub-group of occupied or interned civilians were repatriated from invaded areas voluntarily or by force; they ended up in their own country, but far from their native regions and cut off from their families, who had been left behind. They were often regarded as civilian prisoners, which they were to some extent – in some respect the occupied territories were like huge internment camps – but since they didn't have prisoner status, they didn't appear on the lists of civilian prisoners sporadically furnished by the warring states.

The operations of the Holzminden internment camp allow us to understand how things worked. This camp was created for foreign nationals from enemy countries living in Germany in August 1914. Throughout the entire war, it received deportees from German-occupied territories in Belgium, France and Russia, who were sent to the camp either to punish them for resistant activity or in reprisal, as hostages. The living quarters and activities were like those of prisoner-of-war camps. But the great difference was that women and even a number of children were mixed with the men, though they had separate living quarters. The paradox could not have been greater: though women and children didn't wear uniforms, yet they shared the same fate as men; they hardly had waged war, yet they were the perfect targets in a total war. Once the Germans decided on forced deportation and evacuation of civilians, their authorities also presumed that the civilian camps needn't differ from the military ones. In fact, Red Cross representatives showed no great indignation over this and listed them along with the others without comment.

The story of what happened to the civilian prisoners captured during the invasion period, between August and September 1914, gives us an idea of the extraordinary shock felt by men and women who were suddenly exposed to a war for which they were unprepared. They saw themselves as ordinary civilians, but the enemy soldiers saw them as snipers, or potential ones. Here we have two diametrically opposed systems of representation, both born of hatred and fear of the enemy. Each side had a new role to play. Here were civilians who had recently become sol- diers and were wearing uniforms; perhaps it was logical that they should see the inhabitants of the conquered country as soldiers of another kind. Civilians were intermediaries in the war, and their conflicting representations caused unprecedented acts of violence. Culturally, the war was a total war from the very beginning.

The fate of the civilian prisoners varied. Some spent the entire war in captivity. Their plight can be followed in the Vatican archives, where one finds the appeals of their families, which the Holy See later forwarded to the various belligerent countries and which were then returned to Rome:

> Holy Father,
> Prostrate at the feet of your Holiness I dare implore your paternal
> benevolence for my unfortunate husband taken as a civilian
> prisoner by the Germans in the month of September 1914. The
> dreadful war has taken everything from us. One of my brothers
> was killed, the other is missing, our farm now is nothing but a
> heap of ruins and my husband has been a prisoner in
> Holzminden for three years. Convinced that your Holiness will
> deign to take pity on the anguish of a suffering wife, I venture to
> request your paternal benediction.[5]

When the occupation of Belgium and the war zones in northern France became permanent, all the inhabitants were trapped in captivity. The Western Front is a good illustration of all the problems and paradoxes: for Germany, not only did the war effort there require substantial manpower at a time when all able-bodied men were at the front, but the populations in the territories it occupied had to be fed. Deportation and forced labour of requisitioned Belgians and French allowed Germany to meet this double need – providing manpower, mostly for engineering work near the front, and reducing the population of the large towns, where the gradual ending of all activity had created unemployment and where people needed subsidised aid. Coercion and punishment combined with the practical requirements of war.

With the Zivilarbeiter Bataillonen (ZAB), in 1916 the Germans created a new category of civilian prisoner who was also a forced labourer. His 'uniform' was as simple as could be: a red armband,* which indicated that the wearer was a member of a workers' army battalion.[6] Beginning in 1916, the red armbands, as they were called, were no longer employed on the spot but deported to work camps in occupied areas of France and Belgium.

They were blackmailed in a particularly odious manner. Either they voluntarily agreed to work for the Germans, in which case their situation was one of 'free' salaried employees who were entitled to leaves and to contact with their relatives; or they refused, in which case they were rounded up and subjected to compulsory labour. In the words of one German officer: 'The battalion worker is quartered in barracks. The battalion worker is always supervised in his work, his freedom is thus severely limited ... Choose between the independent and happy life of a free worker or the monotonous, isolated life of the battalion worker.'[7] Since most mayors refused to hand over lists of their town's unemployed, the Germans simply rounded up men in the streets and deported them. These were primarily boys who were too young by a few months or years to have been drafted in 1914, but were now old enough to be conscripted. But they were no longer allowed to respond to their patriotic duty:

*Occasionally, other civilians, for example municipal councillors in occupied territories, had to wear white armbands. These colour-coded armbands, still relatively unsophisticated in 1914–18, were a step in the organisation of a concentration-camp system.

Monsieur le Préfet,

Forgive me for writing to you but I am very distressed by what is happening to me.

I am 21 years old, I am therefore under military obligation, and knowing this the town hall of Lomme sent me an invitation to work for the Germans and I was told it was compulsory.

What should I do? The town hall is forcing me to go, yet they know that's not my duty, and I'm sure you will be just as surprised as me that Frenchmen are sending Frenchmen to work for the enemies. I'd be only too pleased to fight for my country, but working against my brothers makes me weep with rage. Instead of following the example of the mayor of Lille, the Lomme administrators are not energetic enough, it's as though they were afraid, instead of standing up to things. They're all doing their best so we will work. Consider the dreadful consequences for me if I work, and consider the mistake of the Lomme town hall. Monsieur le Préfet, give me advice please, I'll listen to you, for my honour as a Frenchman is worth more than any kind of work for the enemy.

In ending my letter, I beg you to believe, Monsieur le Préfet, in my entire devotion to our dear country, France.[8]

From August 1914 until October 1918, as a war map of the Western Front shows, the occupied territories were at the heart of the German war effort. And the civilian prisoners, at the centre of this heart, were exposed to a concentration-camp life – extremely long work hours, harsh living conditions, bad nutrition, long expeditions, all under military surveillance. Since they had been called up to work but also to help in getting food to occupied towns, feeding the red armbands as much as the German soldiers was out of the question. And since the German soldiers' rations were already minimal, given the dreadful conditions of the blockade, it is easy to believe the prisoners' complaints about their rations and their physical state (most of them were growing adolescents).

The civilian populations were aware of the fate of these red armband prisoners. They saw them as they went by. Sporadically, some families received news and were given the right to send parcels. But the constant movement of most of the red armbands made communication with them or shipping parcels to them extremely difficult; moreover, their families were themselves so destitute that they could hardly be of much help. We know how difficult it was to keep an exact count of the number of deaths throughout the war, even though they were duly inscribed on lists. Understandably, the haphazard organisation of this forced labour, from round-ups or summons issued by town halls into both numbered and unnumbered battalions, did not lead to precise tallies. The imprecision fed alarmist rumours – and the worst of them turned out to be true, unfortunately.

The civilian concentration camps (in the old sense of the term) were particularly well-adapted to meet the needs of the occupying forces: they could keep the rounded up *Zivilarbeiter* and *Zwangsarbeiter* under home guard. Thus the red armbands became double prisoners: there was the immense prison of the areas under military occupation, and within that prison was the prison of the camp, where they were further cut off from their world – from family, region and homeland. Moreover, for the red armbands as for some military prisoners, the camp itself often brought them back into the war, for they were put to work just behind the front lines, where they were threatened by shells fired by their own compatriots; they had become human shields, pathetic defensive weapons in the huge stalemate in which millions of men on both sides of the conflict were caught up. Since their work consisted mainly of digging and reinforcing second-line trenches on the soil of their own country and for the benefit of the enemy, it's not hard to see that their position was morally unbearable. In this Great War defending French soil, not only had they been mobilised in spite of their being civilians, but as prisoners they were made to work against the interests of their 'blood' and 'soil'. 'We have had to build trenches to kill our fathers, our brothers, our cousins,'[9] they said.

The enumeration of family members is revealing here: these

were very young men whose world up to then had revolved around their families and close relatives; now these boys were suddenly at the front. Even though they were a short distance away from the front lines, repairing railway lines and roads, they were nonetheless involved in the logistics of war, helping the occupiers maintain good communications between the front and rear. A deeply moving letter written by a young woman prisoner to her husband completes the picture:

22 July 17

Dear Lucien,

I'm surprised by your silence I havent received news since your cards of 3 and 11 March, yet I would be very happy to get some for I miss you a lot and regardless of my courage and my resignation I don't know if I can stand this suffering of being separated from the whole family as we are if I knew where my little children and my parents are I'd take courage more easily. In spite of everything I'm in good health and so is my little Henri and I hope my letter will find you well also, which is what we must ask for in our sad situation. Rosa is fine still works outside she sends you her greetings but still doesn't know about her misfortune she received another card this week from your parents they sent back to non-occupied France ... all these upheavals of all these families, Rosa doesn't know where Raymond is either.

Dear Lucien if you can try to look into the fate of our poor little children, because for myself I can't and you will write me but write me always as much as possible, that will be a very precious consolation ... I feel like everyone is abandoning me, though, dear husband we must not get too discouraged for we're still needed on earth to bring up our little family. I hope though that there will be an end and that we will all be reunited to live happier days after so many cruel ordeals we certainly deserve to I don't have much else to tell you hello from my comrades to cousin Désiré and to you I hope you are still together.

A thousand loving kisses from afar while waiting to kiss each other close up what a happy day, dear Lucien, but when ... let's hope for God's clemency. Yours for life.

Eugénie Broyart.

(Above all, send me good news from you soon, I forget to tell you I haven't yet received news of the plea for pardon that I asked for I hope).[10]

The young woman who wrote this letter was in an impossible situation. She was a civilian prisoner in a camp in Limburg, and her husband was a civilian prisoner in Battalion 2 of the armbands, probably in an occupied zone in northern France; they did not know what had happened to their children. The Limburg camp was normally a camp for military prisoners, but it ended up housing a few civilians as well, including women and children, the result of chaotic improvisation rather than planning.

War is always, in a basic sense, a process of 'deconstruction' since soldiers are separated from the rest of society and from their families, and since they risk injury and death. Heroism can compensate for the sufferings in part, when there is consent to join the conflict. But here the predicament was different, for both wife and husband were prisoners, completely cut off from their customary world and faced with the newness of a radically different one. How could the wife put together the broken pieces of her identity, especially since she was completely isolated and unaware that on other, different levels her marginal situation was being exploited and used as an anti-German argument by her French compatriots? As an individual persecuted by the new conditions of war, she felt completely alone, as indeed she was. As the (involuntary) member of a group, her great misfortune made her useful for the French propaganda effort against Germany. Unawares, she had been pushed into the middle of the conflict and absorbed into total war.

The same paradox applies to the many military prisoners who were captured during the invasion phase of the war in 1914 and, later, in all the great battles of attrition. Moreover, throughout the four years of conflict, raids were organised with the specific aim of capturing prisoners for interrogation or, conversely, to kill them on the spot, either out of necessity or to terrorise the enemy.[11] This dialectic of terror and exploitation was reproduced in the prisoner camps. After improvising for the first few months, during which time chaos led to human waste, the belligerent states, 'with their legitimate right to violence',[12] grasped that their prisoners constituted a serviceable reserve army that could be put to work replacing the men at the front, so after initially packing the men into jails, they set up organised camps and work detachments.

The chronology of imprisonment follows that of the war: exile, loss of liberty, labour and hunger in the blockaded nations which could not feed them* – these were the many forms of suffering that were aggravated by the duration of internment and by the acts of reprisal waged on the human pawns. In a way, the camp prisoners knew all about total war. They experienced the worst very quickly, indeed while they were being transported to their internment – in cattle cars which took days to reach their destination and in which wounded and able-bodied men, soldiers and civilians, were all piled in together. 'We have the dreadful feeling that they'll never take us out of this wagon, that we've been *forgotten*,' wrote André Warnod, a friend of Blaise Cendrars.[13]

The prisoners experienced this ordeal as a double exile, an exile far from their country and far from their country *at war*. For them, the predicament of imprisonment entailed shame, a feeling of being abandoned and a constant misery. They were condemned to outcast status both objectively and subjectively; the message sent by the authorities – all prisoners are cowards and potential deserters – was completely internalised by the men themselves. Being 'deprived' of the war was being deprived of the whole meaning of life between 1914 and 1918, and they un-

---

*The camps of the Central Powers and Russia were particularly affected by food shortages. While the French and the English sent food parcels to their relatives, the other belligerent parties did not. Many Romanians and Italians literally died of hunger.

derwent increasing physical and mental suffering. They had lost the sense of material and emotional comfort to which they were accustomed, the feeling of continuity with their past. Theirs was an uprooting that could only have meaning if it was provisional, if there would be a future elsewhere. But the continuance of the war, and hence of captivity, quashed even the most tenacious hopes, the more so since real or false news of the captors' victories was deliberately spread within the camps as propaganda.

Were they able to adapt to what was demanded of them or not? The prisoners had to deal with men who had temporarily (they hoped) become their conquerors, and they had to live according to the laws of the enemy state, so it is difficult to answer the question with precision. Officers, or prisoners with special status such as physicians, health-care workers and clergy, were the ones who wrote most about their fate – but for the historian this poses a problem: such people, given their status or cultural background, were best equipped to testify as to their conditions, but they were imprisoned in camps with better facilities and they sometimes even benefited from the presence of orderlies, so their fate was usually enviable compared to that of simple soldiers. Prisoners tended to meet civilians, either because they worked for them (on farms) or with them (in factories or mines). Soldiers on the front nearly always loathed the enemy, though they might respect a specific adversary because he seemed close, just on the other side of the line. Prisoners in permanent contact with their guardians probably made the same distinction: when language proficiency allowed for it, they formed relationships with the commanding officers of their camps and, especially, with their regular guards. Captain Charles de Gaulle, a prisoner as of March 1916, noticed this paradox, and he also pointed out that those guards were never the men who had distinguished themselves on the battlefield by capturing the prisoners.[14]

Neutral agencies, particularly the Red Cross, acted like a protective ring – sometimes from a distance, in Geneva, Rome, Madrid or Washington, sometimes from close quarters, as when their delegates visited the camps. For the military authorities and captor states, prisoners were hostages or bargaining chips. But the jailers knew they had to respect the 'rules of war' and the conventions their nations had ratified, first and foremost the Geneva Convention. This led to contradictions in both the treatment of prisoners inside the camps and in the perceptions that civilians had of them – contradictions that added to the prisoners' suffering. One can understand that the military authorities who were pursuing the war – with so much difficulty – wanted to use every possible weapon against their foes, including prisoners. As for the home populations, the presence of war prisoners among them made them discover a 'misfortune of war' they themselves hadn't experienced at first hand. In Germany, for example, civilians came to look at the prisoners as a mirror image of their country's strength. The 100 labour camps spread throughout Germany brought some of the war home; it meant rubbing shoulders with the enemy, but an unarmed and pitiful enemy. The camps delineated a new and different map of the war, with a front line at home that was very different from the confrontation on the battlefield.

In the principal camps, far from the often harsh conditions of the Kommandos, or work detachments, the prisoners felt crushed and despondent; they also suffered from the monotony of a life with very limited prospects, and they had no desire to re-create a new life for themselves. Real life was elsewhere: it was life at war, war on their home soil. So they tried to keep busy, and joining a group to take part in intellectual, manual or artistic activities or simply to play games was one way of re-creating at least a social life; it also made them feel they weren't just wasting their time in confinement. All kinds of classes were organised, as well as parties, plays, horticultural events, lectures, athletic contests, literary discussions, libraries, games of charade, macramé, parlour games, orchestras, and so on. Professional services were offered by watchmakers, hairdressers, photographers and typographers who could print newspapers. There were competitions to manufacture objects and prizes awarded for making household utensils like outdoor cooking devices or permanent mousetraps. These give a good idea of both the prisoners' craftsmanship and their wish to improve their material and psychological conditions, also of their desire to combat the boredom of endless stretches of time in prison (contrasted with the short time they had actively spent at war). Probably some among them saw the camps as preserving them from the trenches – but they were very few during the war; stories about such prisoners were re-written later. The case of Roger Salengro is significant: a prisoner and patriot from northern France, he published a newspaper in his internment camp and called for resistance against the Germans; post-war calumnies about how easily he had been captured and how contented he was as prisoner led him to commit suicide in 1936.

Torn between rejection of the camp, in other words, rejection of their personal defeat and capture, and the desire to make do with their unhappy circumstances and improve their living conditions as much as possible, the prisoners often fell into what they called 'the doldrums'. For some, especially as the years wore on, this depression changed into a 'barbed-wire psychosis', a non-acceptance of imprisonment that gradually became a genuine psychological illness caused by lack of freedom and separation from family and country.

Thus did the physical limits of the camps become a metaphor for men's imprisonment and double dispossession – of their lives prior to 1914 and, above all, of the real life of patriotic combat in 1914–18. Their feelings are very eloquently expressed by Captain de Gaulle: when he was wounded and captured, he knew that the hell of combat was behind him, and that was precisely what he found unendurable:

> A grief that will end only with my life engulfs me now more completely than ever and I don't think I shall ever experience one so deep and bitter. To be as completely and irremediably useless as I am while we are going through these times, for a person like me who is made for action, and, worse, to be so in the

situation where I find myself, which for a man and a soldier is the most cruel imaginable! Excuse me for having the weakness to complain. It's completely useless, isn't it? Believe me, this merely strengthens my resolve.[15]

That Captain de Gaulle, like the great majority of prisoners, longed to escape makes sense. For escape meant returning to the bosom of the war, moving from the sidelines to the centre. Very few managed it themselves, but in one way or the other all prisoners participated in their comrades' escape attempts.

Although we do not always agree with the methodology of the British historian Niall Ferguson[16] his assumptions about prisoners of war seem to be correct. He argues that it was because of the men's great fear of becoming prisoners that mass surrenders didn't take place – a fear fed by the (all too real) summary executions on the battlefield or by the tales of repatriated aid workers or escaped prisoners, which naturally elaborated on the worst moments of their captivity and which were widely circulated by the propaganda organs. So, to avoid captivity, most soldiers fought to the death. And when they preferred prisoner status, regardless of its hazards, to the continuation of combat, it was because they felt their side had already lost the war. This was the case in Italy at the time of the disastrous Battle of Caporetto, in which the Italians lost 300,000 men, and in Russia in 1917; to a lesser but significant extent it was also true of the German army in late summer 1918.

Forced displacements and reprisals

Compulsory evacuations are another good example of the paradox of the situation in which societies can find themselves during periods of unrelenting national warfare. Finding it impossible to feed the entire occupied civilian population, and with neutral organisations providing only limited help, military authorities sometimes made the decision to evacuate, for a fee, all

civilians who wished to leave and who could pay, and to evacuate the destitute by force. In occupied France, this was how the
Germans economised on their resources and got rid of useless
mouths to feed (bedridden elderly people in hospices, young
children and very poor families). They kept those who could
work, of course. Forced evacuations and detachments of red
armbands had the same function: French civilians had to take
part in the Germans' local war effort or disappear.

It is quite easy to understand the protests of the occupied
population against these evacuations, though at first one might
imagine they would have been happy to be sent away. In spite of
their great suffering, they refused to be evacuated, and this was
partly out of patriotism, partly out of fear of the looting they
were sure would occur once they were not there to guard their
possessions. This is why it is so difficult to make a distinction
between evacuations and deportations.

Travelling conditions, usually in cattle cars, were unpleasant
in both cases. For the deported, there was a labour or disciplinary
camp at the end of the trip, whereas evacuated civilians at least
had the hope of first getting to Switzerland or the Netherlands
and then returning to France. The French government protested
energetically against the compulsory evacuations of indigent
civilians from the occupied eastern and northern *départements*
but not without a certain cynicism; given their physical state
prior to the long trip in cattle cars through Switzerland and
Germany, these evacuees would have been of no use in the war
effort, indeed if they had been, the Germans would never have
allowed them to leave. So it was easy on the one hand to accuse
the German enemy of cruelty while on the other simultaneously
letting the French on the home front call these exhausted fellow
citizens, whose strange journey they didn't understand, 'Boches
of the North'.

This rejection of refugees appears somewhat contradictory:
they were accused of taking jobs away from their hosts, and yet
there was a glaring lack of manpower throughout the war. True,
exhausted women and elderly people inevitably went on the

dole, mostly at the expense of municipalities, whose resources were tight because of the draft. Thus the compulsory evacuees illustrate the complexity of the dilemma: though the enemies were 'executioners' who dislocated local French populations, their cruelty did not make the French as a whole (apart from a few generous exceptions) any more welcoming to those of their compatriots who had been chased from their home by the war.

With the widespread occurrence of reprisals against military prisoners, civilian prisoners and forced labourers, several ages of warfare were in effect going on simultaneously: there was a regression towards the most archaic methods, including quasi-slavery, taking place alongside the use of the latest, most modern techniques of coercion. 'Reprisals! That's the big word! That's the golden calf, the only one that the people in arms worship in common,' wrote an anonymous worker for the Red Cross in 1915:

> But who can't see that it's sophism, a childish argument? Does the
> evil that others commit in any way excuse the evil we commit?
> ... Laws without sanctions are just scraps of paper, we Swiss have
> the right to protest against all the violations ... And we shall do
> so until the conscience of the world rises up and generates,
> through the fertile indignation aroused by these protests, a new
> force in the service of law.[17]

In the camps, punishments were meant to destroy individual resistance, while reprisals and collective punishments were intended to put pressure on the opposing state. All the belligerents, alleging different motives, used these tactics at one time or another – the ill-treatment of prisoners, poor detention facilities and/or food, prisoners used as human shields in the combat zone or on hospital ships. And of course this led to counter-reprisals. Thus civilian and military prisoners were among the first victims in the vicious cycle of total war.

Reprisals ran the whole gamut. Some were benign – though they could have devastating psychological consequences – like the suspension of mail and packages, or food restrictions; others were not, like the bombing of military hospitals near the front, or the torpedoing of hospital ships. Reprisals led to counter-reprisals, complaints to counter-complaints, abuses to counter-abuses – in other words, there were genuine terrorist chain reactions. The first victims of these reprisals were the wounded, who had escaped death on the battlefield, as well as nurses and physicians; the second group of victims were the prisoners.

The Red Cross made many appeals to the belligerent parties and to the neutral countries about reprisals against prisoners. They denounced the systematic recourse to 'an eye for an eye … a barbarian rashness motivated by revenge, for which defenceless innocent people pay the price … War is a terrible enough scourge in itself for other evils not to be added to it by inhuman measures and pointless harshness.'[18] In vain.

An extreme form of reprisal was to send prisoners immediately behind the front lines, for this represented the culmination of the horror of their condition. And this was precisely where a large number of forced labourers were posted, required to work on reinforcing enemy trenches and burying the enemy dead. For the military prisoners sent to those same areas, who had exchanged the status of combatant for that of non-combatant (the first stage in dishonour), and, through their capture, been denied the chance to defend their own soil and their dead, once the focus of their commitment and consent, the dreadful situation they were now placed in had turned everything upside down: French soil was now enemy soil, and the enemy dead were now the bodies they were forced to care for. For men who had once been incarcerated in a 'normal' camp, who had tried to escape precisely because they had felt they were not being useful to their country, and who had been captured again, the situation was deeply humiliating: they were 'combatants' once again – but against their own countrymen. First excluded from the war by their capture, then turned into human shields and pawns for exchange in transactions between the belligerent parties, they were now returned to the centre of war, but without honour. These reprisals were experienced as the worst conceivable outrage;

victims of this treatment were no longer entitled to the 'benefits' that ordinary prisoners enjoyed, like getting mail or parcels; nor were they included on published lists so that their relatives could know they were still alive. They were the living dead. Indeed, the point was to demean them, and the specific objective was to put pressure on their governments.

Violence became cruelty. Sometimes the men were allowed to write about their misfortunes, and then their stories would be exploited:

23 February 1917

To the President of the International Committee of the Red Cross,

Dear sir,

You are no doubt aware of the sad situation inflicted on us in retaliation 7 or 8 kilometres from the front line of fire. The treatment we're subjected to is indescribable. What horrors, what barbarity, war gives rise to. We are crammed into a shed where we can only rest by crouching (for lack of space), and which is exposed to the rain and wind. Every morning we go from there to the front ... carrying material for fortifications. Beasts of burden are less exhausted than we. The saddest sight I have witnessed was seeing the most worn out of our comrades collapse from weakness. The food is very inadequate: in the morning black coffee, in the evening a very watery soup, one piece of bread of around 300 or 400 grammes and a teaspoon of jam. Also, our workplace and quarters are under constant bombardment.

Sir, have pity on us and make a point of having improvements in the situation of prisoners on both sides.

Thank you in advance and with respect.

Albert Bard, Sergeant of the 9th Company in the Camp of Kassel, Germany[19]

On the German side, energetic protests were made about their prisoners being held in the French colonies in Africa. The reprisals, here, were seen through a racist lens:

Our war prisoners, who are European, are working under the orders of fanatic Arabs who amuse themselves debasing Christians. The French have even used blacks as guardians ... The characteristics of the Senegalese are well known, making the atrocities committed against our prisoners a certainty ... You [French prisoners] will be transferred to a disciplinary camp in reprisal ... Warn your families of the reason for this measure: the German government finds it inhuman and degrading for its nationals who are prisoners in Dahomey and Morocco to be guarded by Negroes. If you consider the black race to be your equal, we see it as more or less on the level of monkeys.[20]

Thus we see that invasions, occupations, exactions, expressions of racism, atrocities, reprisals, deportations and the massacres of civilians accompanied the intensification of combat on the battlefields of the Great War. What happened between 1914 and 1918, including the concentration camps, was part and parcel of the process whereby war became total in the twentieth century. And yet, a 'defeat of memory' obliterated these realities; a kind of hyperamnesia occurred about the men in the trenches, who were seen as either heroes or victims, and a general amnesia set in regarding everyone else. This paradox then allowed the culture of brutality and brutalisation of the years 1914–18 to bear fruit in later years, and new victims were born of the repercussions. The violence of war had been rendered commonplace, and its range grew out of all proportion. Worse, people who had suffered in the Great War so thoroughly internalised the banality of violence that for the most part they didn't assert their rights as exceptional victims.

Moreover, people everywhere saw only what they already believed, and for a long time historians simply perpetuated these errors; they didn't describe and analyse what they actually *saw* in the archives, but what they *thought* they saw. If in the 1920s and especially the 1930s the democracies failed vis-à-vis the totalitarian regimes that so skilfully exploited the violence of the Great War and then negated it, it was because they themselves had internalised or repressed that violence and those failures of memory. Given the hypertrophied memory of the combatants' suffering, we have to conclude that it is the amnesia concerning the treatment of civilian victims of the Great War that was at the root of this repression. The prolonged act of forgetting – forgetting both the cruelties towards civilians and the extermination of the Armenians during the Great War – gave impunity to those who later wanted to repeat such acts.

II
CRUSADE

It is striking that in France the fundamental stakes of the Great War, as contemporaries experienced them, have often better been understood by specialists in the study of other subjects or periods – medievalists or modernists, for instance – than by those for whom the war was a chosen subject. Marc Bloch, for example, in his famous article about '*les fausses nouvelles de guerre*' (false news, or rumours, about the war), opened up new avenues of research. His was a much more daring approach than anything attempted later in the 1920s and 1930s, and those new avenues of research would be extended by historians only seventy years later. Pierre Chaunu, to take another example, wrote an essay on France with a dazzling first chapter that begins with the Great War, showing brilliant insight into the meaning the conflict had for its contemporaries; we owe to him the pertinent formulation 'immense emotional investment [...] of the French in France' during the 1914–18 period – an emotional investment that most of the nations in the war also made.[1] Raoul Girardet is another among the select few who seems to have new insights into the 1914–18 conflict; in recalling his slow maturation during the post-war years, he describes a central difficulty in trying to understand the Great War:

> It was not until adolescence that I grew weary of these stories [of the war during childhood]. More years were needed before I became fully aware of the atrocity of the slaughter. And still more years before I could assess its terrifying absurdity: does the history of mankind offer many other examples of such disproportion between an immense sacrifice, acquiesced in, and the actual importance of the initial stakes? With time, I came to realise that this war, triggered so rashly and waged so absurdly, plunged the history of the entire century into horror. Yet as I write these words, I still experience a vague feeling of betrayal.[2]

The extent of this acquiescence is where the whole problem lies – the acquiescence which Girardet had 'inherited' in the post-war years from his own family and which he was so slow to challenge. It was manifest in all the belligerent societies between 1914 and 1918, and it didn't dissipate when the weapons were laid down. There is a huge, almost absurd discrepancy between the meaning of the war for the men and women of 1914 and the striking lack of meaning it has for us today.

We are far from feeling an equivalent disparity about the Second World War, since the struggle against fascism is a motive that is still respected in Western societies today and basic to our common values. On the other hand, a huge chasm separates us from the Great War. Yet it was the matrix; the Second World War developed from its complexities only twenty-two years later. The strangeness of the war, and the strangeness of not comprehending it, was well expressed by François Furet – another historian who has been most perceptive about the Great War's deep significance:

> Today's teenagers cannot even conceive of the national passions that led the peoples of Europe to kill each other for four full years. Through their grandparents, young people may retain a link with that time, but its secrets are lost to them, neither the suffering undergone nor the emotions that justified it makes any sense; nor does what was noble or passive about that suffering and those emotions speak to young people's hearts or minds in the same way that even a second-hand memory might do ... The twentieth century's first war ... remains one of the most enigmatic events of modern history.[3]

Though we might not be able to solve the enigma, let us try at least to shed some light on it.

4

The beginnings of war

Our intention is not to describe exactly how the war began in the summer of 1914 but to examine the reversal, or change of heart, that came about then, for its characteristics continued to affect the great question of acquiescence throughout the conflict.

For Europeans, the beginning of the war was rapid and unexpected, and its speed was a determining factor in the way the groundwork was laid for support of the war.[1] The evidence suggests that this groundwork was established in a few hours, perhaps even less. This was strikingly the case in Great Britain.

Public opinion in England was initially opposed to the war in the main, even after the crisis had reached fever pitch and other nations had entered the conflict. On 2 August, after the other powers had announced a general mobilisation and Germany had officially declared war on Russia, London witnessed an enormous pacifist demonstration. Nothing of this kind took place in any other European country; pacifist opposition movements had collapsed. But in Great Britain, Labour stood firm in its opposition to the war, as did the Liberals and their radical wing, and even a fringe opposition group among the Conservatives. And yet at midnight on 4 August, the United Kingdom entered the war with unanimous popular support, including that of the Irish Catholics, who not only swore unambiguous allegiance to the crown but announced that their armed militias, originally ready to wage a civil war against the Ulster Protestants, would join the latter in guarding the coasts. The change of heart had occurred on the morning of 3 August, as soon as London got word that Germany had handed an ultimatum to Belgium demanding free passage of German troops across Belgian territory. This was a spectacular change, and it is an extreme case, but it is emblematic of the speed with which European public opinion rallied to the war.

Actual war enthusiasm was, however, a weak factor, outside the capitals and big cities, where demonstrations of varying sizes showed an intense war fervour; except in Belgium, there was a distinct split between the rural and urban populations.[2] These demonstrations deserve to be studied more closely, for although they may have expressed the views of a minority, they were the advance guard of a widespread popular support for the war based on resignation, acceptance, sometimes despondency, and later a growing resolve.

The way people were emotionally gripped by a war that was only just beginning remains a phenomenon that probably can't be accounted for in rational terms. The German Socialist deputy Eduard David gave an accurate idea of this irrational dimension when he described in his diary his response to the Reichstag vote of 4 August allocating funds for the war, a vote that was almost unanimously adopted by the SPD deputies (though they had been expected to vote against the bill): 'I shall never forget the incredible enthusiasm of the other parties, the government and the audience, when we stood up to be counted.' In the afternoon, while taking a walk with his child, he noted how hard it was for him to hold back his tears: 'It soothes me to have my daughter with me. If only she wouldn't ask so many useless questions.'[3] Something basic was at work in that intense emotion. Many people (though we have actually very few direct testimonies to this), especially city people, felt moved by a superior force coming from deep within. The speech that Léon Jouhaux made at the grave of the great socialist Jean Jaurès on 4 August is famous in French history books for its Jacobin, bellicose voluntarism (and he was later violently criticised as Secretary General of the CGT labour union). But even more interesting was his effort, when he was publicly questioned in July 1918 about his speech, to justify his improvised comments: 'Through what psychological process, so to speak, did the thought come to me and why was it oriented in that way? I can't really say. There are moments in a man's life when he has thoughts that seem foreign to him and yet that cluster together the traditions he carries within him, and that circumstances make him recall more or less forcefully. Perhaps I was living through one of those moments.'[4] Jouhaux could not express more clearly, or with less embarrassment, that he had spoken almost 'in spite of himself', or rather that 'something' within him spoke, something beyond intellectual control.

We can imagine this same emotional dynamic on a larger scale: what emerged forcefully, between late July and early August 1914, in the hearts of millions of Europeans, sometimes unconsciously and involuntarily, was national sentiment. Patriotic feeling prevailed. International organisations – the international socialist movement, international religious groups (Europe's Protestant churches and the Roman Catholic Church) and international associations of feminists and scientists – retrenched. National defence transcended any feeling of solidarity across borders.

The case of Belgium is especially telling. Though neutrality had been a determining factor in the country's identity ever since 1830, and despite the occasionally anti-French strain of its national sentiments and the highly inflamed struggle between the Flemish and the Walloons earlier in the century, a unanimous movement of defensive patriotism obliterated all internal divisions when the German ultimatum arrived on 2 August. Belgium's decision not to submit and to fight for its honour though it had no chance of success was unanimously supported by a well-informed public.[5] This helps to explain the lack of hesitation in public opinion within the great powers that had greater military means to oppose Germany than Belgium did.

In Belgium, as in France, Germany, Austria, Russia and Serbia, there was a nation and a land to defend. But what meaning did these ideas of defence have in the British Empire's Dominions? They were not threatened as Belgium had been, yet they lapsed into war without even feeling the need (except in Canada) for any formal display of commitment to the 'mother country'. The feeling of a common cause and of an ethnic and cultural unity with Great Britain prevailed over everything else; it even rallied the Boers in South Africa. That the desire to defend Great Britain was so strong is especially strange considering that, of all the powers engaged in the conflict, British territory was the least directly threatened by the Central Powers. Therefore what was being defended was the nation. But there was also something else, something larger: the defence of civilisation, to which we shall return.

Italy's entry into the war, ten months later, is an interesting counter-example.[6] Between August 1914 and May 1915, we know with certainty that the great majority of Italians were 'neutral', i.e., opposed to their nation's joining the war. So Italy's entry into the war in May went against public opinion. What was lacking here was exactly what was present in the other cases: a sense that the nation needed to be defended. Since Italy's traditional enemy, Austria, was not threatening Italy's integrity, the emotional investment in the war that almost all of Europe had made in the summer of 1914 failed to occur in Italy – or at least not until October 1917, when Italian territory was invaded after the defeat at Caporetto. Then defensive reflexes came into play, just as they had with the other European powers in 1914.

In most of the European countries, the call for a general mobilisation and universal conscription created such a huge upheaval that we might forget that the cataclysm of the summer of 1914 owed a great deal to voluntary enlistment. Though we cannot know the exact motivation of the men who signed up, the voluntary enlistments give us a sense of the scale and power of the collective surge of feeling. Nowhere is this more interesting than in England, the only great European power not to have conscription until compulsory military service was instituted in early 1916; until then, its war effort rested entirely on a very restricted professional army and on volunteers. Between August and December 1914, 1 million British men entered the ranks of the army. In fact, the recruitment offices were overwhelmed with an even greater number, but the criteria for acceptance were strict, and there were many stories about young candidates waiting patiently for months before being admitted into a combat unit. In 1915, more than 1.4 million new volunteers joined the recruitment lists; thus a total of 2.4 million Britons, that is almost 30 per cent of the men in the eligible age bracket, volunteered to fight on the continent. In Great Britain alone, excluding Ireland, one man out of four enlisted. The numbers raised by conscription, starting in 1916, were scarcely any higher.[7]

For a more accurate assessment of this tidal wave of volunteers, a few other factors should be considered. First of all, we should note that by September 1914 it could not be said that the men enlisted in complete ignorance of what awaited them at the front. The 'imagined war' had been dispelled with the first casualties, the first tales of combat, the first bereavements, the first arrivals of the wounded. Even the illusion of a short war was dispelled with the stalemate in the trenches in the autumn of 1914. However, the 'real war' did not apparently discourage men from enlisting, quite the contrary: it was *after* the first casualty lists were issued that the wave of enlistment reached its peak, in the summer of 1914; British volunteers enlisted fully aware that gunfire killed, and this was also true of volunteers from the Dominions, who for a long time were hostile to conscription (though, ultimately, with the exception of the Australians, they resigned themselves to it).

Moreover, these volunteers were not *déclassés* men with nothing to lose in the adventure of war but their lives. On the contrary, 'established' men were the first to enlist: among workers, where just under 30 per cent of the eligible age bracket enlisted, skilled and permanently employed workers were in a majority. Middle-class men enlisted in proportionately even greater numbers; in banking, finance and commerce, the level rose to 40 per cent of those eligible for active service. Men often left in groups, without breaking up their social ties from work, leisure activities or neighbourhoods. Workers from a single mine or railway company, members of a sports team, students from the same public school, residents of the same neighbourhood in Manchester or Birmingham constituted the Pals' Battalions in 'Kitchener's army'.

The scale and nature of enlistment in Great Britain and the Dominions suggest the nations' emotional investment in the war. And it was not simply the result of massive propaganda, propaganda that was all the more effective for being deployed in the most urbanised society in the world (the British army being 90 per cent urban and the only army in 1914 in which peasants were not in the majority). Indeed there was mass propaganda, with a profusion of posters with guilt-inducing and brutal messages ('Daddy, what did you do in the Great War?') and many rousing meetings. But the recruiters quickly decided that using the latest forms of mass advertising had a negative effect, devaluing the act of enlisting, and the recruitment campaigns quickly became quite discreet.[8] It has to be said, then, that early in the war, the enlisted British men were for the most part volunteers in the full sense of the word.

Of course, voluntary enlistment was less in countries that had universal conscription, but even there it wasn't nonexistent. It attracted men who were either too young to be called up (seventeen was the minimum age in France) or too old. In France, Germany, Russia and Great Britain, writers, painters and privileged boys in good schools were drawn by the powerful call of 'wartime voluntary service' – avant-garde artists possibly more than the others (the Italian Futurists, for instance), but in any case artists who were not at all bellicose but who felt, like Otto Dix, that they couldn't 'refuse to give themselves to the war'.

There were also foreigners: 30,000 of whom enlisted on the French side at the start of the conflict.[9] The case of Blaise Cendrars, of Swiss nationality, who enlisted in the Foreign Legion in August 1914, was far from unique. Even the gender barrier, impenetrable as it was between men and women in times of war, was occasionally transgressed. In Slavic countries, for instance, many young women volunteered for combat.[10]

It remains to ask how this initial investment outlived the transition from imagined war to real war, how it survived the realisation that the imagined war was actually, as Marc Ferro aptly put it, an 'imaginary' war.[11] For everything points to the fact that the representational frameworks crystallised in late July and early August 1914 – when nothing was yet known about what kind of war would be waged and when most people expected it to be a short war with only limited sacrifices – largely withstood the enormous casualties and the immense sacrifices demanded not only of the troops but, increasingly, of the civilian populations. In a word, they withstood mass bereavement.

During the following four years, Europeans continued to believe that their initial feelings in the summer of 1914 were still justified. This may seem a shocking assertion, since historians have long emphasised – with at times a rather blinkered fascination – that there were many manifestations of resistance to the war. Instances of opposition were indeed numerous and varied, and they allow us to fashion a more subtle chronology and cartography of support for the war, to which we shall return.[12] But on balance they are outweighed by the instances of support, and support *maintained*. The Great War remained until the end a war defined by that consensus. Why wasn't the consensus of those first August days massively questioned in following years? Much of the mystery of the Great War lies in that question: it is part of the mystery of the 'second acceptance' – the acceptance, after the first period was passed, of a long war and great suffering.

For a long time, historians were missing the piece of the puzzle that would convincingly explain this apparently incomprehensible mystery. Now they seem to have found it: it is the phenomenon of the 'atrocities' or, more precisely, the knowledge of the atrocities and the public's perceptions of them (as committed by their enemies). We need to consider the mechanisms by which the imagined 'atrocities' were interpreted.

The first 'news' of atrocities reached people through two channels, which reinforced one another and helped to make the information seem irrefutable: via stories told by refugees from the first offensives and counter-offensives of the war, who had fled the invaded regions of East Prussia, Russian Poland, Galicia and Austrian Bosnia, then of Serbia, Belgium and north-eastern France; and via newspaper articles that elaborated on eyewitness accounts of the invaders' evil deeds and disseminated them far and wide. This process was further strengthened in late 1914 and early 1915 by a kind of second wave of 'news', still more persuasive than the first: it was then that the first reports of the commissions of inquiry on enemy atrocities were published in each of the belligerent countries. The reports of acts of violence which these detailed, against soldiers as well as civilians, were by and large based on fact, and they were very widely circulated, particularly in the nations allied against Germany and Austria.

The French case is a good example. The reports, all addressed to the head of government, were the work of a committee investigating acts committed by the enemy in violation of human rights. The committee, made up principally of lawyers, filed twelve reports[13] between the end of 1914 and the beginning of 1919. The first of these, in December 1914, created a considerable stir. It contained 470 convincingly authentic depositions, often in agreement with each other. The introductory text was published in its entirety by virtually every French newspaper in mid-January 1915, often on the front page: 'Plunder, rape, arson and murder are common practice among our enemies,' asserted the reporters.[14] The text, appearing everywhere simultaneously, convinced the public not just that German atrocities had taken place but also that they were widespread and very grave. These facts were reiterated, summarised, commented upon and illustrated in a great number of other publications, and sometimes even shown in films. It was a huge shock. News of enemy atrocities had an equally great impact, then and a bit later, in other countries that had confronted or were still confronting war, invasion and occupation. We must remember that at some point *all* the belligerents in Europe had the terrifying experience of having the enemy on their soil.

The only exception was Great Britain, which is why the testimony of the British writer Robert Graves is exceptionally interesting. Like so many young upper-class Englishmen, he enlisted in the army one or two days after the declaration of war. 'I was outraged to read of the Germans' cynical violation of Belgian neutrality. Though I discounted perhaps 20 per cent of the atrocity details as wartime exaggeration, that was not, of course, sufficient.'[15] He wrote these lines ten years after the armistice, at a time when he was completely disillusioned by prevailing representations of the war, an especially ironic disillusionment coming from a man who had fought in the trenches. Also, his mother's family was of German descent (his great-uncle was none other than the historian Leopold von Ranke), and until the summer of 1914 he had very close ties with the German members of his family. That a person with his background chose to mention the German atrocities as a major reason for his having enlisted fourteen years earlier clearly shows the meaning for their enemies that the various armies' acts of cruelty gave to the war, in the first days of the conflict.

And the meaning could not be disputed. The facts had confirmed, often beyond the worst initial fears, that the meaning of the combat unquestionably lay in the struggle between civilisation and barbarity. This opposition was considered fundamental by most people, as soon as the atrocities had proven, beyond doubt, the adversary's intrinsic malignancy; and it was never really questioned in subsequent years. In short, we can speak of a 1914–18 war culture, in other words, a collection of representations of the conflict that crystallised into a system of thought which gave the war its deep significance. One cannot dissociate this 'culture' from the emergence of a powerful hatred of the opponent. Deep down, the 1914–18 war culture harboured a true drive to 'exterminate' the enemy. We see clear traces of this everywhere, but it is unusually disturbing when expressed by someone from whom one might expect the opposite message, like the Bishop of London in 1915:

> And first we see Belgium stabbed in the back and ravaged, then Poland, then Serbia, and then the Armenian nation wiped out – 500,000 at a moderate estimate, being actually killed: and then as a necessary consequence, to save Liberty's own self, to save the honour of women and the innocence of children, everything that is noblest in Europe, everything that loves freedom and honour, everyone that puts principle above ease, and life itself beyond mere living, are banded in a great crusade – we cannot deny it – to kill Germans: to kill them not for the sake of killing, but to save the world; to kill the good as well as the bad, to kill the young men as well as the old, to kill those who have shown kindness to our wounded as well as those fiends who crucified the Canadian sergeant, who supervised the Armenian massacres, who sank the *Lusitania*, and who turned the machine-guns on the civilians of Aerschott and Louvain – and to kill them lest the civilisation of the world should itself be killed.[16]

Hatred radically intensifies the violence of war – between soldiers and between soldiers and invaded civilians. Yet historians have tended to underestimate this, and so has the public. Even today, when a testimony attacking the enemy is cited in lectures, on the radio, or in a television programme, it provokes a recognisable audience reaction. Often it is claimed that these kinds of text are mere 'propaganda' and can't at all convey how contemporaries thought. But in fact writings about the enemy in 1914–18 should be taken at face value: they were statements of profound hostility based on an indignant knowledge of the atrocities committed.

As a case in point, one extreme example is especially significant: it concerns the attribution of a specific odour to the enemy

– the perception of an alien smell being connected to one of our most deeply rooted reflexes. The idea that there was a definite difference between the bodily odours of French and Germans – perceptible even on corpses, as soldiers themselves sometimes attested – made its way throughout French society, both on the front lines and the home front. It was most explicitly expressed in the writings of one Dr Bérillon, who wrote a little pamphlet published in 1915 entitled *Bromidrose fétide de la race allemande* (Fetid Bromidrosis of the German Race), presented at a session of France's Academy of Medicine. In it, he put forward the idea that the enemy's basic evilness explained their abnormally abundant defecation, in turn with the emission of a bodily odour in their sweat comparable to that of a polecat. The author concluded:

> The Germans, who haven't achieved control over their instinctive impulses, have also failed to master their vasomotor reactions. In that respect, they are close to some animal species in which fear or anger provokes an exaggerated glandular activity with malodorous secretions …The main organic feature of today's German is that, being unable to eliminate uric elements due to an overworked renal function, he has plantar sweating. This can be expressed by saying that the German urinates through his feet. [17]

Our natural defence against this kind of writing is to laugh it off, but that simply makes its extreme violence less real and spares us the effort of learning from it. Laughter makes us forget that the senior physicians who attended this session of the Academy of Medicine didn't laugh – and that is significant. It makes us forget that hatred and the reflex to animalise the enemy were deeply embedded in the war culture. They were an essential part of the combat.

Erosion, backlash and mobilisation

We do not claim that the belligerents' emotional investment in the war was steady in intensity from the beginning to the end of the conflict, nor that it was identical in all countries, social classes and national groups. But historians have always emphasised the discontinuities rather than the continuities, at the risk of making the duration of the conflict and the scale of the sacrifices incomprehensible, and we should avoid that mistake.

Was there an erosion of support for the war? Unquestionably. Tradition places the great turning point in 1917; today we tend to date the first shift in opinion a year earlier, starting in the second half of 1916, after the slaughter of Verdun, the Somme and the Brusilov offensive (and even earlier among the occupied populations).[18] There are many signs that by then the initial consensus was beginning to wear thin, at least among the Western Allies. The validity of the war was not really questioned (except by a tiny minority), but a significant change took place in what was expected and hoped for, particularly on the home fronts. Consider, for example, the success in Britain of the film *The Battle of the Somme*.[19] The attack of 1 July 1916 had been filmed by several cameramen in the front-line trenches. They could not shoot the combat itself – this was impossible in 1914–18 given the technical requirements of filming and the intensity of the confrontation in no man's land – so the attack scenes were all reconstructed or simulated; on the other hand, the cameramen were able to film the actual return of the wounded and the horrendous consequences of the assault on the German positions in the first hours of the offensive. The footage was brought back to London with record speed, edited, and shown to the British public that autumn. It was one of the first full-length war films and though it certainly had a patriotic tone, it showed no marked hostility towards the enemy. But it did show, mercilessly, some true battlefield realities, particularly the wounded English soldiers making their way, en masse, from the front lines to the first-aid posts. The film was an enormous success: it is estimated that 19 million people saw it in Britain in the first six weeks of its run. After more than two full years of war, the British were evidently ready to witness the reality of the war's brutality. For the first time, civilians felt they had seen the suffering of the combatants. This was a sign of change.

Was there a backlash against the war? Again, the signs, beginning in 1917, cannot be dismissed. Russia is an emblematic case, with the radical break-up of its army on the front: there was refusal to fight, fraternisation with the enemy, mass surrender and desertion. It is surprising that the same kind of break-up didn't occur in the Austro-Hungarian Empire, and that, contrary to all expectations, no strong drive to secede arose among the various national groups (outside émigré circles). Péter Hanák's analysis of intercepted correspondence shows that only very late in 1917 did 'national' sentiment become an important element in popular aspirations[20] – as opposed to loyalty to the Dual Monarchy, which prevailed until then.

In the West, the mutinies that occurred during 1917 were the only concrete examples of a profound decline in support of the war. It is illustrative of historians' long-standing, complacent preference for opposition over consent that the first historical work on the Great War soldiers' world (as opposed to a witness's account) was a study of the exception to the rule – the mutiny of 40,000 men out of the 2 million men on the front at that time.[21] Yet the striking thing about this unquestionably grave crisis was not so much its scale as its limits: we should note that the mutineers did not fraternise with the enemy or desert for home, and they didn't even refuse to remain in the front-line trenches if that was where they were (though they did refuse to return to the front line when they were stationed in the rear). It is not surprising that the German command failed to assess the extent of the crisis in the French ranks. Moreover, the sequence of events shows that the movement ebbed *before* the mutiny was quashed.

In his pioneering study of the French Fifth Infantry Division, a leading player in the spring 1917 insubordination crisis,[22] the American historian Leonard Smith has shown us that a complex equilibrium between the men and their commanding officers existed, an equilibrium based on a constantly re-evaluated and re-adjusted balance of power between resistance and acceptance. The constant 'negotiation' process that went on between the soldiers and their commanders broke down in the spring of 1917, though it led to a new equilibrium in the demands the ones made on the others. The equilibrium was made possible, we should note, by the soldiers' capacity for acquiescence; they remained above all – or rather despite all – citizens in uniform.

If we extend the paradox, it could be said that the mutineers, far from being pacifist opponents of the war – which is what most of the military authorities wanted people to believe and sincerely believed themselves, for they were convinced of a socialist plot – were, on the contrary, in their own way, the most patriotic citizen-soldiers. They wanted victory, and the military command was leading them to defeat, with horrendous, unnecessary losses. Might one not say, then, that these 'mutinies' were in fact refusals to obey bad leaders rather than real mutinies? The troops' compliance in a successful offensive like the one at Malmaison in October 1917 – led by Marshal Pétain, a trusted commander – raises questions about the very idea of a mutiny. Finally, we should not focus on a number of soldiers mutinying in 1917 after the failed offensive at the Chemin des Dames, but on the fact that a much larger movement of insubordination didn't occur much earlier.

Though they never ceased to aspire to peace, the majority of the soldiers in all the armies, like the majority of people on the home fronts, wished first and foremost not to lose the war. The two hopes were not contradictory. Defensive patriotism – defence of the soil and defence of their loved ones – structured the way they thought about the war right to the end. This was true of the German soldiers, too, for though they were occupying forces far beyond their national borders, they stubbornly insisted on thinking of their trench positions, especially in France, in traditional defensive terms as a 'watch on the Rhine' (the *Wacht am Rhein* becoming the *Wacht an der Somme*). In most of the armies (except in Russia), the immense suffering the soldiers endured never rid them of the view that each of them had a *duty. Devoir,* Duty, *Pflicht:* these words were ever-present in the letters, trench diaries and personal notebooks of the combatants.

It is therefore completely erroneous to imagine that the consensus of support for the war eroded in any significant way in the belligerent countries during the conflict. A more detailed chronology reveals further surprising facts. After the initial support there were many new *re*-mobilisations, most astonishingly during the last year of the war.[23] The year 1918 was one of a renewed emotional investment in the conflict. It was also the year of new invasions, such as Germany's last spring offensives on the Western Front. As the French fled from the invaded areas and Paris was bombarded by long-range cannons, the theme of atrocities was revived. The bombing of the church of Saint-Gervais in Paris on Good Friday 1918, which killed several dozen women, children and elderly persons, is forgotten today, but when it happened, the September 1914 bombing of Rheims cathedral was still vividly in mind, and hence Saint-Gervais established a continuity with the earlier desecration and revived people's indignant recollections.[24] As the war was drawing to an end, then, among the Allies at least, the idea that it was a crusade against the barbarous Germans re-emerged with the vigour it had had in its murderous beginnings.

It is often said that propaganda was the determining factor in the warring societies' lasting support for the conflict of 1914–18. The argument is particularly tempting since the Great War period was the first time in which the machinery for mass large-scale propaganda existed, and people were subjected to it in time of war. Newsreels were seen in all the belligerent countries as early as 1915, and they are an important element in the cultural change that has permanently altered the relationship of Western societies to war.[25] It is significant that the same questions that we ask today about the media's treatment of war could be asked in 1914–18, and indeed sometimes were. Yet we should realise that the intervening experience of the propaganda generated by communist and fascist totalitarian regimes – particularly during 1941–5 – distorts our view of propaganda during the Great War.

In fact, in the case of 1914-18, the word propaganda seems inadequate and should perhaps be used in quotation marks.

Our experience at the Historial de Péronne has played a determining role in changing our assumptions and altering our approach to war propaganda. For the historians involved in the Historial, the 'propaganda' objects gradually collected there made for a disturbing discovery – one of the most interesting aspects of which is the extremely wide dissemination of some of these objects between 1914 and 1918 (their prices giving an indication of their rarity or availability). A particular piece of German tableware with an iron cross design, though exceptional at first glance, actually had a rather small sale value, for it had been mass-produced, while other objects, sometimes banal, were quite rare. For researchers whose experience until then had been with archival and library documents, these thousands of objects from the 1914-18 war opened up new vistas. That the 'propaganda' objects in the Historial's stockrooms had been conceived, created, mass-produced in the workshops and factories of all the warring countries led to a new awareness. What this shows is that not only had many people been involved in the design and mass production of such items, many more had bought them.

This obvious truth challenges the historian's broadly accepted 'top down' view of propaganda as something deliberately imposed by governmental and military authorities (like censorship).[26] With these patriotic objects, we are in the realm of supply and demand; there is no ban and no incitement. At which point it becomes abundantly clear that what is called propaganda was not just a vertical process but also a horizontal one, even, to some extent, a great upsurge from below, sustained by a huge number of individuals. Illustrators of children's books, journalists, writers, film-makers, musicians and artists who created posters and postcards, book and newspaper illustrators, primary schoolteachers, high-school teachers, 'intellectuals' and academics, priests in their churches, pastors in their chapels, rabbis in their synagogues – all the cultured elites, on the home front and the front lines, everyone, or nearly everyone, participated in some way in decentralised 'propaganda' that was largely uncontrolled, or at any rate more often spontaneous than organised or imposed.

This suggests a provocative question: what if this 'propaganda discourse' in the widest sense merely translated – or traduced? – the people's prevailing ideas about what the war was? The idea goes against many of our most ingrained convictions, and yet the very logic of the conflict indicates that, for the most part, the mobilisation of public opinion between 1914 and 1918 had nothing to do with coercion, censorship or the authoritarian imposition of certain ways of thinking. No, the reason why the consensus in the belligerent countries was so effective and long-lasting, despite the suffering endured, was that it was basically driven by a spontaneous mobilisation.

We can give only a few examples here. A look at children's lives in 1914–18 gives us a good illustration.[27] Representations of the war intended for children – books and periodicals, images and toys used in schools and churches – everything societies taught their youngest members during the Great War puts us in contact with what people thought was most important, and what each society believed it should communicate about the conflict. The stories for children, the representations offered them, whether suggested or imposed, are like the inner core of the various war cultures.

In our day, when an armed conflict in any part of the world directly involves children, we think of it as a scandal, as something of a desecration. We invariably worry about the psychological effects the violence of war will have on the children exposed to it. This point of view, which seems self-evident to us, is exactly the opposite of the one held in the belligerent countries in 1914–18. In those days it was thought that, by and large, no aspect of the war should be concealed from children; on the contrary, children were supposed to be included in the war. The reasoning was simple: war itself was certainly an evil, but an evil from which good could emerge; thus war 'would be good' for children, and enduringly so, by moulding better adults than in previous generations, adults rid for ever of the obligation to wage war.

The two most important institutions to educate and so-cialise children outside the family, the schools and the churches, as well as all other cultural organisations, set out to bring chil-dren to the heart of the conflict and keep them there. There was a 'mobilisation of children', a mobilisation that even in-cluded a material aspect, since in school appeals were made to their money and work power. But the first thing required of them was an intellectual, moral, emotional and spiritual effort at self-mastery. The brutal forms that this attempt to involve and mobilise children took shows both the extreme tension within the belligerent societies and the strength of their spontaneous support for the war.

The response of French children to the call of the war, to the extent that it is still visible to us in glimpses, is characteristic of this mobilising tension. For the children seem to have fully in-ternalised the demands of the war context. The patchy, fragile and scattered sources – drawings, homework, letters, diaries – show that children, while not the malleable wax creatures their parents and educators thought they were, created for themselves a representation of the war – its violence, its meaning and what was at stake – that was consistent with the view of the world around them. Many of them responded to the demands of their immediate environment by seeing themselves as heroic children. In her imagination, the twelve-year-old Anaïs Nin was a new Joan of Arc leaving New York, in 1914, to free her 'homeland' from the German enemy, and for the first and last time in her writing career she wrote poems, in French, about patriotic suf-fering.[28] Yves Congar[29] was eleven at the beginning of the war and lived in Sedan, a town occupied by the Germans; he be-longed to a secret children's society that organised a 'resistance' against the occupying forces. He sabotaged or stole enemy ma-terial, spat on the occasional soldier he passed in the street, and was finally summoned to the *Kommandantur* for having uttered an insult to one of them.

Some children even saw themselves as combatants: there were cases of primary-school children who ran away from home, alone or with a schoolmate, to join the front lines and fight by their father's, brother's or uncle's side, before they were caught and brought back home. When these runaway children were asked about their motives, they alluded in vague but pertinent terms to the defeat of 1870 and said they couldn't bear to see another defeat, expressing a deep desire to fight for their country. There is evidence that children became convinced that they could help and protect the soldiers by focusing their thoughts on them, and they created prayer circles for that purpose. It was no accident that an organisation of children's prayer groups, founded in a girls' school in Bordeaux in 1915 and enlarged in 1916 and 1917, was called 'the Children's Crusade'.

The behaviour of the children in the belligerent societies is a reliable yardstick of the extent of the spontaneously mobilised support of the war and the extreme, largely self-imposed tension that prevailed during the four-year conflict. The children's involvement is the symptom of the ways in which the Great War was a crusade.

5

Civilisation, barbarism and war fervour

Many contemporaries of the war described the powerful spiritual element that was part of their life between 1914 and 1918. How are we to interpret – and, even more difficult, convey – what these combatants and these civilians meant by 'spirituality'?

During the Great War, people were defending, or believed they were defending, the important values of their country, their region, their family, values that were put to the test of suffering, anguish, injury and death. Each person had a set of emotional and political ties, ranging from those with family and relatives to those with the state. Individual members of families, parishes, professions, neighbourhoods and villages each had their own destinies, as well as a place within the collective destiny of their country and/or church. This brings us to the very heart of the process through which the conflict permeated *all* aspects of the culture of the nations at war. Wartime 'spirituality' can be understood only in the context of the constant flux between the front lines and the home front – of ammunition and food supplies, propaganda and love, religious and patriotic fervour, moments of hope and discouragement, death and mourning, masculine and feminine sensibilities. War slows down some developments in many areas and makes others possible; the development of political and religious fervour is a good example of mobilisation through faith.

Faced with the anguish of temporary separation at the front and the horror of permanent separation through death (compounded because this meant mainly young people dying first, before their parents, contrary to the natural order of things), soldiers and their families revived old forms of devotion, and ancient 'superstitions' arose again among people who were still very close to their rural roots. (This was particularly true of Italy.)[1] A wartime religion developed that included traditional religious services and spiritualism, prayers and amulets, the sufferings of Christ and the intercession of saints, ordinary piety and the belief in supernatural signs.[2] But how can historians rediscover these prayers, this anguish and suffering, given how little space they occupy in the archives? The overwhelming presence of death confers special meaning on all forms of spirituality, and this has been interpreted as a sign of fear; people have smiled upon a 'lightning rod religion' motivated by the omnipresence of death. Yet this view is far too reductive to explain the dramatic increase of religious devotion at the front and at home during 1914–18.

When we read the soldiers' correspondence and diaries, and examine the marks and traces they left behind, even the graffiti on the walls of trenches they lived in, we discover a genuine spirituality of the front. From the writings of people who noticed and described these expressions of religious fervour early in the war, to the smallest local sanctuaries where we can still see today traces of them (especially in the ex-votos), we are struck by an intense life of the soul that might allow us to define a wartime *Homo credens*. Wartime religion is not just a major component in the culture of war but actually a double constituent element of it: it supports God and country, but it also refuses to give that support, on the pacifist grounds that sometimes denounces war as a sign of sin.[3]

In all the countries, the catchphrase was the same: 'God is

with us', '*Dieu est de notre côté*', '*Gott ist mit uns*'. Belief in God and patriotism were usually inseparable; and though this may not mean that everyone was a believer, much less a churchgoer, it is clear that spiritual values and their related vocabulary – good and evil, the mystique of combat, sacred union – sustained people and their ideas about the war, their beliefs that they were taking part in a true crusade. This was a crusade with its roots in the nineteenth century, when the religion of patriotism was born, when nations became sacred and religions became nationalised.[4] And 'chosen peoples', or peoples who saw themselves as such, were now at war with one another.

The historian Alphonse Dupront well understood that the societies at war were saturated with religious hope, that an intense mystique surrounded the very idea of one's mother country. He expressed this in his inimitable way:

> A world in distress, hence deeply anguished. A world in which the Great War would break out, its very name characteristic of a humanity raised, with terror and a secret feeling of fulfilment, to a planetary war ... A Great, World war – that is now the measure. The new war compels us to feel unity. Not the unity of combat among opponents, in other words the metaphysical unity of war, but a cosmic unity, since the whole earth is involved. Hence a religious unity of common salvation. [Charles] Péguy, a tireless discoverer of profundity, announced this in *Clio*: the return of Christendom, summoned by an anguished world. A need for flesh, or for remembrance, in order to live and to comprehend the new world, suddenly open to its full measure yet already shut. What better image is there of its innermost soul ... but the Crusade? Or the related image, temporally and metaphysically, of Christendom? ... Consciousness of a crusade in the Great War is thus located on two levels: the level of historical memory and the level of collective acts. This is to be expected in a crisis of this scale: the extraordinary wakens the extraordinary ... Obviously, the West rediscovered the holy war – or at least God's war – in the Great War ... On both sides, it was necessary to claim God.[5]

In the Great War, people wanted to claim God. And there is no doubt that their determination to fight against barbarism, a goal central to the idea of a war based on law and civilisation, became a holy war. The Great War as holy war and war of holy men formed what was initially a diptych: combatant-knights imitated the saints, particularly the female saints. The war was holy because it was a 'great', long-lasting war, accepted as a trial, and with an eschatological, eternal aim. Depending on one's spiritual affiliation, it took the shape of an Imitation of Christ, an Imitation of the Virgin and the saints, or a patriotic Imitation. The certitude that a 'just peace' would be a revenge against the absolute evil of war and the enemy who had wanted it constituted the third panel of the triptych.[6]

Legitimate war, just war: all the belligerents were convinced of the great truth of their cause. They fought for 'their little country' and for 'their great country'; their resolute if not enthusiastic fervour, combining love of family with love of country, was represented by a whole range of symbols: flags, songs and poems learned at school and in military service. In countries without conscription – the United Kingdom, Australia and New Zealand – enlistment was driven by the same certitudes and by the same unquestioned support. Given the feeling of danger, of aggression, of encirclement, everyone wanted to share the risks out of loyalty to their families and to their 'cultures'. Everywhere enlistment in the war was experienced as a participation in the struggle between life and death, between good and evil. Patriotism became a mystique, and the fervent loyalties it aroused followed rigid national lines.

In Berlin, on August 1 1914, a huge crowd congregated on the Alexanderplatz. It was four in the afternoon and oppressively hot. Everyone waited for news, since 'a state of danger of war' with Russia had been proclaimed the day before. A spokesman for the Kaiser came out on a balcony and announced that the Reich was mobilising troops. In response, the crowd, until then silent and tense, started to sing spontaneously – not the German anthem *Deutschland über alles*, but the Lutheran chorale *Gott, tief im Herz.* The theology of war reached its peak in Germany in 1917, since that was the year of the 400th anniversary of Luther's posting of his 'ninety-five theses'. This *Lutherfeier,* confirming the longevity of German Protestantism, seemed to prove the validity of Germany's cause and of its 'manifest destiny'.[7]

In Paris in 1915, Victor Basch, vice-president of the French Human Rights League, an atheist and freemason, concluded his book *La Guerre de 1914 et le droit* (The War of 1914 and the Law) with the following words: 'This war is the struggle of free peoples wishing to free themselves from militarism and from imperialism ... Understood in this sense, this horrendous war can become a holy war.' That this patriotic mystique was expressed even by the most a-religious commentator can't be just coincidental. Everything becomes useful for the sake of belief, for helping the country hold out and win. On the one hand, a French postcard sent from the front with a Catholic prayer printed next to a four-leaf clover and a picture of Marianne. On the other, a German statuette representing Germania, messenger of the *Gesta Dei per Germanos,* blessing a soldier wearing a spiked helmet. These are only superficially contradictory: both stem from the same patriotic fervour.

The synthesis of religious and patriotic sentiments was not limited to the early months of the war but continued in subsequent years. Many religious meetings helped to mobilise and remobilise the people, through their faith. The various 'Sacred Unions' of church and state in the belligerent countries were meetings of political and spiritual goals. In France, Maurice Barrès, a non-practising Catholic, described their unusual nature in accents borrowed from St Paul:

We shall always remember the extraordinary nature of this union. It was not due simply to the understandable excitement of a people who had been surprised by the war. Let it never be said that any of us temporarily put our faith away like a useless object at the bottom of the cupboard. The soldiers will tell future astonished generations that they never lived their faith better and

that it was never of greater support than when they were
upholding the union ... Catholics will say, 'We saved
Catholicism.' Socialists will say, 'We saved socialism.'
Everyone will be right.

It was in order to defend our faith, our religion, that we each
defended our common country which includes all our religions.[8]

Early in the war, there were stories – some of them hagio-
graphic – about the patriotic and spiritual accomplishments of
the chaplains at the front, of clergymen who had remained on
the home front, of various religious believers. Faith and charity
cemented a union that in France was aptly called 'sacred'. The
Catholic Church, the majority religion in France, benefited from
its advantage in numbers, but the union included Protestants and
Jews.

The phenomenon is especially interesting to study in the
French Jewish community, which had only recently emerged
from the traumas of the Dreyfus affair.*[9] French Jews threw
themselves into the war with passion because it gave them the
opportunity to fight for the Republic, which embodied the
values of the French Revolution that had given them identity and
citizenship. Moreover, they believed that if France won the war it
would emancipate all of Europe, including the oppressed Jews of
Central Europe. This was expressed by Edmond Fleg in 1919:

And you cried when the 'Marseillaise',
Echoing the Hosannahs of the Hebrews,
Brought down other walls of Jericho
To the sound of French trumpets.[10]

For Jewish war witnesses, French Judaism was at the very
heart of the issues that made up the war culture. For, if civilisation was to triumph over barbarism, it was because all the reli-

---

*The right-wing newspaper L'Action française put an end to its 'Affaire
Dreyfus' column two days after the start of the war.

gions of France and the French nation itself were united in combat, in the soldiers' struggle and death: *L'Univers israélite* wrote:

> According to the Talmud, humanity will be saved when the most sublime virtue takes on the most abominable infamies. Above this horrendous spectacle [of death] shines like a growing brightness the justice, kindness and devotion overflowing from the hearts of our soldiers, and these will be victorious: kindness and love will triumph over spite ... A raised square of land, surrounded by a wire held up by four poles, with five wooden emblems: three crosses, a crescent, and the tablets of the law. Our glorious heroes were three Christians, one Muslim and one Jew ... Alas, was war necessary for this union to be fulfilled? Did the sacred have to be based on the profane, the pure on the impure, the highest moral idea on the lowest abjection?[11]

So both national and religious morality underlie the Sacred Union. German immorality was proof of French greatness, and shared hatred bound everyone together. Not only did every man who enlisted in the war become a citizen (foreign volunteers, whether Jewish or not, were naturalised), but he also became a morally superior being, on the side of 'humanity against inhumanity'.

For French Catholics, usually in the majority but a minority in the armed forces during the wars of the secular Third Republic, the Great War was a powerful moment of religious awakening, connected to a shared hatred of the German. For some observers, this 'return to the altar', which saw increased numbers of people taking communion and a rise in religious fervour in the early phase of the war and at certain points later on, can be understood by analogy with the Anglo-American Protestant concept of revival. Patriotic fervour and religious fervour were heightened and intertwined. And the catalyst for this great awakening, which in other times and places had been revivalist preachers or missionaries who stressed the fear of hell and the

sins that led to it, was the war itself. War's new conditions for religious fervour created the awakening.

The inability to regard the enemy as Christian, much less
Catholic, since he was seen as being responsible for the atrocities
and for the rape of the land, explains why both Catholic and
non-Catholic belligerents were puzzled by the Pope. From the
very day he was elected Pope, in September 1914, it was clear
that Benedict XV was acutely aware of the tragedy of the war
and that he had set himself the goal of restoring the peace. Time
and again he exhorted the warring nations to conclude a just
peace and offered his help in arriving at a reconciliation among
all parties (notably in his appeals of 28 July 1915, and especially 1
August 1917). In spite of his repeated failures, he never gave up
trying to mediate a peace, but he was met with almost complete
incomprehension. He claimed to be neutral, even impartial, but
each side interpreted him as lacking political courage, believing
that he actually sided with the opposing side and was being
hypocritically silent. The distrust was perfectly symmetrical:
Clemenceau called him the 'Boche Pope' and Ludendorff 'the
French Pope'. Hatred of the enemy was part of the crusade, and
paradoxically the Pope could not lead it because his flock was in
both camps.

How could Catholics maintain their double allegiance, to
their country at war and to the Pope, when the Pope was advocating two impossible positions – neutrality and peace? In
France, the situation was complicated by anticlericalism and an
'infamous rumour'. This 'infamous rumour' grew out of statements made by a few Catholics, that the war was the Republic's
deserved punishment for having separated church and state in
1905 and having made so many attacks against institutionalised
religion. This was only a small step away from saying that France
deserved to be defeated, clearly a very dangerous idea, since
defeat meant victory for the hated Germany. These few impru-
dent statements must be seen as expressing a certain kind of
moralistic Catholicism that has always made use of catastrophe
and fear to convert people to the cause. The 'infamous rumour'

was related to the 'return to the altar': impressed by the unprecedented religious revival that was occurring in wartime, some
Catholics were tempted to explain it by going even further and
seeing God's designs in the actions of men. Not surprisingly, an-
ticlerical militants seized on this – to them incomprehensible –
theology and used it to calumniate the Catholic Church as a
whole. They were bound to disapprove of churches resonating
with this sudden religious fervour, which they thought had been
in clear decline before 1914.* There is a striking correlation
between the decline in free-thinking during the war and the
new infatuation with religion.[13]

Conversely, signs of religious rapprochement or ecumenism
were believed to prove that spiritual unity would lead to victory.
In all the armies, the chaplains of minority religions (Catholics
and Jews in Germany and Great Britain, Protestants and Jews in
France) held more important positions, proportionately, than the
numbers they actually represented warranted. For whether
Catholic, Protestant or Jewish, the clergy's profession was the
same: to console, encourage and comfort.

Meetings of a kind that would have been improbable before
the war became commonplace in the special circumstances of
the front. Believers from different faiths could have conversations
that were impossible before then. And they mingled with agnos-
tics and free-thinkers who, in turn, witnessed their faith and acts
of faith. The more the road seemed difficult at first, the more re-
warding it was to describe. Though these descriptions were
partly no more than edifying propaganda, there was a genuine
newness to the spiritual encounters, animated by a shared patriotic energy and a shared dislike of the enemy. For example, in
1917, at the request of the family of a Rabbi Bloch who had
'died for France', the Jewish artist Lévy-Dhurmer painted him

*One example of a 'rumour': 'Seeing their churches become empty ...
the priests unleashed a war to make faith blossom again ... It is to the
priests' advantage that the hostilities continue and drag on so that they
can become rich on the many funerals that are a consequence of the war
slaughter.'[12]

holding out a crucifix to a dying soldier, clearly Catholic because he is wearing a medal of the Sacred Heart: a man of faith helping a man of another faith die according to his wish. Though the painting conveys a tragedy, with its sombre colours and flames of warfare, the painter has included a bright window opening on to the sky. Tolerance, the rabbi's willingness to honour a god who is not his, expresses hope in spite of death. Actually, Rabbi Abraham Bloch himself had died in the arms of a Catholic chaplain. Several days before, he had noted in his diary: 'The two priests, the pastor and I travelled in the same car and fraternised very cordially ... Though everyone calls me *monsieur le curé*, they all know that I'm the Jewish *curé*.'[14]

Maurice Barrès's book *Les Diverses Familles spirituelles de la France* is a hymn to the Sacred Union recounting acts of heroism and patriotic piety. That the painting of Rabbi Bloch concludes the chapter on the Jews is revealing: 'The rabbi offering a dying soldier the immortal sign of Christ on the cross is an image that will never perish.'[15] Beyond Barrès the future anti-Semite, there is a whole culture here of French purity permeated with Christian certitudes. Militants of faith – militants in the original military sense of the term – seized power between 1914 and 1918.

Thus were millions of men thrown into an extraordinarily abnormal situation – that of war and of the death of young people who should have had years of life before them. On all the fronts, the tombs were placed so as to be as visible as possible, perhaps to counter the 'invisibility'* of the slaughter and certainly to give back some measure of individual humanity to persons of whom nothing remained, often, but scattered body parts. On the front lines the wooden crosses on these graves were

---

*See Apollinaire's words:
At midnight there are soldiers sawing boards for coffins [...]
There is a cemetery filled with crosses 5 kilometres away
There are crosses everywhere here and there [...]
They think with melancholy on those whom they are not sure of seeing
  again
For in this war the art of invisibility has been carried very far.[16]

made of branches or boards broken in half; wooden crosses became a symbol not just of death but of death in the Great War; soon they became a symbol of the war itself, as in the 1919 novel by Roland Dorgelès, *Wooden Crosses*.[17]

The cross united all combatants, friend and foe, Christian and non-Christian. The crosses aligned along the battlefield were not solely symbols of Christ, for the process of giving a framework to the memory of the war dead also involved an effort to create life out of death, so the idea of the Imitation of Christ did somehow apply to all the belligerents, Christian or not. It was quite logical that for societies where most of the people were Christian, Christianity's message of sacrifice and resurrection should fit so perfectly with this effort, to the point of dominating it almost entirely. After all, isn't memory of the original sacrifice at the centre of the Christian doctrine, as illustrated in the words 'Do this in remembrance of me' (I Cor. 11: 24–5) reported by Saint Paul?

Hence, for Christians, not only did the living combatants imitate Christ on the battlefield, in an ever-renewed Passion, but the dead themselves were re-crucified. The French were firmly convinced that the Germans could not know this *Imitatio Christi*, but George Mosse has shown that for Germans, there was an analogy between death for the fatherland and the Passion of Christ, and it could be traced back to a nineteenth-century tradition. In the words of the very popular poet Walter Flex, war was a 'Last Supper' in which 'Christ's wine is German blood'.[18] So German soldiers, too, even some of the Jewish ones, expected to be buried under a cross: their probable death at war made them consent to a form of Christianity which they accepted not as a religion but as a symbolic system, a political and spiritual 'Imitation of Germany'.*

---

*The situation of the 500,000 Jews in the German army improved considerably during the war – they gained the right to become army officers, for example – but the army's failure to make public the number of Jews mobilised and sent to the front in 1916 had weighty consequences. The figures, which show that Jews enlisted in the same proportion as the

At the same time, all the belligerents tried to show respect for the Jewish and Muslim graves, marking them appropriately whenever the information was available.* And for all belligerents death was connected to the idea of resurrection, given the holiness of the war itself – resurrection of both the homeland and the people within it, of the homeland through the people within it. The long list of Jews who died for France elicited the following comment from the writer André Vervoort: 'They died so that the country could be reborn, more beautiful, greater, more honoured, nobler, and even better. They died for the great traditions of France: justice and liberty.'[20]

Militant Catholics brought this sentiment to a climax, for it fulfilled their vision of God and their country at war. A priest expressed his religious engagement in the war with these words: 'My death will be my last mass, and I will unite my blood with the blood that Jesus shed on the cross.'[21] Catholics whose fervour derived from the most austere Christian doctrine linked their personal sacrifice to their love of their faith. A statement, for example, by Ernest Psichari, a colonial artillery officer who had converted to Catholicism in 1913, sets the tone: 'I go to this war as to a crusade, because I feel it is a question of defending the two great causes to which I dedicated my life.'[22]

These new 'crusaders' like Psichari, of whom it was said that he would 'in the next minute receive communion or die', sacrificed their lives for God and country, and they did so 'joyously', they said, which even very religious Christians would find almost impossible to conceive today. Between 1914 and 1918, this

---

rest of the population nationwide, were calculated and assembled but never publicly released, and all sorts of anti-Semitic hypotheses about Jewish cowardliness, indeed Jewish betrayal, in 1914-18 arose. In fact, 12,000 German Jews died for their country in the Great War.

*One commander, General Petain, wrote, 'I have been told that some graves of Jews were marked with a cross, a fact which might go against the religious sentiment of the families of that religion. Please ... prescribe that in the future all precautions be taken to avoid a cross on the tombs of Jews, which should be marked by a simple inscription.'[19]

spiritual sacrifice was experienced as a supreme religious act, a gift to God in imitation of God: they were ready for martyrdom. The sacrifice was a choice freely made precisely because the price was the very highest one – the sacrifice of one's life.

In France, this heroism of sacrifice was characteristic of militant Catholics in the right-wing organisation Action Française, particularly among converted Catholics, who saw the war as a magnificent opportunity for fulfilling the calling of their newly acquired faith, but it could also be found among much more moderate Catholics and among Protestants: 'I'm not afraid of dying. Now I can say it in all sincerity: I've made the sacrifice of my life,' an enlisted Protestant wrote to his parents.[23] The same was true of Jews, though without the theme of the Imitation of Christ: 'All those who have a Jewish heart in France are prepared for every sacrifice and every form of dedication. To the invaders who dare to tread on the sacred soil, whose every step is marked by pillage, arson and ruination, Jews, like all French, will hold as a rampart their lives as free men.'[24]

If Péguy and Psichari, who died at the front in the very first weeks of the war, became such important figures in the following months and years, it is because their destiny had been mystically prepared for by the premonitions they had of their own deaths. They were prophets who became heroes. In 1916, Psichari's *Le Voyage du Centurion*, about the desert initiation, conversion and death of Maxence, a young military patriot, appeared posthumously. The account of Maxence/Psichari's death was troublingly attractive for those who were imitating both Psichari and Maxence: 'He is the messenger of a people who know full well the worth of the blood of martyrs. He knows what it is to die for an idea. He has 20,000 crusaders behind him ... he is the child of suffering.'[25] In Champagne, Artois and the Ardennes, where Psichari the soldier had died, suffering became literature. Similarly, Péguy's verses were seen as premonitory and quoted over and over again: 'Happy are those who died in a just war,/ Happy the ripened head of grain and the harvested wheat.' Through his exemplary life and death, Psichari is probably the best representative of the mystique of sacrifice that some Catholic intellectuals rediscovered in the war, a mystique that Henri Massis defined as follows:

> Because of the war we shall have lived in incomparable grace ... This is the thought that arises in the cloister of the trenches. No solitary person has meditated more ardently ... What Trappist monastery, what enclosure, offers a comparable barrenness and abandonment, a deeper, truer vision of death, a greater solitude, a society of fraternal souls sustained with such fervour? The holocaust is complete. Whether he chooses the pickaxe that breaks the earth or the shovel that tosses it aside, each of us is digging his grave.[26]

But it was probably the Jesuit stretcher-bearer Pierre Teilhard de Chardin who best expressed the surge of religious feeling in the midst of the disaster of war, the fascination with suffering and its sublimation, the Pascalian theme of the misery and greatness of man:

> The war stripped away the surface banalities and conventions. A window opened up on the secret mechanisms and deep layers of human destiny. There was now an area where it was possible for men to breathe an air suffused with heaven ... Fortunate, perhaps, are those who will have met death in the very act and atmosphere of war, when they were endowed with and, driven by a responsibility, a conscience, a liberty greater than their own – when they were exalted to the edge of the World – very near to God.[27]

The tragic philosophy of these intellectuals was informed by a certain strain in Catholic thought, according to which the Imitation of Jesus can bring miracles and resurrection only through the suffering of the Passion. The war then becomes an immense Good Friday and the front a Golgotha: 'To think that He suffered a hundred times what I see my brothers suffering around me – one brother crushed under sandbags, another clobbered and torn to shreds by a shell, yet another suffering of thirst in his pothole and crying out in vain for his mother.'[28] Some of the items crafted in the trenches – sculpted shells, for example – were fashioned to be put in wayside calvaries on the Golgotha battlefield. Metamorphosed away from their deadly function, they became representations of sacrifice, of Christ on the cross.

The miracle of combat not only made soldiers into Christ figures but it made Christ into a soldier. 'The burial places in the cemetery were hacked to pieces, and under the pieces of marble were yawning black holes,' wrote Henri Ghéon in 1915. 'Christ, at last torn away from that dark lone cross left standing on the flooded plain, lay on the bare ground, arms outstretched. He shared the common fate of our soldiers.'[29]

Ghéon, an *homme né de la guerre* – a man born of the war – was one of the many converts whose faith was revealed to them during the conflict.[30] For many, the war marked the beginning or the end, depending on the case, of a spiritual journey. Also, converts of the 1905–13 years, like Psichari, harbingers of the 'nationalist-Catholic' generation, paid a heavy debt to the war and were the inspirational figures behind other conversions.[31] If the war itself was such an effective proselytiser, it was because it caused the kind of spiritual dereliction needed for a genuine transformation, a conversion in the root sense of the word. Suffering and the nearness of death, indeed the likelihood of death, plunged men into a spiritual state that was conducive to faith.

Hence men were converted to war and converted by war. These conversions were consistent with the ambience of suffering, and militants of the faith were convinced that God was revealed in this suffering. Conversions to Catholicism were the most numerous and best known of these religious transformations, as might expected, given that it was the religion of a majority of the combatants. But it was also the specific nature of Catholicism, the religion of miracle, that drove people to conversion. The conversion experiences were both responses to

God's miracles and miracles in themselves. They were the sign of the mediation of the living or the dead in the war. The war itself, seen in this light, had undergone a conversion and been transformed into a spiritual exercise. A collective Imitation of Christ, it engendered spiritual newborns who imitated Christ individually. Thus several proofs of God's presence appeared concurrently, or so all those who converted before the war believed, and all the more so during the conflict.

While we know of many conversions, loss of faith was rarely discussed during the Great War. Such instances occurred, of course, but the moments of despair, of loss and emptiness, were not made public or recorded in diaries as often as moments of exaltation and faith. Whereas the conversion narrative is an established literary genre, the loss of faith narrative is not. To the question asked by the historian Étienne Fouilloux, 'How can one believe after Tannenberg or Verdun?'[32] one might add a second: 'Can one believe after Tannenberg or Verdun?'

For the most fervently religious, the attainment of grace cannot occur without spiritual abandonment. The naval officer Pierre-Dominique Dupouey's 'beautiful death', for instance, worthy of a medieval knight's, was also a personal and family tragedy: Mireille Dupouey kept in her notebooks a collection of her intimate thoughts and of the letters she continued to write to her late husband. She continued a dialogue of love and faith with the man from whom she felt separated in appearance only:

> Lord Jesus, I begged of the Cross that I might receive love – in response you have led me to Calvary, thank you ... If you tear my heart, may my torn heart adore you ... There is something loftier than heartfelt love, it is the call of France ... I know I loved you more as the soldier Pierre Frenchman first and foremost ... My love, given for France, at the mercy of God's will ... How could my heart agree to be wrenched like this? ... Oh, we must love God with a fearsome love to make such a sacrifice to him. Love him to give my beloved away to him? Love him more than my beloved? ... You are not dead and I am not a widow ... There is

this infinitely dear mourning, because the unchanging deep black of mourning is the image of a solemn, steadfast fidelity ... Now all contact is over; it is a sacrifice, but our hearts embrace each other.[33]

The Dupouey couple had made the transition from sacrificed generation to lost generation.

But this kind of Christian stoicism can seem unbearable; some very sincere believers started to loathe the writers whom they thought prone to abusing the themes of sacrifice and death, composing with a 'charlatan's sarcasm': 'The professionals in the pious journals are determined to let them into the paradise of martyrs,' complained Léon Bloy. 'Listening to them, you would think each person ... gave his life for the love of God, feeling supernaturally detached from all terrestrial affection ... Ah, yes, indeed, even the poor soldiers abandoned on the icy bed of mud that will be their shroud.'[34]

In fact, the war aroused two distinct religious responses simultaneously, which were not experienced as paradoxical: on the one hand, it was seen as a punishment for sin; on the other, it created an immense need for consolation. As sources of spiritual improvement, the two attitudes weren't contradictory. In their spiritual dereliction, the combatants and their families turned to the intercession of those who could bring them temporal comfort in the face of war; the urgent needs of this calamitous time led directly to the core Christian message of sacrifice and resurrection. Yet this increase in religious devotion did not exclude superstitious practices: wartime being such an extraordinary time, extraordinary practices become banal.

These shared religious feelings created a new kind of complicity between the front line and the home front, and between men and women. The men, generally less religious than the women, were surprised by their own religious practices, even by the mere act of attending a comrade's funeral. At the front, which of course was a male world, the soldiers discovered religious practices that in their former lives they had thought of as being in the domain mostly of women. Prayers, religious medals and images, and pious books accompanied the soldiers, and there was a constant flow of such material, which they themselves solicited. The vision of a holy war naturally involved gifts of religious medals and votive offerings, with the intercession of saints proving the holiness of the cause as this letter from a young woman from the Aude illustrates: 'Dear brother, as I write, mother is making a package for you. You'll find a flask of tincture of iodine so that if by misfortune something happens to you, you'll put a bit on and tighten the bandage well. There's a Saint Anthony medal and another medal and you should wear them because Mother is parting with them to give them to you. Wear them, for it will bring you luck.'[35] The philosopher and theologian Jacques Maritain made a similar gesture: 'I'm sending you a medallion of the Holy Virgin. I would be very pleased if you would wear it, not out of superstition, but as a sign of our mutual spiritual affection, and because the most humble concrete signs can be the occasion for God's benediction or grace.'[36]

Votive offerings – mainly to the Virgin but also to the saints – kept in many sanctuaries, were like staged presentations of received graces, prayers as theatre, hymns to life from men and women who were living through mass death. In those little painted or embroidered images, the protectors are in the upper half of the picture, while the war has invaded everywhere else. Flames and cannon fire seem to rise all the way up to the rays beaming from the miracle-givers. These ex-votos proclaim that there is room for miracles even in the most industrial of wars. Soldiers are shown in combat just when the miracle occurs – that is the main theme; the act of grace is signed with their name; and a photograph is very often attached. This photographic proof shows the desire for veracity, which is clear enough from the details of the drawings and the offerings' highly individualistic meanings: here is an individual who has received a special grace – and he attests to it.

The Virgin was worshipped with particular intensity, as were two other heroines of the faith – Joan of Arc, from the remote fifteenth century, and Theresa of Lisieux, who had died recently. In fact, they were both canonised in the 1920s partly because of their popularity during the war; nineteenth-century campaigns for them were taken over by rank-and-file enthusiasts fired with the piety of the trenches and the home front. Joan and Theresa, as well as the Virgin, conferred victory, protected and consoled; they offered the certainty of collective and individual miracles, and presided over religious conversions. Fundamental to this religious fervour was the belief in the reversibility of suffering. From the tragedy of the Crucifixion, from Joan of Arc's martyrdom in Rouen, from Theresa's long dialogue with the Invisible and her death at twenty-four, one could draw the lesson that the greatest pain gave birth to the greatest happiness.

Though Saint Theresa, who gave her life to Christ as a Carmelite nun, might have seemed a less appropriate saint in the trenches than the patriotic Joan of Arc, the war gave both a real function as a rallying point encompassing the Sacred Union and hatred of the enemy. Theresa was called 'the little sister of the trenches', 'the combatants' favourite wartime godmother', 'the poilu's saint'. Believers were clearly inspired by her spiritual struggle, which became their metaphor for the war. Had she not said, 'I would like to die on a battlefield to defend the Church,' and 'My fragrant rain will fall on the militant Church and give her victory'? [37]

Her insistence on family, constancy and the duty to suffer was inevitably moving to young people of that generation, who had not been prepared for those years of suffering yet had no choice but to live through them. She was the 'little sister' at a time when they all had a little sister at home. Like the soldiers, the 'female saints' were young and had suffered; they had sacrificed their lives just as the soldiers were sacrificing their lives for their country. They gave meaning to their war, and it was a meaning with generational overtones. This was true for soldiers in both camps. Mother Agnes, of the Carmelite nunnery of Lisieux, wrote: 'We are being asked from Switzerland [the Red Cross] to send relics for the Germans. We shall do so gladly, because, before God, souls are neither French nor German. They are all precious in the eyes of God.'*[38]

During the war, articles appeared in religious magazines warning readers against the 'superstitions' that had been proliferating since the beginning of the conflict. Both priests and anthropologists tried to understand these phenomena. A Swiss questionnaire that circulated in Italy and France shows the great diversity of spiritual approaches as well as the observers' lucid understanding of them:

1 What means are used to shirk military service (mutilations, superstitions, etc.)?
2 Does recruitment involve any particular practices?
3 Are you aware of strange practices during and after battle (symbolic practices during the declaration of war, the throwing of earth over the head; where and when...)?
4 How is it believed that life can be saved? Are some people considered invincible? Holy objects, holy water, coins or medallions (images and inscriptions?), religious maxims; magical notes, amulets, plants and other magical objects.
5 What are some of the popular remedies used to calm or dissipate certain illnesses?
6 Are there inoffensive or superstitious ways of always reaching the goal (hitting a target or an opponent)?
7 What are the omens of war?
8 Do the people believe in prophecies relating to the war, the destruction of princely families or countries ...?[39]

In the prayer-amulets that soldiers wore, often sewn into the linings of their uniforms, in the prayer chain-letters, in the prophecies, and in the numerical puzzle games played in France

---

*Mother Agnes's wish to influence the canonisation process, then taking place in Rome, made her accept the Germans' affection for Theresa; otherwise it was highly unusual for national barriers to be transcended during the war.

and Italy, the German empire was always defeated mathemati-
cally. 'The black eagle [Germany] will throw itself on the rooster
[France]; the rooster will lose a lot of feathers but strike back
with its spur; it would soon be exhausted if not for the help of
the leopard [England] ... The black eagle will lose his crown and
die in solitude and insanity. Then the universe will enter into a
new era of peace and prosperity. There will be no more war.'

Though there were priests who denounced these 'sheaths
against misfortune', they well understood the origin of the phenomenon: 'It is religion in one of its essential aspects, converted
into a kind of formula against sudden or bloody death ... These
papers [prayer-amulets], which were more or less slumbering,
sewn inside a lining, have come out of their retirement and been
dragged, like everything else, into the universal mobilisation.'[40]
In order to stand firm in the 'universal mobilisation' and live surrounded by death, one needed to be reassured by the affection of
one's family, by one's country and faith, and by superstition as
well. All reinforced rather than cancelled one another in the cru-
cible of the war. Often children who had not been baptised at
birth were now taken for their christenings, the stated motive
being to keep their fathers alive at the front.

Soldiers told many tales about how they had been protected
from death. There were soldiers whose lives had been saved
thanks to a wallet stuffed with letters from a fiancée deflecting
the shrapnel; others were convinced they had been saved by the
Virgin, a saint, an amulet, or a prayer they had recopied. Protestant soldiers, whether churchgoing or not, had a Bible in their
kits; some of them read it, but most of them didn't feel the need,
being reassured not so much by its spiritual content but by its
physical presence, and by contact with it as an object. The Bible
was used as an amulet. This didn't upset an American chaplain:

> I had to search the dead bodies for their little possessions. The
> doctor and I were amazed to find that nearly every man had a
> Bible or cross on him. They do seem religious, he said, these boys;
> I should never have thought they would have 'such things'.

> Perhaps they carried them as a charm, a sort of magic; perhaps
> because they felt more than they knew that 'such things'
> contained the secret of life and death and immortality, perhaps
> because they had a deep love for them. No one can say.[41]

Spiritualism and belief in the premonitions of dreams were a similar kind of response.

All these wartime beliefs testify to the vitality of these men and women, their strong desire to live when confronted with the destructiveness of war. In the face of war's modern rationality, which was of course impossible to understand and internalise, the irrational returned in force to both believers and non-believers. One sees proof of this in all the different national histories of the war.[42] Unsurprisingly, this irrationality seemed completely anachronistic once the war was over, and the mystical determination to fight seemed especially implausible retrospectively, and was swept away in a wave of post-war pacifism. The only possible thing to believe was that it had been a 'war to end all wars', and one should now devote oneself to peace. The religious fervours of the Great War's crusade were all the more repressed since they seemed to belong to the world of the rejected past. From now on, the cult of the New Man, in communism and fascism, grew in strength. But without God.

'Civilising' and 'humanitarian' dimensions of the culture of war

During 1914–18, no one escaped from the war or from being on his country's side, claims to the contrary notwithstanding. Everything was drawn into a contaminating, irreversible chain reaction. Though it would seem that neutrality, humanity and compassion were, point by point, the opposite of enlistment, brutality and reprisal, there were many contradictions. As we have seen, the war was waged with disregard for scruples concerning either civilians or combatants, even though wounded and captured soldiers forced out of combat were supposed to be placed in the care of a neutral party.

Still, the advances made in the Geneva Convention (1864) and the negotiations at the Hague (1899 and 1907) did not go completely unheeded. Wounded soldiers and prisoners of war were better protected by these still inadequate humanitarian conventions than civilians were. The founder of the Red Cross, Henri Dunant, had wanted 'to civilise' warfare, to define a 'human' limit to its brutalities and to prevent it from becoming an 'animalistic' massacre, and his aims were largely realised in 1914–18 thanks to the humanitarian efforts of the International Committee of the Red Cross and many other religious and secular charitable organisations. However, given the exceptional tension of the period, infringements and violations, sparked by terrorist violence, were typical of all the warring countries.

In 1916, for example, the historian Ernest Lavisse gave the Red Cross a prize on behalf of the Institut de France. He used the occasion to describe the war – particularly the war waged against occupied civilians – as proof of Germany's intrinsic barbarism, which he had already had ample opportunity to observe in the *département* of Aisne in 1870 (once making the comment: 'Hatred of the Germans is a virtue that the Germans themselves have made easy, and the extent of our misfortune has made forgetting impossible').[43] Extolling charity, compassion and the 'spirit of Geneva' was merely a pretext for showering praise on the French Republic, and republican messianism merges with humanitarian messianism:

> It [the Red Cross] repatriates the civilians that Germany, having torn them from their native soil in one of its most odious and typically barbaric crimes, agrees to release. Geneva has watched troops of these unfortunate people arrive, exhausted by famine and misery ... has given them food, and flowers, and tears of brotherly compassion. The Committee performs its enormous task in a marvellously orderly fashion; everything works with the precision of Swiss clockwork ... We are comforted to see that in

spite of today's regression to the barbarism of ancient times, humanity still exists ... Of all the fighting nations, France is the one that suffered most and was in the greatest peril. It is she that the enemy wanted to destroy first and foremost, as the necessary prelude to world enslavement. The enemy was right ...
Superhuman Germany is actually inhuman. It was right therefore to want to destroy France, where human rights and the rights of peoples have been proclaimed.[44]

And yet there was a glaring difference: in Geneva, the Red Cross gratefully acknowledged the Institut's 20,000 francs, but was careful not to reproduce Lavisse's speech. For he expressed a truth from the perspective of his own country: France on the side of humanity. The Red Cross was neutral: from its perspective humanity was stateless.

While millions of men and women waged war so zealously, how could a few individuals and organisations ensure respect for a certain kind of humanity? Because of their intrinsically international and supranational stature, the Red Cross in Geneva and the papacy in Rome, as represented by Benedict XV and his nuncios worldwide, thought the 'charitable' or 'humanitarian' task was up to them. They were repaid with incomprehension everywhere: not only, as might be expected, from the belligerent and bellicose, who included most of the world population, but also from militant pacifists, a tiny minority. One reason for scepticism was the Red Cross's narrow legalism, its obstinate determination to work only within the limits of the ratified conventions lest the belligerents bar them from all action. Occasionally, the Red Cross overlooked a decision taken by one side so that it could act in another sector; sometimes it also had to accept on the one hand what it necessarily condemned on the other. It could not be outspokenly critical of those responsible for a belligerent country's malfeasance lest it jeopardise the few humanitarian actions, such as repatriation or assistance, that the malefactors authorised.

In France especially, the brutal war being waged against

Germany was always seen as justified by Germany's crimes; the barbarian who was bringing death and desolation had to be stopped at all costs from pursuing his vile acts. His evil deeds and the many deaths were proof of the legitimacy of the struggle, and this led to escalating brutality in the reprisals. For the French, the map of the war on the Western Front was proof enough of the enemy's intrinsic barbarism and grounds enough for violent hatred. Had not the Germans violated both France's sacred soil and their women's sacred bodies? Never had the words of the 'Marseillaise', the national anthem of the triumphant Third Republic, seemed so meaningful and real: the enemy had marched right in 'to slit the throats of our daughters and women'. The great difficulty the humanitarian organisations encountered in their missions arose from the fact that there was a gulf between people who sought the truth and those who knew, or thought they knew, the 'truth', for whom the enemy was by definition barbarian.

Since a world war essentially ruled out neutrality, the only possible conclusion for the Red Cross and the papacy was that peace had to be made. They were thus doubly out of sync with the belligerents, and their position seemed doubly untenable: there they were advocating neutrality and peace while war, which made both impossible, was raging. Yet they kept a lucidity about their aims, often tinged with bitterness, as in the following statements made by Red Cross delegates:

> The preoccupation with the harm one hopes to inflict on the enemy is so strong that it prevails all too often over what could be beneficial to oneself; this is the mentality of war, one recovers from it ... [but] later, sometimes when it is too late ... Even in normal times, telling the truth is no easy task ... but the task becomes so much more difficult in these critical times when passions are overexcited by war and people are blinded with hatred. When a Frenchman commented on my mission by saying, 'Someone who is neutral, a spectator of a war like this one, can't see things from the perspective of a belligerent who is in the

mêlée,' he was certainly and *fortunately* right. If a neutral person
were to judge things in war from the belligerent's perspective, he
would no longer be neutral ... Yet may the neutral person be
allowed a humble prayer, that he may be trusted, lest his work be
useless and in vain.[45]

But what can be done in a world where the premise is that
the other person is lying, and that 'Germany has no conscience',
or that 'France and England are hypocrites'? How could countries both wage all-out war and respect the spirit of the international conventions that had been ratified before the war? Both
sides believed that the Red Cross delegates were being deceived,
that they were shown things selectively when they visited the
camps and that they were selective in what they published –
either that or they were purposely withholding shameful secrets
to protect the enemy.

Besides, the perversity of the system was such that the Red
Cross actually needed the war which had become its *raison d'être*.
And this inevitably revealed other contradictions. The Red Cross
was organised along military lines, imposing obedience, belief in
discipline and a code of honour. Did it merely want to harness
violence or did it want to make it disappear?

The first humanitarian task was to enable military and civilian prisoners to correspond with their families, reestablishing
contact between the front lines and the home front. But in a
sense the two fronts had changed places: prisoners' families were
now on the 'front lines', fighting to get information and to give
help and love, while the prisoners seemed in the rear, feeling
useless or being made to work guiltily for the enemy war effort.
To be of any real assistance, the humanitarian organisations had
to persuade both the prisoners and their families that they were
now set apart, that they had become neutral, like themselves;
they had to show the prisoners they had rights and duties not as
German, French or British nationals but as prisoners. This was
where the great ambiguity of humanitarian action presented
itself, for the prisoners and their families could never divorce

their ways of thinking from their national origin. Not only were they deeply convinced that the enemy was evil and perpetrated evil, but they also suspected the humanitarian organisations of siding with the enemy and selectively choosing witnesses' testimonies. Prisoners on all sides were sometimes killed on the battlefield. Other prisoners witnessed this violence and they never forgot it throughout the entire term of their internment. For them, the very concept of neutrality was questionable. On each side, people were so convinced of the legitimacy of their struggle for law and civilisation that neutrality, or aloofness from combat, was inconceivable to them – except to conceal a secret partiality. Though they willingly accepted the Red Cross's help with the mail, for example, they refused to believe its statements or actions whenever they might be interpreted as discriminatory: since both sides believed that *only* the enemy powers treated their prisoners badly, the French refused to accept the idea that the Red Cross might investigate French camps in Morocco, and the Germans that it should investigate the German ones in East Prussia. It was impossible to *think* in neutral terms, hence neutrality was *unthinkable*.

Secondly, there was the paradox of peace and war, and the strange circumstance that the Red Cross, by a kind of intrinsic perversity, was living off war and its atrocities. This reproach was made by observers, notably militant pacifists who were hardly benevolent about the Red Cross. (As we have said, these pacifists were as rare between 1914 and 1918 as they were legion after the war.)

Already, in 1901, when Henri Dunant was given the Nobel Peace Prize, pacifists felt that this was a betrayal of Alfred Nobel's will. For them, humanitarianism was not about peace. And this dispute arose again when the International Committee of the Red Cross received the Nobel Prize in 1917. Because of the war, the peace prize had not been awarded since 1914, a decision which pacifists regarded as implicitly supporting the war, leaving the worldwide violence unchallenged (though the 1916 Nobel Prize in Literature was awarded to Romain Rolland, then a resident of Switzerland, probably principally for his book *Above the Battle*). Now that the peace prize was again being awarded, in 1917, it was given to an humanitarian cause once more. As far as the pacifist movement was concerned, humanitarianism was like a poultice applied to a wooden leg. The Swedish pacifists turned their frustration into a joke, expressing regret that the Red Cross had failed to win the Nobel Prize in Medicine.

No one, and certainly not the Red Cross, challenged the truth that the war was an unspeakable horror in every respect. But a new and radical way of thinking about war in 1914–18 did reach those who were trying to help prisoners and to stop the victimisation of civilians. The humanitarian revolution of the twentieth century dates back to the Great War, but it took another eighty years of the most terrible atrocities before the 'right to interfere' became a daring possibility and before people attempted to assert it on war terrain. Conversely, what the militant pacifists who criticised the Red Cross primarily objected to were the so-called humane rules of warfare, for like their turn-of-the-century predecessors they believed that these would merely encourage the waging of war by making it not more humane, but easier, and easier on consciences as well. In a sense, they advocated the worst-case scenario in order to achieve their goal – the permanent absence of war.

The paradox was, of course, that this peace utopia abandoned the weakest victims to their fate – the newest victims of war, children, women, civilians in general and prisoners of war. An ideology that stressed peace at all costs and saw humanitarianism as pernicious was tantamount to one that cleared the way for brutality. And that is what the Red Cross couldn't accept. Yet it was agreeing to shut its eyes to infringements on, indeed the demise of, codes of honour between armies in wartime, and it would confront the same tragedy repeatedly in the twentieth century.[46] Was the idea of 'making war civilised' another dangerous utopia, founded on the outdated, erroneous hypothesis of mutual respect between enemies?

The Red Cross appealed to ethical conduct, whereas total war was proof to each side that the enemy obeyed no rules, and even refused to respect the difference in status between combatants and non-combatants, which set the latter apart. The warrior's honour, which respected non-combatants and a fallen enemy, had been replaced worldwide by a determination to use any means necessary to overpower the adversary. And this was cloaked in the hypocrisy – though it was not consciously experienced as such – of believing in the enemy's complete responsibility for the conflict. Stories the soldiers told were full of details about infringements of the rules of warfare that had once been valued in the West, which were always attributed to the enemy, as in this description of a young French officer's death at Verdun in 1916: 'Five German officers surrendered to the sub-lieutenant and he stepped forward, trustingly, to take them into custody; one of them drew his gun and murdered him point blank. This act of odious betrayal cost an excellent soldier his life.'[47]

Honour, when it still existed, was exercised only along national lines, never otherwise. Hence, in prisoner-of-war camps, escape alone was honourable, even if there was a dangerous risk of being recaptured and transferred to a disciplinary camp. The countless escape attempts made from all the camps are a good indication of this. All prisoners devoted untold energy to their efforts to escape because they considered it their duty to re-join the struggle however they could. But this honour as the prisoners conceived it contradicted the legalistic position of the Red Cross, which demanded that one should respect one's condition as prisoner so that one's guards would, reciprocally, honour it too.* While prisoners accepted the minimal rules of humanitarian neutrality, such as having their names on file in Geneva and being supervised by the Red Cross, which enabled them to cor-

---

*In Jean Renoir's film *La Grande Illusion*, released in 1937, a French officer and a German officer are seen to share the same sense of honour, but they know their world is fast disappearing. Humanitarianism is treated with contempt, as when the Russian soldiers look upon the books sent by the Tsarina with disgust and set them on fire.

respond with their families and receive packages, they never felt that these rules obliged them to remain neutral in the conflict. They even found it normal to take reprisals on enemy prisoners: Charles de Gaulle, writing to his mother in September 1916, said, 'We hope, for example, that the hundreds of German officers taken prisoner on the Somme in the next few weeks will be properly and delicately shipped off to Dahomey. In my opinion that is the only way of compelling the enemy to give us what it owes us here.'[48] Hence the same prisoners who felt that the Geneva Convention should be diligently applied to them considered that violations vis-à-vis the enemy committed by authorities in their own country were perfectly justified. This remarkable display of national superiority completely contradicted the spirit of the international conventions. In fact, neither neutrality, internationalism or supranationalism could hold out against the perverse dynamic of total war.

Science in combat and racial prejudice

Intellectuals had the dangerous power of being able to promote and orchestrate the perversion of total war. Whether on the front lines or the home front, they had no doubt that their intelligence had something special to offer their country in hardship: the war was a continuation of intellectual activity by other means. The physical involvement of intellectuals who became soldiers was only one aspect of the self-sacrificing patriotism at the core of the war culture, a culture of 'authentic martyrs of the national ideal'.[49] As both intellectuals and soldiers, in turn or simultaneously, they gave themselves over to their two vocations with equal ardour.

In the very first months of the war, Sigmund Freud, in his *Thoughts for the Times on War and Death*, set down what he saw as the onset of total war. The discovery that Europeans were behaving like 'barbarians', locked in reciprocal hatreds, was 'a disillusionment': 'Science herself has lost her passionless impartiality;

her deeply embittered servants seek for weapons from her with which to contribute towards the struggle with the enemy. Anthropologists feel driven to declare him inferior and degenerate, psychiatrists issue a diagnosis of his disease of mind or spirit.'[50] Though he was an Austrian patriot whose sons were on the front, Freud was the first in a long line of intellectuals to discover that modern war produced extraordinarily traumatic situations that neither the societies themselves nor their professional analysts were prepared to confront. During the nineteenth century, the 'human sciences' and modern medicine had developed as part of humanity's 'positive progress', whereas brutality and brutalisation – internalised feelings of violence that were easy to act on because they expressed one's visceral patriotism – were symptoms of this new kind of war. Intellectuals, far from being detached from this view, in fact provided the explanatory matrix for it. The belligerents on both sides called on two groups of 'experts' to testify against the enemy – scientists and 'neutral persons', the guarantee of scientific objectivity being viewed as a form of neutrality – and invited various researchers, preferably from non-warring nations like Spain, the United States (before 1917) or Greece, to publish their supposedly irrefutable testimonies. This allowed for the elaboration of reliably tautological testimonies made by reliably neutral people.

The elites of all countries shaped their nations' support for the war, depicting an ideal of sacrifice and abnegation and reinforcing the people's certainty that they were an organic part of a threatened nation. The Germans, the English, the French – all reasoned identically in this respect. The Germans were convinced that the French and the English, in contrast to them and German *Kultur*, placed self-interest above collective interest. Conversely, for the French, France's universal humanistic culture, its sense of patriotism and history growing out of the nation's long tradition as the 'Church's elder daughter' and out of the universal values of the Rights of Man and the Republic, were at the heart of the anti-German struggle. And this universality *à la française* was supposed to represent truth and enlightenment as against German *Kultur*'s sectarianism, its intrinsic falsehood and its brutal, i.e. 'barbarian', violence. For the French who were most gifted at giving this idea meaning, i.e. the intellectuals, France was indeed waging a war of a superior civilisation against barbarism, of heroes sacrificed to a battle against the 'odious enemy' (as de Gaulle called Germany).

The youngest of the well-educated social elite in all the belligerent countries became officers when they were called up. And both non-commissioned officers and officers, fighting at the head of their troops, were most exposed to danger and usually had a higher casualty rate than their men. After the war, one theme was reiterated tirelessly: 'We will suffer for ever from this wound to the head.' [51] In France it was believed the loss of the nation's best minds was a specifically French tragedy, and it was noted that a number of writers had been struck down by 'the symbolic wound of the intellectual, a bullet in the forehead'.

The graduates of the École des Chartes are an interesting example: as historians and archivists with a particular love for medieval history, they endowed their battlefield patriotism with an energy fuelled by their historical and humanistic culture; they saw themselves as modern 'valiant knights', members of an intellectual and ethical knighthood.[52] In sources like the *Song of Roland* and texts about Joan of Arc, the *chartistes* found resources for the love of their country, for its creation and defence. Their patriotic duty and professional duties mutually reinforced each other and drove them to 'nationalise truth'[53] forsaking the universality of science and research.

But of course this contradiction was not apparent during the conflict itself: the need to maintain a division of the world into good and evil swept all before it. Since the universality represented by France and her allies was good, everything else was evil, and evil pervaded everything German. The archivist and palaeographer Claude Cochin wrote in 1917:

> Every day German shells pound the soil of our nation. They are also erasing the past of our race. Churches and fortified castles

that had been spared the ravages of time are being crushed by
Krupp's steel. Modern explosives are destroying buildings that had
defied the centuries and seemed indestructible. The written
monuments of French history have suffered as well. But their pain
is obscure ... The red leprosy on the ruins of Rheims is far more
pitiful than old papers blackened by fire, whose disappearance is
less eloquent and moves us less. Yet one day this will be included
in the bill of indictment to which intellectual Germany will have
to answer. Among the archives destroyed, the most disastrous loss,
without a doubt, are the departmental archives of the Pas-de-
Calais ... The history of one of our most beautiful provinces has
gone up in smoke.[54]

Another *chartiste* breathed life into the cathedrals of northern
and eastern France and portrayed them as exemplary victims of
the Germans:

Rheims cathedral is burning. I am choked with grief ... I talk
with the soldiers. The fierce battle is no longer important. The
people are infused with fifteen centuries of faith and love and
they feel struck at the heart. I am pleased by their anger. They
release a volley of curses. Blessed fury! So the race is not dead! It
vibrates with intensity, recognises itself and finds its destiny again.
Faith against faith, thought against thought, race against race.
Every falling stone is a soul dying, slipping away, laden with anger
and hope, begetting artists and believers. France's earth shudders
with pain and desire. The dreadful chaos is changing into a
building site; the blaze into an apotheosis. Our hatred will watch
over this rubble. Sacred ruins are needed to attest to the
barbarism, legitimise the victory, bring about the resurrection.[55]

War brutalises men in both senses of the word: it injures their
flesh and their souls, and it renders them brutal, too. These young
officers, whose combat was constantly re-legitimised in their
own eyes by the military and cultural barbarism of the enemy,
forgot that they had once been peace-loving students and quiet

scholars. Love of France and hatred of the enemy sustained them and stimulated them to struggle for a victory they considered as legitimate and therefore good. They fought with all their weapons, cultural hatred of the adversary being among the most important. Augustin Cochin, cousin of Claude, wrote from the trenches just a month before he died there:

> We are for the time being lodged in the ruins of their incredible
> constructions of forts and underground villages. What a race of
> slaves and serfs! Never would the fear of heavy shells or
> punishments make our men do one tenth of this … Dreadful,
> dreadful race; the more we see them from close up, the more we
> loathe them. The bands of prisoners are revolting to see, vile, trying
> too hard to be liked, delighted to be caught … It is annoying to get
> killed behind the parapet by such animals. They have a peculiar,
> powerful odour, which we can't escape from, living as we are on
> their lines, special lice, too — the famous large, iron-cross lice.[56]

He uttered the crucial word: race.

In the first days of August 1914, when a plan was being considered in France to expurgate German intellectuals from the lists of all universities, laboratories and other institutions they had been associated with, the philosopher Henri Bergson analysed the question very clearly:

> The struggle against Germany is the struggle of civilisation
> against barbarism. This is everyone's feeling, but our Academy [of
> Moral and Political Sciences] is particularly qualified to make the
> statement. Largely dedicated to the study of psychological, ethical
> and social issues, our Academy is fulfilling a scientific duty in
> pointing out that Germany's brutality and cynicism, its contempt
> for justice and truth, signals a regression to a state of savagery.[57]

The Germans' barbarism was believed to have been substantiated as soon as they declared war and violated Belgium's neutrality; intellectual 'knowledge' of their atavism predated knowledge of the invasion. Germany at war was a national incarnation of barbarism. The atrocities, far from being thought to reveal a specific German crime, were considered merely to confirm pre-established convictions.

How could such ideas be accepted among scholars who had not long before admired, even envied, German culture? Why didn't they show any scepticism or see any inconsistency? Their conviction of the superiority of their 'race' swept away all scruple and opened the door to their new Manichaean views. Now there were the Germans and then everyone else, those who were barbarians and those who were civilised. Édouard Herriot, later to be prime minister, wrote in 1916:

> What had seemed to us German thought collapsed under the wave of violence. All independence of mind disappeared before this Prussian savagery. The present war will have revealed, once again, the conflict in Germany between theory and practice, thought and deed ... Bluntschli, the former professor of law at the University of Heidelberg, may say: 'Among civilised nations, war cannot have as its aim destruction and carnage, but only the restoration and preservation of the law. The useless killing of even an armed enemy is forbidden.' Admirable doctrine! But look at the acts committed by the German army every day in Belgium and France! There is a gulf between theory and practice; and the basic sophism on which all of so-called German culture is built can be found in this permanent contradiction. That is, literally, *the German lie*. [58]

So the lie, now, was Germany. But in contrast, as the preface to a French book on German science put it:

> It is not just France that they [scholars] intend to serve, but truth. Contrary to the Germans, they believe that defending truth is the best way of serving their country ... Our country should be grateful to the authors of this book for having demonstrated the truth, not a truth in the service of the state. Impartial judgement is the best homage that can be paid to French genius. [59]

The war of 1914–18 offered this kind of cultural ammunition, and it gave an intellectual foundation to a war culture. It is no surprise that a great number of scientists' comments were fashioned into intellectual artillery directed against the enemy, for the French believed it was the enemy who had wanted the conflict, who bore entire responsibility for it, and who was pursuing it with the diabolical purpose of destroying the opposing 'race' by waging total war.

It is not clear whether French or British intellectuals really grasped the complexities of German national thought. Usually they made no distinction between the militants of the Pan-German League – whose ranks did indeed swell during the war – the German people as a whole, and Germany's intellectual, political and military elites. One Frenchman wrote, 'Everything will be done scientifically! *Deutsche Kultur* is "organised" barbarism, a barbarism that has reinforced itself by harnessing the forces of civilisation.'[60] This understanding of pan-Germanism among the Allies inevitably broadened the war and intensified its brutalities, for *Kultur* was seen not only as the origin of the Germans' will to wage war but as responsible for their way of waging it.

In October 1914, ninety-three German scholars published an 'Appeal to the Civilised World'; it was followed by counter-appeals and counter-petitions from France, England and Russia, while pro-German and pro-Allies intellectuals in the neutral countries also waged a war of manifestos. The German scholars had two arguments: first, they emphasised the vigour of Germany's intellectual life and the universal qualities of famous German philosophers, musicians, writers and scientists; and they replied to the accusation of barbarism by pointing out that their adversaries harboured uncivilised peoples in their huge colonial empires and, moreover, used colonial troops on Europe's battlefields. War as a civilising force was an idea now advanced by Germans: 'Rest assured that we shall struggle to the end, as a civilised people, a people for whom the heritage of a Goethe, a Beethoven, a Kant is as sacred as our own selves and our own homes. We shall answer for it on our name and honour.'[61] But it was impossible for the Germans to win this dispute, for their adversaries had set up a false syllogism: since a German had no honour, if Goethe was German then he was not part of universal culture. Exclusionist French universality relegated German culture to being a mere sectarian *Kultur*, and that is how the French derisively referred to it once the war began.

On one side there was a universal culture and civilisation, with its Greek origins, its subsequent attainments and its acme reached in France, and on the other, a German singularity that had no claims to anything. 'Why would it be an advantage to mankind to preserve German civilisation?' asked Louis Dimier, commenting on the German scholars' manifesto. 'On the contrary, wouldn't it be an advantage to erase it from the earth? Don't the intellectuals see that those very words, German civilisation, *Deutsche Kultur,* express a usurpation?'[62] Hence, as the scholar Pierre-André Taguieff has pointed out, 'One is either a man or a German. That's the universalist's method of exclusion.'[63] Being good and human is universal, and being evil must be consigned to the inhuman, even non-human; hence the fiction of the dehumanised enemy, first struck off from the civilised category and made into a savage or barbarian, then reduced to the level of a noxious animal or vermin.

In various essays written during the war and its aftermath, Sigmund Freud pondered over what he called 'the narcissism of minor differences', a term he applied to the small differences between the male and female genders or between families, circles of friends, peoples and nations. Basing himself on the remarks of a British anthropologist, he wrote:

> Crawley, in language which differs only slightly from the current terminology of psycho-analysis, declares that each individual is separated from the others by a 'taboo of personal isolation', and that it is precisely the minor differences in people who are otherwise alike that form the basis of feelings of strangeness and hostility between them. It would be tempting to pursue this line

of thought and to derive from this 'narcissism of minor differences' the hostility which in every human relation we see fighting successfully against feelings of fellowship, overpowering the commandment that all men should love one another.[64]

Freud rightly asserted, 'We are no longer astonished that greater differences should lead to an almost insuperable repugnance, such as that which the Gallic people feel for the German, the Aryan for the Semite, and the white races for the coloured.'[65] But what struck him was that fear and hatred could develop and culminate in aggression even when similarities were stronger than differences. Hence Freud anticipated subsequent discoveries in anthropology: that differences that seem minor from the outside can seem major from the inside. He related this perception of difference, which can become unbearable, to narcissism. When we recognise ourselves all too well in someone else and yet perceive them as different and dangerous, we have feelings of aggressiveness compounded by strong feelings of guilt.

For some years now, writers have been taking the view that the 1914–18 war was a fratricidal one, a European civil war. They have summoned Abel and Cain to explain a Europe that destroyed itself in hatred. But the analysis by Freud, a 'neutral' scholar as well as a father of soldiers in the Austrian army, allows us to go a step further.[66] We should perhaps suggest that the entire culture of war may rest on a kind of narcissism, turning minor distinctions into major areas of contention, with symbolic elements seen as all the more important because the real differences are insignificant.

We should keep this in mind as we consider the way that the racial arguments were brought into the debate in 1914–18. From the very beginning, the intellectual and propaganda skirmishes revolved around the concept of barbarism and were seen from its vantage point.[67] Not only did the Germans challenge the accusation as it was applied to them, but they accused their opponents of being barbaric themselves in their use of colonial troops and their alliance with forces that they didn't consider commendable:

'It is not true that we wage war in violation of human rights,' protested the scholars in their 'Appeal to the Civilised World':

> Our soldiers commit neither undisciplined acts nor cruelties. On the other hand, to the east of our country, the earth is soaked with the blood of women and children slaughtered by the Russian hordes, and on the Oise battlefields, our opponents' dum-dum bullets tear into the chests of our brave soldiers. A people allied to Russians and Serbs, who have no fear of inflaming Mongols and Negroes against the white race – offering the civilised world the most shameful imaginable spectacle – is certainly the last one to be able to claim that it is the defender of European civilisation.[68]

There was more to come. In July 1915, the German government sent a paper on 'the Violation of peoples' rights by England and France in using troops of colour in the European theatre of war'. That is, nearly a year later, we have the German state making use of the same racial argument and asserting that the French and English colonial troops were the cause of the depravity of the war:

> These people, natives of countries where war is especially cruel even today, have brought the customs of their countries to Europe, and under the eyes of the high command of the Anglo-French armies, engage in acts of cruelty that not only violate the recognised laws of warfare but also defy the laws of morality and humanity ... The coloured auxiliaries ... have the savage habit of making war trophies of the heads and cut-off fingers of German soldiers and of wearing necklaces of cut-off ears. With underhanded perfidiousness, they steal their way among the wounded Germans on the battlefield to gouge out their eyes, lacerate their faces with knives and slit their throats. The Hindus accomplish their infamies with sharpened daggers ... Some Turks, even when wounded themselves, crawl around the battlefields and murder defenceless wounded Germans with bestial savagery. It is

hard to understand how French commanders, well aware of the
barbarous and cruel habits of Senegalese Negroes, could have
assigned these men the task of escorting wounded German
prisoners and in so doing make them guilty of murder ... The
moral feeling of any civilised man is revolted to see that the
behaviour of the French military authorities is so lacking in
propriety that they have placed under the guardianship of these
people and sacrificed to their brutal passion women who had the
misfortune of being in France at the beginning of the war.[69]

Hence the Germans turned the accusations made against
them during their invasion of Belgium and northern France
against the Allies' colonial troops, and they were not without
some justification, for the murder of wounded men and prisoners, and other acts of cruelty did occur.* A parallel can also be established concerning the knowledge of real atrocities and
fantasies about them. Soldiers from African and Asian colonies
were used as a focal point in the Germans' polemics on barbarism, civilisation and culture:

Admittedly human rights do not unequivocally forbid employing
tribes of colour in the struggle between civilised nations, but
under one condition, however: that the troops of colour
employed in this way ... be submitted to a discipline that
excludes violation of the customs accepted among civilised
people ... It is therefore with the interest of humanity and
civilisation in mind that the German government energetically

---

*Proof of these acts of cruelty can be found in French documents. But
the colonial troops were not the only soldiers to commit such acts, as we
have seen. Moreover, evaluation of the atrocities committed by African
troops must take into account that 'whites' regarded as atrocities types of
combat that were part of the cultural practices of men who were used to
fighting with bladed weapons. Also, it is true that the Allied military
command armed African troops with machetes (objects of terror for the
Germans) and that they were used to 'clean the trenches' after battle.[70]

demands that troops of colour cease to be used in the theatre of war in Europe.[71]

The Germans gathered information from prisoner-of-war camps where they kept non-European troops and the (to them) equally terrifying Russians and used it for racist propaganda purposes. Their fascination with racial types is apparent from the hierarchical classifications they used in collections of photographs taken on the different front lines, and some of the anthropometric photos were retouched to give men low foreheads and menacing scowls. The African, Asian and Russian prisoners terrified the Germans and reminded them that their nation was surrounded; the entire world was in league against them, and losing the war would lead to the death of their civilisation. According to this fraudulent anthropology,[72] Germany's aggressors were numerous, ubiquitous and vile. Some of the captions were more explicit:'Types of combatants in the present war ... warrior from the coast of Guinea (Africa) whose native land still has regions populated with anthropophagi.'[73] Others, of photographs taken at the camps in Münster and Friedrichsfeld that held prisoners from the French colonies in West and North Africa, were ironical: 'Combatants for liberty and civilisation', 'Our opponents' brothers-in-arms' or 'Champions of civilisation from all countries'.[74] We need comment no further; the barbarians were not those who were labelled as such.

These arguments were all the more effective because the stereotypes had been shared by Europeans for centuries. Since the Germans weren't deploying colonial troops in Europe, they took full advantage of racist representations and used the most primitive expression of white superiority, saying that the colour black was a sign of intrinsic inferiority, of moral blackness. German soldiers might be accused of waging a barbarian war, but the French and the English were guilty of having 'real' barbarians in their ranks. This racist view of Africans made the myth about the cut-off ears easy to generalise, a myth adduced from few actual, though exceptional, battlefield practices. On both sides of the front, Africans had long been thought of as cannibals who dismembered people and cut off heads. In fact, France didn't even bother to refute the claims. A 'humorous' anti-German postcard showed a Senegalese soldier trying to eat a 'Kraut' raw: 'He tastes bad, just like pig.'[75] (That the soldier was probably Muslim and would never have eaten pork didn't disturb the cannibal stereotype.)

Thus the Great War was represented, on a deep level, as a struggle between two opposing 'races', and this has greater implications than a war of civilisations. It was thought that the differences between the French and the Germans could and should be drawn from a biological standpoint, since race was identified with the nation, and that the Germans were aware of this (or so the French believed) since they were waging a war that was meant to weaken the French 'race'. War, especially for the pan-German theoreticians, would allow Germany to shield itself from aggression and to guarantee that its 'ethnic body' [76] would be permanently protected. Alsace-Lorraine, which the French always describe as having been 'occupied' by Germany between 1871 and 1918, then liberated and returned to its original Frenchness, is a case in point. The French were convinced that it was impossible to make the inhabitants of Alsace-Lorraine into Germans, given that all their 'racial' characteristics were French, even by olfactory criteria.

> There's a reason why the populations of Alsace-Lorraine have been so resistant in recent times to Germanic assimilation. It is because there's a racial odour that deeply separates the indigenous race from the invading race. The odour of the German race has always produced very unpleasant sensations on the olfactory function of our compatriots in Alsace-Lorraine.[77]

Similarly, fetishistic practices, the spiked helmet, the skulls on the *kalpack** of the hussar death squads, and especially the custom

---

*'A felt cap of triangular form worn by Turks, Tartars, etc. Also an oriental cap generally' (*OED*).

of hammering nails into commemorative war statues, such as the statue of Hindenburg in Berlin, were seen as significant flaws: 'Doesn't German *Kultur,* seem to hark back to the fetishes of Africa?'[78] These practices, indeed, are encountered today only 'among the half-savage tribes of central Africa and Congo. [Associated with other] mental predispositions denoting a poor ability in exerting cerebral control, they show a pronounced inferiority in both the psychological and ethical areas.'[79] For the French, the message was clear: the German race was degenerate; it had regressed to the level of the 'inferior' peoples, though perhaps it had always partially and secretly been there. And what was to be done when the Germans occupied territories belonging to the French race? The dreadful fear arose that perhaps the invaded people might be contaminated by the invaders. Perhaps the German methods of occupation led to a kind of impregnation. Telegony* – a completely outdated, supposedly scientific theory – was revived and used as part of the ideology of race.

This kind of polemic shook the French scientific community throughout the war. The contributions of the Germans to modern scientific thought were considered of minor importance, and in addition tainted and contemptuous of human rights. German scientific expertise resulted only in destructive modernity, like the chemistry of gases, 'that shameful product of modern science'.80 In fact, though it was true that Germany's most brilliant chemist, Fritz Haber, had succeeded in convincing the German high command to use chlorine gas as a weapon in 1915, many German senior officers felt it was contrary to their code of honour and were reluctant to do so: 'The instruction to poison the enemy as you would poison rats had the same effect on me as it would have on any honest soldier: it disgusted me,' wrote General Berthold von Deimling, who was ordered to carry out the first trial on 22 April 1915. 81 This shows that military tradition could give rise to moral doubts, contrary to what

---

*This held that the father of a child could biologically affect the progeny subsequently born of the same mother but fathered by other men.

many intellectuals asserted, but the doubts were overcome when certain thresholds were crossed and total war gained ascendancy.

But in those years, scientific nationalism replaced true intelligence, and the French dutifully refuted every German theory, regardless of its content and even if they basically agreed with it; this meant that they risked falling behind in certain areas, which would work against them in the future.*

In the circumstances, Gustave Le Bon rewrote all the prefaces to his earlier books and updated his theories for his new works on the intermixing and struggle of the races. Of course, given the war, he stressed the differences between the French and German 'races', even if he reluctantly categorised both as 'superior'; for they were 'historical races' whose natural (i.e. inferior) characteristics had been swept away by history, by civilisation. Le Bon emphasised that in so far as the German race was concerned, the civilising process was superficial: 'Social constraints conceal ancestral barbarism in some peoples, but since it is merely masked, it reappears as soon as these constraints dissolve.'[82] And elsewhere, adjusting his theory to the circumstances of war, he added:

> As for the ferocity the Germans have exhibited during this
> campaign, it is the result of their natural dispositions and racial
> hatreds ... German philosophers ... using Darwin's concepts,
> today somewhat outdated ... asserted that the principles of
> survival of the fittest and selection ruling the animal kingdom also
> ruled the peoples of the world ... Naturally, the Germans are the
> superior race destined to dominate the world. Being the fittest,

---

*This was the case in evolutionary theory. The French rejection of all German scientific contributions was also due to ignorance; the extreme complexity of the phenomena concerned could evidently not be deciphered. With all the good will in the world, how could it be understood in 1914–18 that biological 'selectionism', with its *völkish* connotations, was very different from general pan-Germanism? (Militant anti-Semitism became part of the Pan-German League's programme only in 1919.)

they alone have the right to survive. The weak must be reduced
to slavery or be annihilated.[83]

Le Bon's books were bestsellers, but there were also other,
less important writers who quickly contributed their expertise
to the anti-German struggle. They may have denied it, but the
French shared with their enemies a Darwinian vision that made
it legitimate to take theories from the life sciences and apply
them to the social sciences.[84] They all saw political bodies as reacting and functioning like living creatures, and France's struggle
against German barbarism illustrated this. Indeed, there was an
'ethnicising of historical and political consciousness'[85] through
the twisting of scientific research. This was science serving the
objectives of a war of civilisations instead of civilisation serving
science. The data the scientists compiled confirmed results that
they 'knew', and the war became a vast laboratory of biased experiments designed to prove the greatness of the homeland and
the vileness of the enemy.

Though racial and racist arguments were useful in proving
on which side one belonged, good or bad, experiments still had
to be made on large groups of people. That was how the detention camps on both sides, with their concentrations of human
beings, began to be used as laboratories.

This 'scientific research' conducted in the detention camps or
based on stories from the occupied territories led to obvious
conclusions. For the French, the German 'race' was inferior,
comparable to that of the worst African tribes, and all-out war
was more than justified, it was vital. The analyses made by physicians were typical of the general determination to see political
standards prevail over scientific ones. Some psychiatrists noticed,
for instance, that Germans were more prone to neuroses than the
French, which proved they had 'chaotic characters'; in battle they
showed themselves to be 'eminently impressionable when facing
cannon fire, and had frightened dazed expressions.'[86] Dr André
Gilles added:

This imperfect psycho-physiological background, combined with contemporary history, as well as with the deliberate evolution of their minds in a brutal cult of materialism, gives today's Germans an unbalanced element; the placid German is a mask concealing the German beast which the war has revealed to us; under his smug layer of fat, his *Gemütlich* smile (his bonhomie can be likened to the sated satisfaction one has after a big meal), Germans are essentially passionate people, which is why those who tell us they are primitive, uncivilised and barbarian are right. However ... they are knowledgeable savages ... Hence, added to the brutality of the individual, which is an instinct of his race, is a collective brutality that has been systematised in a doctrine which, depending on how it is applied, can be called *Kultur* or pan-Germanism, and which has conceived of war as the means of achieving its ends, a war ferociously intensified by massacres, pillages and rapes. From the collective depravities, applied militarily, stem individual depravities and, among them, psychological neurosis.[87]

The French, on the other hand, were supposed to have resisted remarkably well the Darwinian test of war: 'If you can't adapt you're finished. Well, let's say it loud and clear, our French race adapted instantly and admirably to this unforeseen danger ... War is the best reagent of a race's nerves and resistance. Though the test was difficult, it turned out in our honour and testified to the fact that the French race has not degenerated.'[88]

6

Great expectations, eschatology, demobilisation

The central paradox of the Great War is that from the beginning, and probably even most strongly during the bleak periods when the belligerents were discouraged, when determination sagged – as it did everywhere after the two big battles of Verdun and the Somme in 1916 – each side believed they were waging war because it would bring a new and radiant world in the future, a purified world rid of its central flaw: war. This belief predated the popularisation of President Woodrow Wilson's statement that it was a 'war to end all wars', which he made when the United States entered the conflict in late 1917. There was a genuine eschatology of peace, of the triumph at long last of redeemed humanity over the forces of evil.

The French rallied around this eschatological banner with great conviction, believing that war was being waged so it would never have to be waged again. We can see this from the writings of personalities as diverse as the actor-mime Jacques Copeau and the cartoonist Gustave Hervé: 'Here is the admirable thing: a peaceful and pacifist nation, victorious over fearsome militarism,

waging a fearsome war, destroying war with war,'[1] said Copeau.
And Hervé wrote:

> Our ancestors who were at Valmy [the battle where
> Revolutionary French forces defeated Prussia in 1792] ... have
> entrusted us with the Rights of Man and the Rights of Nations,
> the gospels of modern times. They have bequeathed us the
> sublime task of creating peace on earth, of crushing all forms of
> militarism, overthrowing all kings, and abolishing all birth
> privileges. To defend all this, the poor souls go joyously to their
> deaths ... After these horrors, we shall continue shouting our
> hatred of war louder than ever; perhaps people will have the
> decency to stop calling us stateless when they'll see our ranks
> filled with so many joyous veterans with wooden legs![2]

For at least a century, the French had used their landscape,
their art, music and literature to define the nation. The garden of
France, with its harmonious universal values, was contrasted
with the black forests of Johann Fichte's vaunted nation of
genius. To shed blood was a warrior's act, but, more importantly,
it was a way of sealing the representations of the nation. The
Great War was to bring the fulfilment of France's messianic
promise. The French, more than any of the other belligerents,
believed in the mystical power of the war; history seemed to vin-
dicate Charles Péguy, and his death was seen as confirmation of
that 'manifest destiny'.

On 14 July 1915, a powerful symbol was chosen to mark the
French national holiday: the remains of Rouget de Lisle, author
of the national anthem the 'Marseillaise', were transferred to the
Invalides. In his speech at the ceremony, President Poincaré referred once again to the deadly battles as a struggle for the life of
a just and universal nation:

> There isn't a single soldier, a single citizen or a single woman of
> France who doesn't clearly see that the whole future of our race,
> not just its honour but its very existence, hinges on the grim

> moments of this inexorable war ... Moral strength and
> perseverance will be our prize in the final victory ... The day of
> glory celebrated in the 'Marseillaise' has already brightened the
> horizon; in a period of several months the people have already
> enriched our annals with a multitude of marvellous exploits and
> epic tales. It will not have been in vain that these admirable
> popular virtues will have risen up en masse, from all parts of
> France. May they be allowed to accomplish their holy mission.
> They clear the way to victory and justice.[3]

France more than the other countries managed the tour de
force of consistently condemning the war as an absolute evil *and*
attributing the evil to Germany, so that only victory in war would
bring the truth of peace. Henri Barbusse's *Under Fire*, a novel
published in 1916 that was praised by readers both at the front and
at home until the end of the war, succeeded because it described
the deathly, brutal horrors of combat so well, bringing these realities from the front lines to the home front. But Barbusse also af-
firmed the central contradiction of the war culture *à la française*,
which was the backbone of his last chapter; 'The Dawn' admirably expressed both French support for the war and the fact
that such support couldn't possibly continue indefinitely. Support
was based on the determination to kill the 'Prussian' militarism
that was opposed to French messianism. Yet if the French felt that
goal wasn't achieved would they not later feel betrayed? In *Under
Fire* the men in the squad, huddled in the mud, say this:

> 'We're made to live, not to be done in like this!'
> 'Men are made to be husbands, fathers – *men*, what the devil!
> – not beasts that hunt each other and cut each other's throats and
> stink.' ...
> 'And likewise, what have *we* been for two years now?
> Incredibly pitiful wretches, and savages as well, brutes, robbers and
> dirty devils.' ...
> 'There will be no more war,' growls a soldier, 'when there is no
> more Germany.'

'That's not the right thing to say!' cries another. 'It isn't enough. There'll be no more war when the spirit of war is defeated.'...

'If the spirit of war isn't killed, there'll be scuffles throughout the ages.'...

'We must fight!'...

'We've got to give all we have, our strength and our skins and our hearts, all our life and what pleasures are left us. The life of prisoners that we have, we've got to take it in both hands. You've got to endure everything, even injustice – and *that's* the king that's reigning now – and the shameful and disgusting sights we see, so as to come out on top and win. But if we've got to make such a sacrifice ... it's because we're fighting for progress, not for a country; against error, not against a country.'

'War must be killed,' said the first speaker, 'war must be killed in the belly of Germany!'...

'That's all silly talk. What diff does it make whether you think this or that? We've got to be winners, that's all.'[4]

Most of the soldiers who read Barbusse, alarmed by their own violence as they may have been, went no further. But Barbusse tried to do so, along with the pacifists who were still a small minority in 1916. 'But the others had begun to reflect. They wanted to know and to see further than today.'[5] Barbusse's conversion to complete pacifism had been set in motion.

However, in order to understand the messianic intensity of the war in France, we should certainly not view it through the prism of a tautological history that features mutinies of the French soldiers and the Bolshevik Revolution. Nor should the Barbusse of 1916 be interpreted in the light of his subsequent conversion to communism by 'the great glow from the East'. For the fervours of the war were largely overshadowed by the militant pacifism of the post-war years. The eschatology of pacifism replaced the eschatology of victory at any price. Soldiers returning from the war converted to the creed of peace. A conceptual screen was created in the 1920s by literature, eyewitness accounts and cinema: the tragedy couldn't possibly have been supported by those who endured it, people now said, much less supported with such spiritual fervour.

Avant-garde artists are notable in this respect. Like all other belligerents, not only had they been mobilised (in the passive sense of the term) but they had also supported the idea of a just war. Even before 1914, many of them were eager for a war which they hoped would lead humanity towards a purer, more modern world. The Berlin artist Ludwig Meidner and the Italian Futurists were 'bombarding' the world with their impatient, unfortunate enthusiasm. Everywhere, artists welcomed the declaration of war in 1914 with a kind of elation. Hence Apollinaire:

> *We arrived in Paris*
> *At the moment when they were posting the mobilisation order*
> *We understood my comrade and me*
> *That the little car had taken us to a new age*
> *And that though we were both mature men*
> *We had just been born.*[6]

Though the mobilised artists, extending their Cubist, Vorticist or Expressionist investigations,* found inspiration in the spectacle of war, their perception of the conflict soon evolved along with everyone else's. After the brief illusions of the war's early phase,[7] they focused on expressions of suffering and individual tragedy. Disillusionment, upheaval, a shattered world (what the German Expressionists call *Zerreissenheit*) began to shape their work. Marc Chagall, Otto Dix, Steinlen, Nash and many others were able to bear witness to the soldiers' extraordinary descent into the hell of war. The 'holy war' that Malevich

---

*Camouflage studios, created in France at the initiative of the painter Guirand de Scevola, allowed a number of Cubist painters, like André Mare and Fernand Léger, to put their art, otherwise reviled as 'Kraut Kubism', at the service of their country. The avant-garde's extreme modernism was thus put at the service of the war, and vice versa.

and so many other artists had sought (in Apollinaire's words),
wanting to overthrow the 'old world' of which they had grown
'weary',[8] turned out to be a time of death and division. Yet
during the years of conflict, the artists either could not or would
not represent the violence realistically: the horrible realities of
modern death, the bodies torn to pieces, the hundreds of thousands of unknown soldiers – unknown for the first time in
history, Unknown with a capital 'U'. This is nevertheless what
the works conveyed, though the artists dared not represent it
until well into the post-war period.

We ought to be able to understand this contradiction. How
can we expect the artists, painters, musicians, scholars and intellectuals who had been 'mobilised' like all their male contemporaries – to represent the unbearable effects of a war in which
they were themselves actors? It is always very difficult to represent death, even when you can point to the killer. It is almost impossible when you know you are complicitous in making the
violence commonplace. There were a great many French representations of German atrocities on Belgian and French soil; far
from being works by brainwashed patriots or by artists who were
repressing the reality of death, they were works that represented
the intensity of the conflict the only way they could – by placing
the blame on German 'barbarism'. The thousands of pictures of
destroyed churches – starting with the omnipresent cathedral of
Rheims, which the French government considered not restoring
and keeping right there in the heart of France, so that it might
remain as the everlasting proof of Germany's ignominy – are
proof of the support the artists gave both to the idea of sacrifice
for one's country and to hatred of the Other.

Creating art for peace and against barbarism was the only
way that disenchanted avant-garde artists could survive the conflict. The composer Albert Roussel explained the paradox clearly
in a letter to his wife in 1916:

> You'll find my letter very lyrical and grandiloquent, but, you see,
> the life we lead here makes us develop a very special mentality.

We're constantly rubbing shoulders with the coarsest prosaic life and the most astounding idealism (if you know how to wrest it from the small facts of daily life). You live in near-total materialism, and then suddenly, right next to you, you notice sheer heroism and words or acts whose antique grandeur is the stuff of dreams. So when you reflect a bit and stay at a distance, as I do, in order to be free to have a personal vision, you feel a great breath of idealism rising up and welling up inside you; for many this will be the great benefit of this abominable war and, let us hope, a benefit that will survive it. All these energies it will have liberated will come together and be condensed in peacetime works and in every expression of artistic thought. There are still beautiful days ahead, my dearest, and radiant springtimes for those whose hearts remain young and who can express it.[9]

The diary of the German painter Franz Marc for those same Verdun days vividly illustrates the same state of mind, in which one could be tormented by the daily spectacle of death and simultaneously enthusiastic about battle:

Here we are in the middle of the most tremendous day of the war. Someone who hasn't participated in this German advance can't have any idea of the mad frenzy and gigantic force of the advance. We are generally in pursuit. The poor horses! But ... the incredible thing is, we have succeeded (and will continue to succeed) on the strongest spot of the French front, Verdun – no one would have believed it, it's incredible ... We are feverishly tense here about the outcome of this enormous struggle that words could never describe. I don't doubt for a minute the fall of Verdun and our incursion into the heart of the country.[10]

Marc, having written those last sentences, was killed later on the same day – one of the many of the lost generation, a generation that kept their illusions until death. For the survivors, only lost illusions would remain.

Less study has been devoted to the final phase of the Great War than to its beginnings*[11] – so that we tend to forget that it was only on the Western Front that the war ended on 11 November 1918. Shock waves from the war, even on the strictly diplomatic and geo-strategic levels, continued through the early 1920s, gradually subsiding and then taking on the shape of peripheral conflicts directly related to the Great War: the Baltic war, the Russo-Polish war, the Greek-Turkish war of 1919–22. This absence of a gap between the Great War and the succeeding aftershocks had a cultural dimension as well; when they faced their Turkish adversaries between 1919 and 1922, the Greek soldiers bore the memory of the Balkan conflicts of 1912–13 and also of their intervention in 1917–18 on the Allied side on the Eastern Front.[13] It wasn't just that the great battles on the Western Front, particularly the Battle of Verdun, were a point of reference. Many of the Greek soldiers' practices had been learned in the trenches of the Eastern Front from contact with French troops – such as the custom of having female penfriends, or writing and reading trench newspapers.

The tragic legacy of the conflict for the next half-century stems from the way the final phase of the 1914–18 war was experienced and represented. The culture of war did not die with the armistice. One of the very first questions that should be explored and understood is that of the return of the soldiers. Unfortunately, we have only sketchy knowledge of the demobilisation – a slow process that lasted until 1920 – and even less knowledge of how soldiers resumed their peacetime lives with

---

*How the Great War broke out captured the attention of historians very early on. It could even be said that the 'causes' of the war were the favoured angle of study, especially in the years 1918–39, but also for a long time even after 1945. There are countless books on this question in all countries. They are still being written. Unfortunately, such a concentration of historiographical energy seems not to take into account the excellent observation made by François Furet concerning the Great War and apparently suggested to him by his long study of the French Revolution: 'The more significant the consequences of an event, the more difficult it is to think about it from the perspective of its causes.'[12]

their emotional, family, social and professional connections. And this goes for both soldiers on the various fronts and prisoners who returned from the camps. It seems obvious that the joy of returning home alive could not have erased all the heartbreak and pain; the severing of ties with comrades at the front, 'survivor's guilt', and the after-effects of battlefield traumas are all subjects which require further study.[14]

The post-war experience of soldiers who were hospitalised is a similar subject. We have scant knowledge of the sufferings of those who rejoined the civilian world blind, disfigured, as amputees or with burned lungs. The case of veterans with mutilated faces (the '*gueules cassées*' or 'smashed mugs') is perhaps more familiar. In France, associations were created where veterans with facial wounds could spend long periods of time with their comrades in specialised facilities; for these victims, who had lost a part (perhaps the essential part) of their personal identities along with their faces, there never really was a demobilisation after 1918.[15]

Parallel to the soldiers' return was the return of refugees and deported civilians from the concentration camps to their destroyed home cities and villages. Here again we are steeped in ignorance. We know little of the impact of the human losses. We know even less concerning the other losses, the loss of houses, villages or towns for the people who had lived in them, and also the loss of furniture, personal effects and photographs. Though hundreds of thousands of individuals in Europe were affected by material destruction, our knowledge of their experience is very limited. But the complexity of the problem can be surmised from the variety of reactions to it. In northern France, in the *département* of the Meuse, thousands of acres remained in the 'red zone' (zones where many villages were never rebuilt, or from which they were rebuilt in other locations), but in some regions of the Pas-de-Calais and Picardy – particularly in the *département* of the Somme – the inhabitants rejected the idea of a red zone; they set about salvaging a land they had considered lost, and they resettled in very precarious conditions on the ruins of razed pre-war villages; there wasn't a single village that wasn't rebuilt, and almost invariably in its exact pre-1914 location.[16] Actually, in post-1918 France, the word 'rebuilt' was not used in this context; it was said that the buildings or villages were 'reconstituted'. The wishes of the contemporaries are revealing: in Albert, an important town to the rear of where British forces had fought, the nineteenth-century church built by the architect Dutoit had been completely destroyed by bombs; in the 1920s, his son 're-constituted' it exactly as it had been. In Arras, too, a similar 'reconstitution' took place. What do these words conceal, and what do the actions signify?

Mobilisation played a large part in societies in Europe (and more generally in the West) in determining the length of the war, the forms of its violence, and the scale of the sacrifices the people accepted. The intensity of this mobilisation was such that we must of course inquire about the intensity of the demobilisation, including its cultural aspect. We can be certain that the demobilisations differed on the winning and losing sides. For the Germans, the fact that the defeat was an external one, as it were – inasmuch as it had taken place outside the country and the German population had not had to contend with the physical presence of the enemy on its soil prior to the cessation of combat – underpins their refusal to accept the military catastrophe that was their defeat. On 12 November 1918, Hindenburg wrote to the troops saying, 'You have kept the enemy away from our frontiers and you have saved your country from the misfortunes and disasters of war ... Proud and with our heads held high, we bring to an end the struggle in which we have held out for four years against a world filled with enemies.'[17] Hindenburg's dispatch must not be interpreted as the hollow boast of a vanquished leader; it must be taken literally. His perception of the war as a defensive war had been shared by most Germans throughout the conflict, and thus the troops were thanked as though they were returning home victorious.

These words were translated into actions in the days that followed. In many German towns, the soldiers were welcomed like conquerors by both the civilian populations and the authorities.

One example was the future president of Germany, the Social Democratic leader Friedrich Ebert, in Berlin, where as elsewhere the regiments were greeted as they passed with celebrations, not commiseration. (It should be said that in some Social Democratic milieu, however, the officers were greeted with contempt and their epaulettes were stripped from their uniforms.) The Germans truly refused to draw from 11 November 1918 the same consequences as their conquerors. As a result, not only did their defeat seem incomprehensible to them, not only was it rejected or attributed to betrayal (the myth of the 'stab in the back'), but it was sometimes quite literally suppressed. During the Weimar Republic, the German defeat was not mentioned in some school textbooks: chapters on the Great War ended with the final German offensives in the spring of 1918.[18]

The denial of defeat also translated into a feeling that the war had not come to an end with the armistice: 'The war against the German people continues. The First World War was merely its bloody beginning,' declared a Freikorps officer named Oberlindober in 1918.[19] (It is relevant that Oberlindober later became head of the veterans' association under the Nazis.) The Freikorps' cruelty in crushing the Spartacus League in 1919 and the extreme right's terrorism under the Weimar Republic should be understood in the light of this continued war 'against the German people'. Many veterans shifted their brutal front-line practices to the home front and went on waging war. Distance in time seemed to have little effect on this denial of defeat and pursuance of combat. A most revealing indication of how the extreme right became radicalised, partly through its interpretation of the war experience, can be seen in the difference between Ernst Jünger's *Storm of Steel*, published in Germany in 1920, and his *Copse 125*,[20] written in 1932: over the twelve years, the 'iron man' of the trenches changed into the 'new man'.

The brutalisation of German soldiers through their experience as combatants and their denial of defeat are crucial issues that deserve to be examined further. In his important book *Ordinary Men*,[21] Christopher Browning rejects a historicised explanation for the radical violence of the German reserve police battalion 101, whose actions in the Second World War are the subject of his book. He plausibly notes that the men involved were too old to have been socialised under Nazism and were not in battle after 1939, and he uses psychological and sociological parameters to explain their behaviour. Hence his title and his pessimistic conclusion on the potential for extreme violence in every human being. But there is one hypothesis he does not fully explore: the possibility, indeed probability, that some of these men may have fought in the Great War and were too old to be on the front lines in 1939. One can see here that the lack of historiographical connection between the mobilisations of 1914–18 and those of the Second World War is a serious deficiency. In any case, if this hypothesis is accurate, some if not all of Browning's policemen were not 'ordinary men' but 'ordinary Germans'[22] – that is, Germans who never felt 'demobilised' after 1918.

On the winning side, the conclusion of the Great War was experienced differently. In both France and Great Britain, there were different phases in the cultural demobilisation process. The first phase probably occurred in 1919, with the Peace of Versailles marking a first disappointment. The historian Serge Bernstein believes another, second phase was reached in France around 1924–5, when public opinion realised that the parenthesis that the Great War had opened would never be closed.[23] It seems reasonable to distinguish yet a third phase in the late 1920s and early 1930s, when novels and eyewitness accounts of the war subtly changed and it became possible to write about fear (Gabriel Chevallier), cowardice (Céline) and deliberate mutilation (Jean Giono).[24] In a radical inversion of the culture of war that had predominated during the conflict, the rejection of courage could now be highlighted, indeed justified, as the only true form of courage.[25] Demobilisation within French culture seemed, ten years after the end of the war, to have taken a decisive turn; the hardened pacifism of veterans during the 1930s was another symptom of this.[26] That is one of the great paradoxes of the Great War: it was *accepted* in 1914–18 and much later *rejected*. Could it be that, at the end of a collective mourning process, an aggressive hatred of the war replaced the initial emotional investment in it? The writer Maurice Genevoix, who had been an exemplary officer during the war, put it in the following terms in 1923:

> You have all been killed, and that is the greatest of crimes. You gave your life, and you are the most unfortunate. I know nothing but the gestures we made, our suffering and our gaiety, the words we spoke, our faces among other faces, and your death ... I have nothing left but myself, and the picture of you that you gave me.
>
> Almost nothing: three smiles in a tiny little photo, a living person between two dead ones, his hand on their shoulders. All three blink because of the springtime sun. But in the sun, what remains of the little grey photo?[27]

Was there a 'Great War syndrome' comparable to the 'Vichy syndrome'[28] that developed after 1945? If so, how did it emerge and under what circumstances and conditions? The general disenchantment that set in during the 1920s with the crusading spirit that had animated and motivated the combatants of 1914–18 remains essentially opaque to us.

III
MOURNING

For eighty years, historians of the Great War overlooked the long, painful scars of grief that followed after the conflict was over.[1] True, the mass deaths were recorded (not without difficulty), but the bereavement, the mourning process went unrecorded. It was as if historians thought that simply stating the number of dead, breaking them down into categories by age, year and military unit, was equivalent to acknowledging the scale of the catastrophe. They put the catastrophe into a demographic context but not into the equally important context of collective grief. Yet little in twentieth-century history can be understood unless close attention is paid to the immense grief experienced during and after 1914–18. This is an issue that transcends the history of the conflict per se. At issue here is the history of Western attitudes to war, to death in war, and perhaps to death in general.

7

Historicising grief

Grief, bereavement and mourning are the backdrop to many studies concerned with the Great War and its aftermath – but although veterans and veterans' organisations, commemorations, the various inter-war pacifist movements, 'pilgrimages to the tombs' and battlefield 'tourism' are all subjects intimately connected to mass death, only passing references are made to grief itself, which is neither described nor analysed. Yet *how* did people suffer?

If we have failed to answer this question, it is probably because most historians have felt that this kind of grief did not lend itself to the historical treatment. So demographic and social analyses have taken precedence over other types of historical approaches: the compilation of the number of widows and orphans, studies of the criteria for receiving state aid and pensions, post-war changes in social status, the new role of women after the deaths of so many men, new marriage strategies and the social life of the bereaved. These are all interesting subjects, but useful only if grief is given attention as well.

In contrast, consider the state of Israel. Here is a society that has gone through several conflicts since its war of independence in 1948, with the nation's survival being at stake in each one, and war therefore having a strong defensive legitimacy. Especially since 1967, Israel has been the subject of psychiatric epidemiological studies intended to determine the scale and intensity of grief after each conflict and to help the bereaved come to terms with their loss.[1] No comparable study was made in Europe after either the First or Second World War, but we must try to reconstitute the impact of the 1914–18 catastrophe retrospectively, despite the difficulties and even though our tools are inadequate.

Psychological suffering, after 1914–18, was unexpressed – unexpressed, first of all, due to a lack of appropriate words. In French, for instance, there are words describing bereavement only for the wives and children of the dead: 'war widows', 'war orphans'(usually designated as *pupilles de la nation*', or wards of the nation). A new term was coined for betrothed women whose fiancés were killed: '*veuves blanches*', white widows (apparently derived from the fifteenth-century expression 'white queen', designating a childless royal widow).[2] As far as we know, this is the only example of semantic innovation in French produced by the war, and significantly it did not remain in the language. This case apart, there are no specific terms in either French, English or German to designate the father or mother of a deceased person, or the brother and sister, grandfather and grandmother. There are also no words to describe their grief, and thus grieving was denied a true status – so much so that we often fail to realise that war bereavement affected not just the parents, wives and children of the dead: brothers and sisters, grandparents, uncles and aunts, nieces and nephews, cousins, sons- and daughters-in-law, and sisters- and brothers-in-law, friends and girlfriends were the unacknowledged mourners of 1914–18.

The English language is slightly richer than the French in this area, though it is no more specific in designating the different categories of bereaved persons according to their relationship to the deceased. But English does distinguish *bereavement* (the objective observation of loss, dispossession and separation), *grief* (psychological suffering, and the sorrow and pain it causes) and *mourning*, 'a set of acts and gestures through which survivors express grief and pass through stages of bereavement'.[3] French

has only the last word, mourning, or *deuil*, to express the phenomenon. The possibilities in German are also limited: the only
terms are *Trauer* and *trauernd* (to mourn, a bereaved person) and
Verlust (loss). The inadequacy of language contrasting with the
magnitude and gravity of the bereavement is the first explanation for the great silence that prevailed after 1914–18.

There are other explanations, too. Paradoxically, grief, unlike
pleasure, tends to be expressed, and often profusely, but only
within certain limits. And it was precisely those limits that were
transgressed by the mass mourning in the years during and after
the Great War. The psychological suffering of bereavement at its
most intimate level was stifled, buried, hidden, repressed. Great
trauma, we now know, is compatible with feelings of guilt, and
always entails a strong impulse to remain silent. An extreme but
telling case about the Great War is that in some families it was
explicitly or implicitly forbidden to make any reference to the
relative who had died on the battlefield.

At the same time, the grief of those in mourning because of
the Great War was emphasised, sometimes even flaunted. In
France, England and Germany, reminders of the deaths sup-
planted commemorations of victory so often that psychiatrists
might speak of a 'show' of mourning, so conspicuously was it *displayed*. It was publicly conspicuous but also conspicuous within
families, as in the ostentatious death announcements and the ex-
travagant displays around the portraits of the deceased hanging
on living-room walls. Here is a German example among many:
on a canvas serving as a structural support for the ensemble is
placed a portrait of the 'dear departed brother' between a Prussian and a Bavarian flag and framed by two large pictures of
Prince Ruprecht of Bavaria and Kaiser William II; above is a
crucified Christ with two kneeling angels at his feet. An inscribed ribbon surrounds the entire assemblage: 'In memory of
our beloved brother. The hero who died for the salvation of the
Homeland!' A great many compositions like these were created
in German families using standardised components sold in
stores.[4] And here is a French example: a naïve, sentimental text

composed by a war widow reproduced on a plaque and placed on the grave of the deceased for everyone to read:

> TO MY BELOVED HUSBAND. DREADFUL WAR, you took my beloved away from me and gave me nothing but tears instead; you did not want us to be happy. You made me remove my wifely dress and put on the veil of a weeping widow. Why? Were you jealous of our happiness? At thirty-eight, beloved husband, you departed from your dear wife to avenge your country, leaving me little hope; and at thirty-nine, after a year of suffering, you departed from me for ever, alas, leaving me with a broken heart. Now I can only console myself by kneeling on this icy stone. Farewell, my beloved husband. I will weep for you as long as I live.[5]

In this instance, a simple enamel plaque. But for soldiers whose families could bring the bodies home, large monuments – a last swan song of the nineteenth-century cult of the dead – were erected in many cemeteries, with bronze or stone statuary showing the face, bust or entire body of the deceased, and sometimes his widow or mother or children as well. Yet – and this is only an apparent paradox – this display of bereavement conceals the most important thing, which is intimate grief. The neglect of this hidden truth is in itself suspicious, and suggests its importance.

We believe that the grief of bereavement from the war of 1914–18 can be tracked down with the historian's tools, despite the many difficulties. 'Tales of mourning' *can* be told, provided that we adopt a micro-historical scale and are patient; bereaved lives and the many threads that connect them can be reconstituted. Of course, many of the threads are abruptly cut off, lost or frayed, leaving sketchy, discouraging dotted lines. Rarely can the biographical paths be followed to the end of the mourning process, which in many cases ended only at the death of the bereaved person. All too often we have to be content with fragments, reconstitute missing pieces, and accept that we cannot be completely certain. Yet it is possible to glimpse grief at the most intimate level.

Death and mourning were such completely repressed themes after the Great War, their existence was so pervasively denied, that they almost became socially invisible. The diagnosis of this 'interdict laid upon death by industrialised societies', as Philippe Ariès called it, was made years ago by Ariès himself and by the anthropologist Geoffrey Gorer.[6] It is not unreasonable to suggest that this taboo also affected how historians have viewed the Great War.

Gorer was probably the first person after the Second World War to grasp, in studying his own country, not only the Western taboo on death but also the influence of the First World War in creating it. In an autobiographical preface to his work, written in 1963, he mentions a strange development: in 1915, when he was still a child, he noticed that mourning clothes were increasingly frequent on the street, so that his widowed mother 'no longer stood out in the crowd',[7]* but then quite unexpectedly they became rare in 1917–18. It would seem that a sartorial ritual of mourning subsided just when the number of bereaved was on the rise. This was not merely a child's impression; a specialist noticed a decline in the use of black clothes in France and Great Britain starting in the middle of the war: 'It was the terrible slaughter of the First World War that undoubtedly caused the major breakdown in funeral and mourning etiquette.'[8] Another scholar believes that 'one thing is irrefutable: the rituals of mourning fell apart in a continuous process that can be traced back to the period just after the First World War'.[9] An ostentatious display of mourning seemed increasingly inappropriate as the mass slaughter of the Great War continued.

Thus the war was a decisive turning point in the relationship of Westerners to death, and showed a shift in attitude that had probably started just before 1914.[10] Yet the causes for this paradoxical change remain rather obscure.

---

*The preface explains that Gorer's father died (according to eyewitness accounts, heroically, an important detail) in the sinking of the *Lusitania*, in May 1915.

The grief people felt for the men who died in the Great War has left perceptible traces even today. Many people who were orphaned by the war are still alive, thanks to the long life-spans in the West, and some rare oral histories have captured their views.[11] Recently, the daughter of Lieutenant Imbert, who was killed in September 1914 and buried by the Germans with the writer Alain-Fournier, took her father's remains to a cemetery in the Meuse; in a televised documentary, she explained how she was finally able to complete her mourning process or, more accurately, able finally to fill the void of an interminable absence.[12] There are countless men born after the Great War who were given the names of dead combatants by relatives who didn't want the cherished young soldiers' names to fall into oblivion. The historian Raoul Girardet, for instance, was named after his father's brother, killed in September 1914. Clearly, many European families bore the scars of mourning for a long time. Even today, the traces of bereavement have not entirely disappeared. Here is a 1997 letter by the niece of a soldier killed at the beginning of the war, written in response to a request for people who could give evidence about just this subject:

> Unfortunately I have no manuscript to give you on the death of my uncle M.P. who was killed when he arrived at the front in December 1914 ... He was my father's older brother, and my father always told us that their father didn't allow anyone to talk to him about his dead son. He would have found it unbearable and he refused to have his body sent home. Though the family was large, no one ever went to the scene of the tragedy, and no one knew in which cemetery my uncle had been buried until I wanted to tell the story of my father's life in 1989-90 (my father died in 1990). At that point, I wanted to lift the veil. Starting with the death certificate (transcribed in Roussillon, his birthplace), I wrote to the mayor of Montzéville (Meuse), where the first death certificate had been issued. And this was how in April 1993 I discovered his burial place: Esnes-en-Argonne, grave no. 280. My sister went there the following summer, and my eldest daughter in

August 1994. For health reasons, I myself was unable to go, but because of this research and discovery, I felt retrospectively all the grief that had been repressed for so long. It was like an echo, a vibration through time, both of that young life cut off at its prime in all its beauty and of my grandparents' grief. I think I have really lived through this bereavement and I still feel it.[13]

A portrait of this uncle, whom it was forbidden to mention, and a photograph of his grave were enclosed with the letter.

If there had been no Great War, said another witness, 'I would probably have been different.'[14] This is not a pointless conjecture: without the lasting grief of bereavement, many descendants of those who lost a relative during the Great War would indeed have been different.

8

Collective mourning

In *Thoughts for the Times on War and Death*, Sigmund Freud expressed his revulsion with the implementation of total war, the extremism of which he immediately detected and theorized at the onset of hostilities. His 'thoughts on death', both the primary and final consequence of war, are just as powerful. Before 1914, people had wanted to forget death, 'eliminate it from life'. But war brought it back on an industrial scale and it was unbearable. Hence Freud's wisdom in suggesting that death be reincorporated into life: 'To tolerate life remains, after all, the first duty of all living beings ... We recall the old saying: *Si vis pacem, para bellum*. If you want to preserve peace, prepare for war. It would be in keeping with the times to alter it: *Si vis vitam, para mortem*. If you want to endure life, prepare for death.'[1]

No one in 1914 was prepared for the slaughter. Yet by 1918 nearly 10 million people were dead. To describe the mourning of the 1920s and 1930s, one could paraphrase Freud: 'If you want to endure life, commemorate death.' Contrary to history, which is constructed of immutable facts by historians, memory evolves and is constantly being reconstructed by all of us. Hence, to write a history of memory brings our reflections to their point of maximum tension.

In 1918, Marcel Proust recalled the cathedrals north of Paris he had visited before the war: 'I admire and weep more for the soldiers than for the churches, which were only the recording of an heroic gesture that today is reenacted at every moment.'[2] It is not surprising that Proust so aptly expressed what most people felt in Europe and even beyond Europe. After the war, the cathedrals could be rebuilt, but what remained of the dead beyond the dual injunction, repeated *ad infinitum*, never to forget and never to allow such a catastrophe to happen again? Freud well described the 'complete collapse when death has struck down someone whom we love – a parent or a partner in marriage, a brother or sister, a child or a close friend. Our hopes, our desires and our pleasures lie in the grave with them, we will not be consoled, we will not fill the lost one's place.'[3] In 1918, this could be said of most of the survivors of the war, veterans from the front lines as well as men, women and children on the home front. They couldn't replace what they had lost, so they became what they had lost or, more specifically, they became what they had loved and lost.[4]

Marcel Proust, Sigmund Freud and the sociologist Maurice Halbwachs, with their deep understanding of bereavement, the mourning process and the workings of memory, are excellent guides to the complex private and public attempts to transfigure mass death. What they wrote, in the shadow of the war or in the years when it was still a recent memory, offers a contemporary intellectual context and raises important questions. The central proposition of Halbwachs's *The Collective Memory* (distorted in a posthumous edition, but now republished in a corrected edition) is one we can appreciate today: 'It would seem appropriate to distinguish two memories, one that could be called interior or internal, the other exterior; in other words, a personal memory and a social memory.'[5] Halbwachs believes that individual memory always crystallises in a social framework, but he also realises that 'personal' memory maintains traces that are unique to each individual. Depending on the case, these blend with common and collective memories or resist blending. Collective memory and oblivion, individual memory and oblivion: such is the double tension within which commemorations of the Great War must be understood.

The collective presence of the dead, or their constant 'return', went through many forms of representation. As soon as the slaughter started, in the summer of 1914, and with even greater care after 1918, *each one* of the war dead was *remembered* in his family, his village, his parish, his workplace. In all the belligerent countries he was also *remembered* by the state at both local and national levels. The words spoken at ceremonies, the images offered in inscriptions and commemorative monuments, the stained-glass windows, the cemeteries and ossuaries, have lasted to this day and through them we can recall these endless commemorations where political liturgy and private bereavement were complementary. The death 'of oneself', as Ariès calls it, and death of the Other, the burial of relatives and burial of others, the connection to God, to the nation and to propaganda, are inextricably and painfully intertwined. The Roman Catholic Church allowed a prayer to be added to the mass in 'memory' of a less important saint whose day was the same as the dead person who was being honoured. It was as if, in and through memory, the soldiers of the Great War became new 'saints', alluded to in the liturgical calendar more discreetly than the official saints, but mentioned constantly in the 1920s and 1930s.

The geography and chronology of war commemorations are significant. The basic pattern was set up right after the war – in monuments to the dead, and various ceremonies of remembrance, both at the battlefields and at home. The majority of the soldiers in the Great War – the British, including combatants from the Dominions, troops from the colonies, the Americans and the Germans – fought and died far from home. Conquerors and conquered thus shared the same duality: 'realms of memory' were erected on sites where the men had fought and died as well as on their home territory, at both their collective and individual places of belonging, national and local, public and private, secular and religious. Thus conscious and unconscious desires had the effect of 'nationalising' certain sectors of French, Belgian and

Turkish soil, which, having swallowed up combatants from all countries, were now areas reserved for recollecting them. They also had the effect of bringing the Great War to nations that had been spared the war itself, like the United States, Australia, Canada or South Africa.[6] The commemorations were a way for the home front to bring the front lines home. In France, soil from Verdun was often placed in urns at the monuments or in town halls, vividly illustrating with the soil itself the phenomenon of spatial appropriation in mourning.

The chronology of all this activity raises many unanswered questions. How did people move on from supporting the war to supporting the memory of lost soldiers? Most of the monuments were erected at the precise time when, the war having ended, support for it was shattered for good, having been in decline since 1916 and, even more sharply, since 1917, though it had picked up again during the re-mobilisation of 1918. This meant that in France, for example, the Sacred Union was given expression in stone and bronze just when the terrible human toll was being assessed. The deliberations of the committees in charge of building the monuments, like the inaugural speeches at the unveiling of the monuments, show this tension between identity in war and identity in mourning. In every country, the local monuments to the dead were a fundamental link between capital cities and the provinces, and the battlefields and the home fronts.

George Mosse in the United States,[7] Antoine Prost in France, Reinhart Kosseleck in Germany and Ken Inglis in Australia were the first historians to study war memorials and the commemorative ceremonies that took place around them. In the 1970s, these pioneering historians 'invented' war memorials as a historical subject. Decades later, their successors are no longer considered marginal, for their studies are in keeping with the new perception of death and mourning in total war.

In France, two works – one individual, by Maurice Agulhon, the other collective, *Realms of Memory*, edited by Pierre Nora[8] – were landmark studies both in substance and methodology. Their approach should encourage a comprehensive history of memory in which figurative representations are understood as essential: the war memorials are sculptured, constructed works that occupy specific places in the rural or urban landscape; they are an expression of governmental power, of 'mentalities', of consensus and rejection.

For the generation lost in the war, an entity was created that perfectly obeyed the classical precepts of tragedy: unity of time, 11 November; unity of place, the war memorial; unity of action, the commemorative ceremony. In the eleventh hour of the eleventh day of the eleventh month in the fifth year of the war, the arms fell silent, opening the field to tears. Whether 11 November became an official national holiday or not depended on the country, but the day itself, or the previous Sunday, is everywhere a day of reflection and remembrance. In Britain two minutes of silence are observed, during which everything stops – from production lines to buses in the streets.[9] In most countries, the commemorations crystallise in one of the rare successful expressions of what has been called 'civil religion'.[10] The gatherings around the war memorials at eleven o'clock, the flags and black crepe, the flowers and speeches create opportunities for a moral and civic pedagogy that reunites the dead and the living for the duration of the ceremony. Deceased and veterans, husbands and widows, fathers and orphans seem to come together again through the symbolism of the procession and silence. Added to this, in France, has been the reading out of the names of the fallen, followed by the reply, 'Dead for France'. These liturgical elements have sometimes ended with fireworks and illuminations, banquets and athletic contests – pre-war practices and social occasions revived and adapted for the commemoration of the dead.

During the war itself, a distinction was made between the religious and the sacred, and this has been maintained. Parish monuments to the fallen soldiers, for instance, are not necessarily more religious than monuments built by civic authorities, but they are all equally sacred. Through their bereavement, freethinkers became adept at making the secular sacred, and in the post-war societies this automatically meant that the Judeo-Christian forms were recast in national terms, whether at the Arc de Triomphe, in Westminster Abbey, in Arlington National Cemetery, or at grave sites in military or parish cemeteries.

In French, 'monument to the dead', in English, 'war memorial': whereas the French stress death, the English choose to recall the *war* — the war as cause of death, but also as the source of an enormous upheaval in people's lives that didn't necessarily end in death. The English term is therefore more all-encompassing: the monuments were built in memory of both the war dead and the war itself. France rejected the kind of memorials that were widespread among the other former belligerents, 'utilitarian' memorials in the form of fellowships, stadiums, libraries and clocks. And there, it was only the dead who were entitled to having their names inscribed on the monuments, in other words, to having their heroism recognised and proclaimed, and the only form of remembrance was a statue in the middle of a public space, in a place 'honoured by an entire community because the collective memory has infused [it] with sacred content and beliefs have become stronger by taking root there'.[11]

The fact that so many of the American and English soldiers were enlisted men explains both the semantic differences and the 'utilitarian' aspects of some commemorations of the war in the Anglo-Saxon countries. The logic of conscription meant that it was not necessary to recall the names of everyone who had participated in the war, but it was different when the heroes were volunteers. In Australia — the only country that rejected conscription throughout the war — the monuments always bear the names of *all* the enlisted men, whether they returned alive or not. Swimming pools and meeting halls became places of remembrance of those who had sacrificed themselves as well as gathering places for veterans and for society in general.[12] In Australia, 25 April, the anniversary of the landing of the troops in Gallipoli, is designated for commemoration of the dead as ANZAC Day. (In the 1920s, some veterans used to get so inebriated on ANZAC Day that they were asked not to appear at the war memorials.) Thus the ways of mourning and of remembering sacrifices are inextricably connected. War memorials are where the survivors identify with the heroes and justify their sacrifice;[13] they are stone monuments designed by the sculptors who got the commissions to do so, but they are re-designed, as it were, by the participants in the ceremonies that subsequently take place there.

Monuments had been erected after the American Civil War, after various colonial wars, after the Franco-Prussian war of 1870-71, but it was after the Great War that they became universal, recalling the omnipresence of the 1914-18 tragedy throughout the world of the former belligerents (except in Russia, which had then become the Soviet Union). Both conquerors and conquered partook of the same commemorative frenzy and the forms hardly differed, in style, size, symbols or allegories. The public space allotted to the memory of the war was homogenised, worldwide: whether in England or Germany, Saint George and the archangel Gabriel slayed the same dragon. Noting that in 1925 the artist and war veteran Adolf Hitler designed a project to honour his former comrades, a much larger arch of triumph than the one in Paris, Ken Inglis points out that the creators of war memorials tend to forget and invent as much as they remember.[14] The number of citations to dead soldiers on public monuments should be multiplied by at least four or five (in France this would means multiplying the number of the 36,000 town memorials) to get an adequate idea of the full commemorative impulse of the 1920s, for each dead soldier was entitled to have his name publicly engraved not only in his town but also in his workplace, his school and his parish; and the living rooms of millions of homes became family altars exhibiting photos and mementos.

In France, the town cenotaph was most often a stele, similar to those used on tombs in cemeteries; they were the least expensive, and conformed to the spirit of the period. Business had never been better for architects, stonemasons and undertakers. Shrewd wholesalers put out catalogues with a choice of ornaments for the upright stone slab – palms, laurels, the Military Cross, or the statue of an infantryman. The words most frequently used in the inscriptions were: 'children', 'They answered the call', 'dead', 'heroes', '*Caduti per la patria*', 'war', 'Fallen Heroes', '1914–1918', 'duty', 'sacrifice', 'martyrs', 'memory'. In all countries, the rhetoric of 'high diction' – including Horace's omnipresent '*Dulce et decorum est pro patria mori*' – usually prevailed.

Only very few openly pacifist monuments were built – in France, for example, there are about ten – and when they were, only one inscription (usually 'Cursed be the war') was chosen. But in every other respect their style is the same as that of the other monuments. While there were strong pacifist currents in society after 1918, why wasn't this reflected in the monuments? It is not because the monuments were chosen by state authorities. Monuments were also built spontaneously everywhere, overseen by the veterans themselves or their families – in other words by society in general. Thus the evidence is that the building of monuments was determined by the scale of the mourning, the immeasurable bereavement experienced, and not by the desire to suggest that war should never happen again.

In France the law separating church and state prohibits religious ornaments on public property. Yet the monuments to the dead after the Great War were routinely adorned with crucifixes in Catholic towns, and very often in other regions as well, even when they weren't within the cemeteries. The list of dead, the second component of the memorial, completed the funereal impression. The alphabetical order most often adopted reinforced a uniformity of treatment, mirroring the uniformity in the military cemeteries where the dead were buried. Naming was the important thing: the names recalled the individuals and granted them an existence against the oblivion to which they had been consigned on the battlefields. Inscribing the names, reading them, touching the inscriptions, as we can see mourners doing in photographs from the 1920s, brought men out of the anonymous unreality of loss and emptiness.

The sculptures for the monuments, works of art at the service of memory, depict one of three tragic subjects: the courageous warrior, the martyr, or death. There are many statues of soldiers (*poilus*, tommies, diggers, sammies – the nicknames show the warm familiarity with which they were considered), so that the men are brought back to their native environment and into the circle of their family, and their local and political milieux. Their stances are brave, even swaggering, because it is known that they were heroic, even if they lost the war. Their uniforms and weapons are represented with great precision. They stand on their pedestals, doomed to pursue for all eternity the exemplary combat for which they gave their lives. Their war is sanitised. No mud, no lice, no blood: they are as clean and fresh as toy soldiers, operetta soldiers playing and replaying the part that was theirs – the heroic defence of a great cause.

Yet these monuments are tombs, empty tombs. And as cenotaphs they remind us that they are built on bodies, like so many posthumous merit lists. On some of the battlefields and in big cities, generals got their own monuments, but everyone else was commemorated in one monument. *War memorial* glorifies the fact of having fought in the war; *monument to the dead* that of dying in the war. But since death can't be glorified or exalted – it is always intolerable, no matter what its cause – all the monuments choose to deny death by showing soldiers who are eternally alive, resurrected in bronze. (Very occasionally the taboo against represented death is lifted, and a valiant knight resting in his tomb is depicted, but this is quite rare.)

The war memorials in France, Italy, Germany and Bohemia glorified not only the combatants but the civilians on the home front, without whom it would have been impossible, either materially or psychologically, to hold out for the duration of the war. And of course they proclaimed grief. We can agree with the veteran Georges Dumézil, who wrote several speeches inaugurating monuments in the 1920s: the sculptures expressed the triple function of the Sacred Union – it was essential to believe, to fight and to work in order to persevere, so the monuments illustrated this triple theme in stone and bronze. At the top, a rooster, a lion, a Saint George or an eagle representing the homeland; in the centre, the soldier; and at the foot of the monument, civilians – the elderly, women and children – either looking up at the soldier in admiration or attending to their daily tasks, farm work (still the main livelihood at the time) or factory work. Though the memorials glorified the courage of the survivors and united them in their ordeal, they were above all places of mourning, where bereavement and religious and patriotic fervour were complementary. There, as on the stained-glass memorial windows in churches, the Christian soldier was likened, in his sacrifice, to Christ in an *Imitatio Christi*. When his mother, the new Virgin Mary, was reunited with her son and held him in her arms, the monument became a pietà. *Stabat mater dolorosa*.

The places of death, the battlefields themselves, were also converted into commemorative sites through the creation of a network of military cemeteries, landscaped memorial parks and large battlefield monuments – all of these 'compensat[ing] for powerlessness with pathos'.[15] In its adaptation of the articles in the Treaty of Frankfurt that had organised the first European military cemeteries in 1871 (similar ones had been created in the United States in 1847–8 after the Mexican–American War and many times over after the Civil War),[16] Article 225 of the Treaty of Versailles stipulates: 'The Allied Governments and the German Government will cause to be respected and maintained the graves of the soldiers and sailors buried in their respective territories.'[17] The former belligerents did indeed transform the land into so many 'reliquaries' of sacrifice, so many 'heroes' gardens'.[18] But the apparent uniformity of the military cemeteries hides an essential distinction: in France the dead conquerors, who died for justice, were given light-coloured steles, the colour of purity, while the defeated Germans were given dark-coloured steles or crosses as a reminder of their black objectives. They were also forced to bury their soldiers en masse in assigned spaces, probably so they would occupy and 'contaminate' French national soil as little as possible. We see this in the German cemeteries in

France, for example, or the Austrian ones in Italy, necropolises that group together tens of thousands of bodies, mostly in communal graves.

All the former belligerents were obsessed with identifying the tombs. Some chose to unite their own dead in one area – the Americans, for example, quite consciously compensated for their late entry into the conflict and their relatively small losses with large cemeteries. Others spread the tombs of their soldiers around so that their dead would be everywhere. This was the decision made by the Imperial War Graves Commission: rather than bring home the British Empire's 1,019,882 war dead whose graves had been registered, they buried them permanently as closely as possible to the spot where they had fallen. The belief seemed to be that remembrance of the dead would be better served there, giving impetus to further commemorations throughout the Empire. Winston Churchill expressed it in these terms:

> The cemeteries ... will be entirely different from the ordinary cemeteries which mark the resting place of those who pass away in the common flow of human fate from year to year. They will be supported and sustained by the wealth of this great nation and empire, as long as we remain a nation and an empire, and there is no reason at all why, in periods as remote from our own as we are from the Tudors, the graveyards in France of this Great War, shall not remain an abiding and supreme memorial to the efforts and glory of the British Army, and the sacrifices made in the great cause.[19]

In memory of the son he had lost in the war, Rudyard Kipling designed an immense 'cross of sacrifice', based on a sword motif, and the 'memory stone', a kind of interdenominational altar adorned with the verse from Ecclesiastes 'Their name liveth for evermore' which were used by countless English memorialists.*

---

*The body of Kipling's only son was found only in the 1990s. Up until his own death in 1936, Kipling never ceased to believe that he might continue to communicate with him through spiritualism.

The British were the only nation to allow families a space on the base of the steles where they could have whatever words they wanted engraved. Since no bodies were sent home, and Australia and South Africa were too far away for relatives of the dead to have any hope of ever paying their respects at the grave sites, the engraved words substituted for their presence. The cemeteries were all made to look as British as possible, with the planting of lawns and flowers. Plants from Australia and India were acclimatised in northern France. Thus the empire dead rested on soil that looked distinctly British – thanks to the uniform architecture of the cemeteries – and distinctly national as well, with engravings of Canadian maple leaves on the steles or with actual Australian eucalyptus trees.

Unlike the British, the Americans and the French were upset by the military authorities' refusal to return their dead. In France, a public outcry led to a proposal, strongly advocated in the veterans' newspapers and voted on by the Chamber of Deputies, to allow the exhuming and transportation of the sacrificed heroes. There was a fundamental political and symbolic issue at stake: the state wished to keep together all those who had worked and died for victory, whereas many of the families felt that the sacrifice of their children was enough, and now it was time for them to be returned.

Whatever the policies of the respective countries, in the end the majority of the dead remained buried on the battlefields, if only because the conditions of combat had made for a great many unknown soldiers, and had turned the battle sites into cemeteries as enormous as the conflict had been. In the ossuaries, men whose nationalities could be identified thanks to remnants of their uniforms were grouped together.* The four French battlefield ossuaries, Douaumont, Lorette, Dormans and

---

*Often the deaths had been so brutal that not even this could be ascertained about the corpses, although it was acknowledged only very late. Until recently, the largest and most symbolic French ossuary, Douaumont, was supposed to contain only precious French remains: this was obviously not the case.

Hartmanwillerkopf, together with the chapel at Rancourt, have national characteristics which all the soldiers shared superimposed on regional characteristics. They have acquired a certain celebrity, the celebrity of heroism and sacrifice: the wish was to recall – on the most prominent parts of the sites where the most difficult, horrendous offensives were fought, on the hilltops that had witnessed death, from the highest and most far-flung points – the nature of the Great War. Though the monuments are empty tombs, the ossuaries store the remains of tens of thousands of men whose identities were swallowed up by earth and fire.

Right after the war, all the former belligerent countries assigned days for remembering the soldiers' sacrifices. There were processions and arches of triumph (even for the defeated German soldiers, who were welcomed, as President Friedrich Ebert put it, as having been 'unvanquished on the battlefields'). The erection of both temporary cenotaphs (on 14 and 19 July 1919, in Paris and London) and permanent ones (the several Tombs of the Unknown Soldier) had the same purpose. Everywhere death was meant to pervade the social fabric.

The sequence of events in Paris on 14 July 1919 and 11 November 1920 sheds light on the popular state of mind right after the Great War. It could be said that the 1,350,000 dead Frenchmen largely invaded the entire symbolic and emotional space. In 1919, victory was celebrated, but the weight of the French losses prevailed. In 1920, the burial of the Unknown Soldier was meant to give a unique place to the dead heroes among all the heroes, the fallen soldiers among all the combatants, but the definition of hero can vary and controversy over this became just as intense as the ardent grief. There may have been differences among the national commemorative events, but they all shared a fervour born of the war and related to the millions of dead and wounded, a fervour stemming from messianic feelings for the homeland.

On 14 July 1919, the huge procession that filed under the Arc de Triomphe was intended to glorify the army and offer a reminder that the love of France involved a willingness to die in its defence. Yet the tens of thousands of tricoloured and Allied flags, the coloured ribbons and blazes of light, the cheers during the military procession (which included Allied troops) failed to convey the tenor of that day. For before celebrating the victory, it had been deemed appropriate to recall the dead. A watch was kept all night from the 13th to the 14th at the foot of the cenotaph – a huge, empty coffin of gilded plaster reinforcing the idea of the almost obscenely temporary aspect of life. Then Bastille Day itself was given over to the living. But no one was taken in: the military procession was headed by a thousand disabled veterans representing the million severely wounded veterans who had survived the war. Death certainly hovered over the victory, as hundreds of thousands of bereaved people filed past the cenotaph in silence or in tears. On 19 July, London witnessed the same behaviour during the Victory Parade: people wanted to stay as close as possible to the empty coffin, symbol of the void left behind by the millions of lost soldiers. The dead stole the day of glory from the survivors.

For some, however, these festivities and military displays were a political betrayal and an insult to the dead. The French Socialist Party, for example, offered a 'separate, refined' alternative – an afternoon of poetry and music – to honour the dead along with their own hero, Jean Jaurès, who had been assassinated on 31 July 1914; they called him their 'first war casualty': 'We are certain that our readers will contribute, with their collective fervour to the grandeur of a solemn occasion that is religious (in the best sense of the word) more than it is political ... If there are more important duties than visiting a tomb, there is certainly no nobler duty than the one bringing the dead into the chorus of the living so as to draw from their union a lesson for the future.'[20]

In 1919, what remained of the Sacred Union was that great breath of collective fervour which had been born in 1914 and had endured with intensity and anguish throughout the war years, and which national commemorations reactivated everywhere by honouring the sacrifice and, often, inducing horror at its pointlessness.

All the former belligerents staged national ceremonies for the burial of an unknown soldier.[21] This cult of the Unknown Soldier was the Great War's commemorative invention *par excellence*, and a gift to posterity bestowed by war's brutalisation: anonymity guaranteed everyone's heroism and allowed everyone to be mourned. These tombs became altars of the homeland. Starting on 11 November 1920, when the first two ceremonies took place in London and Paris, this international ritual became a focus for every national power. In 1921, it was the turn of Washington, Rome[22] and Brussels; in 1922, Prague and Belgrade, followed by Warsaw and Athens.

The new states that had been created by the treaties at Versailles were particularly keen on the ritual. They had been born of and from the war and the sacrifice of their people; their very existence testified to the blood that had been shed. Whether conquering or conquered states, they all instituted the same cult, death making the memory uniform. After Sofia buried its Unknown Soldier in 1923, Bucharest and Vienna followed suit. (There were two exceptions: in Germany during the Weimar Republic, the mayor of Cologne, Konrad Adenauer, was opposed when in 1925 he proposed having an unknown soldier buried on the banks of the Rhine. And indeed, what would it have meant so far from Berlin, Germany's decapitated capital? There were various other German burial sites for unknown soldiers, but only as of 1933 was this kind of cult instituted by Germany's unknown corporal, Adolf Hitler.[23] And in Bolshevik Russia, the only major tomb welcomed in Moscow was Lenin's; there was no memorial for the Russian soldiers who had died prior to 1917.)

In France, the choice of resting places and the organising of ceremonies caused heated disputes, though the principles of burying an unknown soldier and celebrating it on 11 November were more or less unanimously accepted. For the year 1920 was also the fiftieth anniversary of the Third Republic. From minds so branded by the war that the only ritual imaginable was burial in a symbolic location came the idea of placing in the Pantheon, along with the body of the Unknown Soldier, the heart of Leon

Gambetta. Thus the heart of the Republican patriot of 1870 would rest next to the anonymous patriot who had voluntarily sacrificed himself for his country, for the very Republic which had now successfully recovered from Germany the provinces it had lost in 1870–71. The Pantheon seemed be the natural place; after all, wasn't there an inscription on its pediment expressing the country's gratitude for its great men: '*Aux grands hommes la patrie reconnaissante*'?

This idea failed to take into account what the French people thought of the enormous national effort that had been made in the years 1914–18. Veterans and their families, in other words most French people, believed that the soldiers were *not* the usual 'great men', destined in a rather banal way – like the 'good students' of the previous decades of the Third Republic – for the military, political, literary or scientific acclaim of being put in the Pantheon.[24] The Ministry of Education, responsible for organising the 11 November ceremony, therefore ended up splitting the ceremony in two: 'Transport to the Pantheon, and burial under the Arc de Triomphe of the remains of an unidentified *poilu* fallen during the Great War'.

In the end, the real 'miracle' of the Unknown Soldier was that he rallied everyone – from socialists, most of whom had become communist between the ceremony of 11 November and the permanent burial in January 1921, to Catholic Republicans. And the Archbishop of Paris was asked to bless the Unknown Soldier's coffin – a great innovation. Though most of France was Catholic, who could say if the Unknown Soldier wasn't Protestant, Jewish or atheist? In any case, a Protestant minister had foreseen what would happen as early as 1915: 'Jesus Christ will have the last word. He will live through a new era under the Arc de Triomphe with a humanised humanity.'[25] And a rabbi put into verse the messianic Republican fervour of mourning, recalling that often what was most painful for the families was their not knowing where their departed relative was buried. The Tomb of the Unknown Soldier, simultaneously unique and collective, was specifically intended to respond to that anguish:

Tell me, passer-by, the name
Of that old man or youth
Who will sleep his slumber
In such triumph?
He is called 'conqueror', he is called 'symbol'
His name is repeated from one end of the earth to the other
He is called 'honour', the 'unknown soldier'
'The anonymous hero' lost in the crowd!
Partisan of a fertile oeuvre
He has saved the world.
He died for liberty
And for humanity ...
Oh, France dear France!
Forever be blessed
For having erased the grief
That was breaking our hearts!
Every wife, today, every sister, every mother
Exalting the career of her dear 'departed',
Will proudly say to herself, without illusion:
He is surely the one who is going to the Pantheon!
Oh, poilu, go take your place
There in the glorious monument,
Soldiers of your race require
A giant's granite resting place![26]

On 10 November, the Unknown Soldier's coffin arrived in
Paris by special train from Verdun, where he had been chosen
from among eight others, and was placed for one night at the
Place Denfert-Rochereau. A wake was organised. The next day,
the coffin was brought from Denfert-Rochereau (named for an
heroic French commander of 1871) to the Pantheon and then to
the Arc de Triomphe. The route through Paris that was chosen
for the procession served the organisers' intentions superbly: the
Republic's revenge for its defeat of 1870 was linked for ever to
the victory it had just achieved, while the price the French had
paid was taken fully into account. The Unknown Soldier, his

coffin draped with the French tricolour and placed on a gun car-
riage, was surrounded by disabled veterans; as those who had in-
augurated the procession of 14 July 1919, they were reminders of
the tragedy of war. It had destroyed men; it had destroyed families; the commemoration was to make them live again, and the
burial of the Unknown Soldier, his adoption by the entire
nation, were *his* and *their* resurrection.

The coffin was accompanied throughout the day by a ficti-
tious family: a war widow, a mother and father who had lost a
son and a child who had lost his father. The war had reversed the
logical sequence of generations, and the commemoration was
intended to set things right; each person was to adopt the
Unknown Soldier as his father or son*, just as the village war
memorials sometimes had sculptures of schoolchildren admiring
the 'child of the village' who was none other than their father. A
strange genealogy was engendered by the war.

The ceremonies of 11 November 1920 brought to the streets
of Paris hundreds of thousands of people in tears, convinced they
were seeing their lost relative go by. The Republic could congrat-
ulate itself for the fervour of those anonymous people who had
defended and saved it. The reporter for *L'Humanité*, though he
says he followed the procession 'out of professional obligation',
wrote a most poignant description of the Unknown Soldier, the
soldier known to all those who had loved and lost a dear one: 'Did
he perhaps fall near me in Artois, Champagne, or Verdun? Was it
he who showed me pictures of his father and mother, his wife and
children during our long martyrdom in the trenches?'[27]

The burial in the permanent tomb took place in January 1921.
The inscription was a reminder that the victorious Republic was

---

*In a detective story of the time, *La Dent d'Hercule Petitgris*, by Maurice
Leblanc, a mother is 'saved' by the conviction that her own son is the
Unknown Soldier:

'Not for a day, not for an hour, will I leave Paris.'

'Why is that, Madame?'

'Because *he* is there, in the tomb.'

(First edition, 1923, republished, Paris: R. Laffont, 1988.)

identified with the French nation: 'Here lies a French soldier who died for his country. 1914–1918. 4 September 1870: the Republic is proclaimed. 11 November 1918: Alsace-Lorraine is returned to France.' For years, the tomb of the Arc de Triomphe was the first place that visitors to Paris from the provinces or abroad would visit; it became 'the centre of official public spirit-edness',[28] ahead of the Pantheon or the Invalides. 'The culmination of it all was the eternal flame, blessed sacrament of the nation ... A wondrous ritual, this nation made into man, dead and resurrected on the patriotic Easter of 11 November.'[29]

Beyond the official ceremonies and military processions, the various Unknown Soldiers did successfully crystallise the values of sacrifice and the tragedy linked to the war. And in a reversal that probably pleased the small minority of people who had criticised the ceremonies, the tombs eventually became symbolic focuses for the expression of pacifism.

Hence, everyone everywhere found their place – or nearly everyone, since some were excluded, or at least kept on the sidelines during commemorations of the Great War. War prisoners, deported civilians, soldiers from regions that had been transferred to another nation as a result of the war (Alsatians, Lorrains, Poles, Czechs, for example) – these were all people who experienced in anticipation the tragedies of the next war. They are the missing link between the excessively celebrated heroes of the Great War and the victims of the Second World War. The unanimity of the Sacred Union had covered up all potential divisions during the Great War, and the unanimous ceremonies of remembrance were similarly centred on a single experience – that of the soldiers in the trenches – an experience that tended to discount or overlook the exceptional sufferings of other minority groups, whether defined by gender (women), age (the elderly and children), status (prisoners) or geography (citizens of occupied territories).

Civilians in occupied territories and, even more, prisoners of war and civilians who had been deported were groups who lived through the conflict outside the national territory, either geographically or symbolically, and hence they became victims of denial, insofar as the duty to remember was concerned. The war had been waged in defence of the nation's now sacred soil, the soil symbolised by the trenches, where the blood of the dead had mixed with the earth, and it seemed almost inevitable that those who had spent the war far from that soil would now be excluded from that particular memory.

How does one commemorate victims who are not heroes? How can one commemorate the suffering of hunger, cold, forced labour, rape, being taken hostage, requisitions? The characteristics of collective suffering were sometimes listed on commemorative monuments in northern and eastern France and in Belgium, with the entire trail of misfortunes caused by total war being presented like an indictment. But since the point was to denounce German crimes rather than to highlight the suffering in and of itself, the tragedy of the forced labourers, one of the new misfortunes of modern war, was scarcely or never alluded to. The memory of those labourers' suffering was camouflaged, as much as possible, precisely to make the difference between them and the others bearable. Hence, in northern France and in the Ardennes, 'ordinary' monuments to the dead were erected very soon after the armistice, as a way of announcing that these regions were reclaiming their place in France and that the four years of war fought on their soil had been a mere parenthesis.

As might be expected, the inhabitants chose Sacred Union monuments in bronze and stone, showing fighting *poilus*, triumphant roosters and home-front civilians struggling together for the victory of France. The 'normality' of these monuments is indicative of the normalisation of suffering in the post-war years. The inhabitants in these disaster areas had to be seen as French like everyone else and as having died for their country like everyone else. In Alsace, soldiers are often represented naked on the monuments; for how can a German be distinguished from a Frenchman if he isn't wearing a uniform? The Strasbourg pietà has the bodies of two lifeless sons on her knees; and the inscription 'To our dead', though it doesn't deny the reality of death, omits the usual 'for our country'. For indeed, which country was it?

If the truth about these Alsatian soldiers, who are either conquerors or conquered, can't be acknowledged, what about the soldiers who really *were* defeated? The same collective repression of catastrophe took place in Germany as had taken place in France after 1871. Defeat was never mentioned in the commemorations; soldiers were always referred to as heroes who had been outnumbered or betrayed. On the monument to commemorate the Battle of Sedan, where Germany had defeated France in 1870, was inscribed the motto '*Impavidus numero Victis*'; now the new motto was '*Im Felde Unbesiegt*' (In the Field Unvanquished). When, eventually, a name was actually ascribed to those responsible for the German defeat – communists, Jews, the liberal state, and so on – the political and cultural consequences were tragic. For what could not be repressed anywhere was death, the void. Taking collective revenge on that void became a primary objective of the fascist regimes.

9

Personal bereavement

In the aftermath of the Great War, who were the people in mourning and how many of them were there? We must answer these questions if we are to understand the period between the two world wars, and indeed if we are to understand twentieth-century history as a whole.

The historian Jay Winter has suggested the interesting concept of 'communities in mourning' as a means to grasp the sheer scale of the mourning after the end of the Great War. Every social structure in Europe went into mourning for the men who had fallen in 1914–18: businesses, companies, schools, universities and athletic clubs built their own war memorials complement-ing the ones in churches and town squares; they organised their own commemorative ceremonies and published their own memory books. In these books, the obituaries were usually written by the deceased's closest friends; information was pro-vided by the families themselves, who could decide what they wanted to have written about the deceased. The tone of these memorials seems conventional and formal to us today, for the lo-cutions of bereavement have changed. But on second reading their emotionally charged content is apparent; in the yearbook of the École Normale Supérieure, for example, on 31 August 1915, here is Paul Morillot, the father, signing the obituary of his son, Georges Morillot, killed in 1914: 'A father is going to speak about his child: may he be forgiven for that ... I wish to write about the short life of a son of France, a young soldier, a graduate of the Normale in 1914, similar no doubt to many others.'[1]

The actual presence of communities in mourning – communities *of* mourning, perhaps – reminds us that the mourning was collective, and endured collectively. Veterans' groups were also associations of bereaved people (the full title of one of the two large veterans associations in France, the Union Fédérale, was 'Federal Union of French Associations of Disabled and Discharged Veterans of the Great War and of their Widows, Orphans and Descendants'). The grief of the bereaved was therefore recognised and alleviated by the creation of social structures aiming, implicitly or explicitly, at helping survivors. Similarly, support was provided to orphans, thanks to the work of various philanthropic institutions, some of them set up at the very beginning of the conflict.[2]

The first circle of mourning was undoubtedly composed of the soldiers themselves. In their war writings – letters, personal notebooks and trench newspapers – which express wartime emotions as they occurred, it is striking to note the extent to which the primary combatant groups were themselves communities in mourning and communities of mourning. The omnipresence of death at the front made the most atrocious sights commonplace, and all the combatants realised, usually with a touch of terror and guilt, their capacity to be hardened about the death of others, yet the small groups of men who constituted the fabric of the armies of the Great War often took great risks and expended considerable energy to honour, under horrific circumstances, their own dead.

In the French case, it would be more accurate to say that the soldiers *imposed* this practice. Marshal Joffre, in a directive of 19 July 1915, followed a well-established nineteenth-century tradition (even though it had been subverted since 1870) when he continued to order the digging of communal graves that could contain around a hundred corpses of men in the ranks, but the soldiers themselves took the initiative of building individual graves.[3] And on the German side, extreme care was often taken even to make tombstones; one can see examples in museums as well as, for instance, in certain forgotten areas of the Verdun battlefield. The Germans also built cemeteries with individual graves in some of the French and Belgian cities they occupied.

And that was not all. According to all eyewitness accounts, the soldiers maintained, as best they could, the graves of the comrades to whom they felt close, and sometimes placed flowers on them. They went to the trouble of informing the dead comrade's family of the location of the burial place and describing the funeral tribute that had been made; often they included a map of the grave's exact location. Below is the letter which, together with a sketch, a Breton infantryman, Auguste P——, sent on 27 November 1915 to the family of a comrade who had been killed. The author clearly went to great trouble to write it:

> My dear Friends, I answer your letter that I received last night I
> had already written to you the day before yesterday and put a
> stamp so as I could be sure it would arrive, an then a pal who was
> going on furlough to the Côtes-du-nord took it and will put it in
> a box at home. Ernest was not board at all between our hours of
> misery we had fun anyway he never talked of not returning on
> the contrary we said to each other that once the War was done
> weed spend a week at each other's house to get used to civilian
> life again and he was always very cheerful weed promised
> ourselves many things for the end of the War. As for the letter you
> rote he didn't get it it came Monday and poor Ernest died in the
> nite of Wednesday to Thursday. It's a military Cemetery you could
> say since there are only soldiers but it was also a field of Apple
> trees Four at his feet there is a little Apple tree and two or three
> metres from his head there is also a big Apple tree full of Apples
> since i had to take them away to dig the grave I'm sure because I
> buried him only since then it mite have been Bombed thursday
> I had went to bring a Cross and the Bottle on the cross and
> engraved his Baptism certificate in ink and on a Payper in the

Bottle which i put top down on the tomb and it can't be seen without taking away some earth, for I stuck it in pretty strong, coffin, my poor lady, there aren't any i wrapped his head in his Greatcoat poor fellow and that's how he went. We left the next Tuesday of Saint Tomas. As for his things I'm not surprised for it's a real messy Regiment but I'll take care of it for the chaplin with the Rank of captain who gave him his last Prayers is still with us he came to see us again last Monday so as soon as I see him again i'll talk to him about it so he'll make sure to send you the package, i asked in my last letter for his picteur, he always had mine on him, you will be very kind to send to me it very soon Four i expect to go on furlough and i'll take it home with me madame you have no cause to thank me what I do is my duty God commands me to do it. Goodbye my Friends. Hoping to have News from you. A Friend who will never forget you.[4]

It was not unusual for soldiers on leave to feel that they should visit the relatives of a dead comrade. The writer Maurice Genevoix remembers it with horror in a book written more than half a century after the war:

When misfortune strikes, each one of us experiences his suffering alone. But on that day ... between Benoist's father and mother, it seemed to me that I felt – it even flowed through me – the grief of the parents of a soldier who had been killed ... Between his rare words, the father let his eyes wander in the distance ... And suddenly his jaws would tighten, and I could see the muscles tremble. The mother stared at me constantly. And then I had to look away. What I saw in her eyes was in the end unbearable to me.[5]

These two texts demonstrate the same thing; it is striking how strongly this primary group carried their memories of the dead. Everything we know about the conversations among soldiers shows how frequently the survivors talked about those who had been killed; in personal notebooks, for example, the other men's deaths are very present. Even first-person accounts com-

posed after the war show this; the comrades who were killed in
the war are named, described, written about at length; very
often, the narratives are dedicated to them. Genevoix was shattered by the death, in 1915, of Lieutenant Pourchon, a young
graduate of the Saint-Cyr military academy, and he dedicated his
book *Ceux de 1914* (Those of 1914) to him. Half a century later,
he dedicated *Trente mille jours* (Thirty thousand days) to the same
young man. Of course, these first circles of mourning, made up
of the relatively small community of soldiers, necessarily splin-
tered rather quickly: rapid troop rotations between 1914 and
1918 regularly broke up the primary groups and then demobilisation dispersed them completely.

The circles of mourning on the home front were perforce
longer lasting. We might think of them as a series of concentric
circles, whose contours become increasingly difficult to trace as
we move away from the most strongly affected relatives. The first
circle was by far the bleakest: the dead man's parents, grandparents, children, wife and siblings. Then there was a second circle
of mourning, whose contours are roughly those of the larger
family group – uncles and aunts, cousins, nieces and nephews,
brothers- and sisters-in-law. These first two circles correspond
more or less to what demographers today call 'the immediate
family'. Though the relationships in the second circle are not as
close as in the first, we should not underestimate the grieving of
these relatives: the young Françoise Mariette (better known later
as the child psychiatrist Françoise Dolto) was deeply affected by
the death of her uncle in the war when she was still a child; she
saw herself as a 'war widow' and experienced her bereavement as
a tragedy.[6] The following text, written by a primary-school pupil
who was asked to describe his day of 1 January 1915 speaks
volumes about the impact of the death of his cousin on his
parents and on the rest of the family:

> The year that is starting finds everyone steeped in sadness because
> of this dreadful war that is making so many victims. In our family,
> we were particularly unhappy, for just the day before we received

very bad news: one of our cousins had been killed on theYser battlefield, in the line of duty of a good Frenchman. On the morning of 1 January, we were more in the mood to weep as we greeted one another than to extend wishes for a happy new year ... In the evening ... we stayed by the fireplace, barely talking, and we thought about our dear cousin whom we shall no longer see and also about all our valiant soldiers fighting so heroically to defend our country. I will remember that day of 1 January 1915 for the rest of my life ... and I will always feel hatred for those accursed Germans.[7]

Beyond this second circle of mourning is a third made up of 'distant' family members, but this circle is impossible to reconstitute.[8] (Along with the immediate family, it makes up what is called the extended family.) On the other hand, there is another, more clearly apparent circle around each war dead: the circle of 'chosen' relationships, of male and female friends. Needless to say, they are never mentioned as victims of the Great War, yet we all know that grieving for a friend can be just as painful as grieving for a close relative. Here is the obituary written by Maurice Genevoix for one of his friends from the École Normale, Paul-Raymond Benoist, killed at twenty-five on 15 January 1915, whom he remembered along with other disappeared classmates:

We had fought often, during those long months of war, and each engagement had created voids around me. All the good friends at the beginning, whom I had chosen, who had lightened my hours, and to whom I wanted to give back the strength they had given me, had fallen, one after the other, all of them, until I was alone in a crowd of indifferent men. So, I, who had not let a single day go by without recalling the École and the faces of my classmates, right away found a safe haven in such recollection. My hope lay in it, and I was invigorated by it. But then letters came to me that were so many deep shocks. One told me, 'Casamajor is dead' and the other, 'Rigal is dead.You knew them, they were strong, ardent, young, rich in heart and mind.You loved them. They are dead. That's it. You'll never see them again.' And I thought about them, I wept for them within myself; and I had a frantic desire to keep them alive, with their living faces, their living gazes, and the sound of their voices, and the sight of their familiar gestures ... And among those whose support I wished for, to make this cult of our dead more fervent, was Benoist, dearest to my heart and most valued friend ... I said to myself, 'He at least will be saved.' And I believed it. Then one morning, in the white hospital room, the mail orderly handed me a card. And on this card I read, 'Benoist is dead.' I felt an all-encompassing and crushing sorrow. I couldn't understand it; it didn't make sense ... And I could see the little house again, the parents who had waited for him and who now no longer were waiting for him. I decided to go to them so they would know that other hearts were suffering humbly from the same despair, and to keep within myself, piously, a bit of that anguish greater than all other anguishes. They made me come into the bedroom he loved. I saw his last portrait, mountain-climbing, and his Military Cross fastened on the frame. His father and mother were crying. And he was between them ... But after we had closed the door on the peace of the bedroom, the father spoke, as if to himself and very slowly: 'Poor fellow,' he said. 'Life will not have weighed heavily on him. At least we did everything we could.' ... Isn't it true, my friend, that life will not have weighed heavily on you?[9]

By writing of circles of mourning we do not mean to establish a hierarchy of grief but to clarify how each death devastated emotional worlds, in a wide-ranging gradation of aftershocks. The notion of 'entourage', which demographers use to describe the relational sphere that surrounds each individual, can be used here, so long as we also include relationships of love and friendship. These 'entourages' are affected by mourning in varying degrees, depending on the relationship with the deceased when he was still alive. It is almost impossible to estimate the number of mourners in the countries whose soldiers fought in the Great War; available statistics do not refer to the bereaved but only to relatives entitled to benefits among the deceased's ascendants and descendants (and in some of the belligerent countries, such as Russia after 1917, there is no reliable number at all). And aside from the fact that the number mentioned is always smaller than the true number of people affected by bereavement, the people entitled to benefits varied according to the country's benefits rules. In France, for example, during the period between the wars, war widows who remarried lost their benefits, but obviously remarriage didn't erase the fact that they had suffered the loss of a previous husband. Meanwhile, other women acquired the status of war widow when disabled war veterans whom they had married *after* the war subsequently died. Similar difficulties apply to orphans; when they came of age, they vanished from the statistics, which is why they rapidly 'diminished' in number in Europe after 1919. Yet they will have felt the absence of their fathers to the end of their lives.

To get a measure of the extent of the first circle of mourning in Europe, one should begin with the number of widows and orphans. There were 525,000 war widows in Germany in 1920, 200,000 in Italy, 600,000 in France, 240,000 in Great Britain.*[10] On the assumption that 30 per cent of the men killed in the Great War left widows behind, this comes to about 3 million women for the belligerent parties as a whole. (There were more than 1 million orphans in Germany, at least 760,000 in France,[11] 350,000 each in Great Britain and Romania and 300,000 in Italy.) If you count an average of two children per widow, as Jay Winter does, you arrive at a total of 6 million orphans.

The numbers are even less certain if we try to estimate the number of bereaved parents; in Germany, there were 192,000 financially dependent parents or grandparents who received compensation, but this represents only a tiny fraction of bereaved German parents.[12] We know somewhat more in the case of France, thanks to Antoine Prost's calculations: by the end of the

---

*The German figure declined to 371,000 by 1924; and the French one increased to 700,000 by 1933, of whom 262,500 had remarried.

1920s the number of fathers and mothers having lost at least one son in the war was 1.3 million – the number was higher immediately after the war; in other words there were as many bereaved parents as there were soldiers killed. This leads to an estimate of 2.5 million non-military French 'war victims', i.e. bereaved close relatives.[13] But this figure hardly encompasses the scale of the mourning in its entirety: it omits grandparents, brothers and sisters,* uncles and aunts, nephews and cousins, relatives by marriage, and, of course, male and female friends and surviving comrades from the front, not to mention more distant social relationships.

Perhaps it would not be far-fetched to base estimates on what we know of a Frenchman's 'entourage' today: 'All individuals, regardless of age or type of household, seem to be surrounded by a minimum of ten people in their immediate family and a maximum of around twenty.'[14] The shorter life expectancy at the beginning of the twentieth century would mean that for people affected by the Great War we should lower these numbers; they then match, more or less, the numbers in the first circle of mourning as they appear in micro-historical studies.

The case of one soldier among many, the young officer cadet Maurice Gallé, who died on the Somme in 1916, can serve as an emblematic example. He was an only child, unmarried, with only a few relatives; yet his immediate family included seven people (a grandmother, two parents, an uncle, an aunt and two cousins). When he was buried for the second time in 1922, nine people received condolences and the ceremony was attended by around thirty people. This gives us an idea of the 'entourage' of one particular soldier who died in the war.[15]

---

*A quick, albeit arbitrary, calculation shows the importance of the sibling group: according to the 1881 census in France, three out of five children belonged to families that had at least four children. It can therefore be estimated – leaving aside the possibility of two bereavements in the same family – that 780,000 dead French soldiers had at least three brothers or sisters, which amounts to at least 2.3 million bereaved siblings.

Extrapolating from the rough figures, we arrive at the following plausible conclusion: if we add up immediate family, distant relatives and wider entourage, it seems that by the end of the Great War, the various circles of mourning included, in France, the quasi-totality of the population. Virtually an entire society was probably in mourning; an entire society formed a community of mourning. Except for the small nations, where the number of casualties was proportionately greater – and consequently mourning even more extensive – France was the belligerent country with the greatest number of mourners, given what we know about the proportion of men killed in the total population. Germany followed close behind. Then came Austria-Hungary, followed by Great Britain, and then Italy and Russia. *

Not only have historians failed properly to consider the scale of mourning caused by the Great War, they haven't studied its content either. Primo Levi warned that we must be wary of the lazy use of certain words, like 'cold' and 'hunger' to describe the concentration camp experience; so too, with a few exceptions, mourning caused by war has very little in common with mourning in peacetime. What forms of grief lie behind the word? *How* did people mourn? What was their suffering *like*?

Bereavements caused by war are very specific. First of all, it is worth repeating this truism: death in combat, particularly mass deaths of the youngest men in a society, reverses the normal succession of generations. A mother whose son, Lieutenant Paul Colmant, was killed in September 1915, explained this with poignant simplicity to her son's superior: 'No matter how proud as Frenchwomen we poor mothers may be of our sons, we nevertheless carry wounds in our heart that nothing can heal. It is strongly contrary to nature for our children to depart before us,

---

*The number of men killed in France represented 3.4 per cent of the total population, as opposed to 3 per cent in Germany, 1.9 per cent in Austria-Hungary, 1.6 per cent in Great Britain and Italy, 1.1 per cent in Russia – they were 5.7 per cent in Serbia and 3.7 per cent in Turkey.[16]

since God gave them to us so they would shut our eyes.'[17] The writer Maurice Barrès, in an article devoted to the heroic actions of an eighteen-year-old soldier, wondered, 'Why should the old people remain alive, when the children who might have initiated the most beautiful era in French history march off to the sacrifice!'[18] For readers today, these words may seem tinged with unbearable cynicism and impudence. But in the context of 1914, with its pervasive atmosphere of sacrifice, the regret that Barrès expresses so grandiloquently was completely sincere. As someone who was good at detecting the emotions of the war period, he was clearly expressing the feelings of guilt of an entire generation that was too old to take up arms and had to resign itself to seeing its children die. It is very likely that some of the men who were ineligible for the draft but who nonetheless enlisted were motivated by feelings of guilt towards the younger men, who were almost exclusively bearing the burden of war and death.

Similarly, one can perhaps explain the mobilisation of leading writers and intellectuals into propaganda service by their visceral need not to leave the entire burden of the country's defence to the next generation. Barrès, the historian Ernest Lavisse, the sociologist Émile Durkheim and Rudyard Kipling, all had sons at the front. Their political commitments at the time and their writings – later so violently criticised – must be read knowing that they saw their own children exposed to death while they themselves were safe.[19] Kipling, whose only son died at Loos in 1915 and who refused, against all evidence, to list him as missing in action until 1919, wrote a poem that well expressed the shame of the surviving older generation about the death of the young: the young soldier in the poem says, 'If any question why we died/Tell them, because our fathers lied.' And perhaps it was that same shame that put an end to the pre-war pomp surrounding death and funerals; after all, given how many young people had been killed, it seemed indecent to build large tombs for their parents.

There were more survivors than there were dead, true, but

for those living at the time, the normal succession from one generation to the next had been reversed on a vast scale, and the shock of this made the mourning process even more difficult, harder than we can even imagine today. The shock was all the more traumatic since, with the decline in mortality of the previous century, it had become unusual for the young to die before their elders. A comparative study of the death rate in the older populations of London, Paris and Berlin during 1914–18 offers an interesting insight. In each of the capital cities, there was an increase in the mortality of 'elderly people' that cannot be explained by the material conditions of life in wartime – or at least not entirely. It can be explained only by the psychological shock and unprecedented suffering caused by the death of young people, particularly for grandparents faced with the deaths of their grandsons.[20] In fact, death from bereavement was not unusual: Émile Durkheim died of grief one year after his son's death, in December 1915.

This specific mortality, directly linked to bereavement, may come as a surprise to readers in societies that are unaccustomed to the idea of death in war. Knowledge acquired from contemporary psychiatry can be of help in understanding it. If the death of a child, regardless of his or her age, is an 'everlasting bereavement', the pain of the loss is even greater with a child who has reached adulthood: 'Elderly parents who have lost an adult child,' writes one expert, 'are much more traumatised and present a state of chronic bereavement with psychological, somatic, etc. disturbances. The death of this child becomes the foremost subject in their mind and conversation for the rest of their lives.'[21] One spectacular example of parental grief in 1914–18 and subsequent years is that of the German artist Käthe Köllwitz, who in 1931 sculpted a kneeling parental couple, crushed by bereavement, to be placed in front of the tomb of her son Peter, near Ypres.

Thus it isn't surprising that, according to an American system of classification which measures adult psycho-social stress (and whatever one may think of it as a system), the death of a child is ranked sixth in intensity, corresponding to 'catastrophic'. The same system ranks the death of a parent, for a child or an adolescent, at the fifth level ('extreme'). [22] These two situations were precisely what a growing number of parents, grandparents and children of soldiers experienced beginning in 1914.

The war bereavements of 1914–18 had other tragic features. Only the wounded who were hospitalised could be visited by relatives before they died; in the great majority of cases, no relatives were present to attend to the dying men in their final moments. So the soldiers often died alone, and if not alone, almost always without the support of close family members. All the stages that prepare a person for bereavement were thereby eliminated, as were all the rituals that ordinarily accompany the first moments of loss. And what was especially cruel for the people bereaved by the Great War was that they lacked the *bodies* of those who had died.

After 1918, as we know, the bodies remained on the battlefields in military cemeteries established in the combat areas. The Americans and the French were the only ones who by national law or decree had the right to request that bodies be sent home for private burial. The movement to have this happen didn't begin until the summer of 1922 and culminated, after several years, in the repatriation of nearly 240,000 coffins, [23] which is about 30 per cent of the 700,000 identified bodies whose families were entitled to ask for them – a significant proportion.

This need to bring back the bodies of relatives one had lost, even spending a huge amount of energy to disinter bodies when the law did not yet allow one to do so, shows the acute psychological suffering caused by distance and prolonged absence. Jane Catulle-Mendès, the widow of the poet Catulle Mendès (who had died in 1909), used all her social connections and contacts to get behind the front lines at the Chemin des Dames, as early as 1917, to have the body of her youngest son, who had enlisted at seventeen, exhumed at night. [24] During and after the war, fathers disobeyed the regulations to carry out such operations by night and clandestinely in the temporary cemeteries. When the French government finally gave permission to repatriate the bodies in 1920, wives, parents and sisters had to go through the dreadful experience of exhuming the skeletons of their husbands, sons or brothers, so the bodies could be officially identified and they could get them back. The anger of the politican Louis Barthou before the National Commission on Military Burials, on 31 May 1919, when the government still opposed the return of the soldiers' mortal remains — in his case, his son's — speaks volumes about the bereavement of war and the particular grief caused by not having the corpse:

> Fine, it's all very well to say that our children will be equal in death, but I don't see what principle of equality requires that a hard and fast rule be established as far as families are concerned. There is my son, who was killed in 1914, five years ago. He's in a tomb, his mother and I are waiting for him; and because others have not been found, you tell me that you forbid me to take my son and bring him to Père-Lachaise [a cemetery in Paris]? Well, I tell you that you have no right to do this. You explain it by saying that hundreds of thousands of soldiers have been killed and you haven't identified them? But mine was. You speak of identification? Well, mine was identified. Of the transportation shortage? But I can bring back my son on my own, without asking anything of the government. This is not what I understand by equality and I think the proposed government bill is a mistake. That's why I, for my part, won't accept it.[25]

The grief of bereavement was increased by the recurrence of loss. The length of the conflict and the number of dead often led — though it is impossible to cite numbers — to multiple painful bereavements. The case of General Castelnau, who lost his three sons in the war, was famous in France, but it was not unusual. The four sons of Paul Doumer, the French statesman who was later President of the Republic (and assassinated in 1932) were all killed. Vera Brittain, a young student at Oxford and nurse during the war, who later became an ardent militant feminist, Labourite and pacifist, lost her fiancé in 1915, two other friends in 1917, including a severely wounded friend whom she had considered marrying, and finally her brother on the Italian front in 1918.[26] The monument to the dead in the Forêt du Temple, north of the Creuse, bears the name of a mother, Emma Bujardet, who 'died of grief' in 1917 after losing her three sons.

The lack of details about the fate of loved ones was another characteristic that countless tens of thousands endured in the 1914–18 war. Its unique conditions of combat increased both the number of missing and the number of unidentifiable bodies for all the belligerent parties. In France, *half* of all the corpses were in this category. The relatives were not able to have a grave or burial place where they could grieve and begin their mourning; they had only the ossuaries, like the one at Douaumont,* or the Tomb of the Unknown Soldier. This deeply traumatised them. 'The symbolisation of the dead person is fundamental, by whatever means: a grave, a cenotaph, or something that belonged to the person,' writes a specialist on this subject. 'The metonymy ... in other words, the shift in meaning from the thing contained to the container (from the corpse to the tomb), is essential for mourning: it allows the living to focus their grief on a support that gradually becomes a substitute for the body of the deceased.'[28]

For relatives, knowing of the soldiers' enormous suffering of mortal agony on the front added yet another torment. Families could well imagine that suffering, just as they could imagine their dying sons' animal solitude and anguish. This excerpt from the diary of a war widow, published in 1919 but written during the war in memory of her husband, who was killed in 1914, is revealing:

---

*During the inauguration of the first part of the monument in 1927, Monsignor Ginisty was explicit: 'You whom we have seen wandering so many times through this labyrinth of death, in search of the name, the trace of your loved one, calling to him in a sobbing voice, come to the ossuary. Here is the tomb that probably contains some of him.'[27]

He dies all alone, over there, like a dog … And this horrible, pitiful death we call 'death on the field of honour'! What irony! … Where are the honours we pay to that poor unknown who will not even have a coffin for his eternal rest? … He will lie for days and days, forgotten, on the bare earth, with a smashed skull or chest, and German crows will steal away his dearest memories. Nothing! He will have nothing. Not even a pauper's grave, not even a stone, not even a cross. All of this is too little for Him who died on the Field of Honour. Christ could be resurrected from the tomb, for he had a tomb. As for him, He will have the earth, like the animals.[29]

The widow was not writing in pacifist protest. She did not deny the need for patriotic sacrifice. But she expressed, with unusual bluntness, the additional pain that the conditions of death in the war caused the loved ones of the soldiers who were killed.

We can understand the families' insistent questions in their letters to fellow soldiers or commanders of the men they had lost. What were the loved one's last moments like? What were the exact circumstances of his death? Where was he wounded? How much did he suffer? People also want to know if he had died alone and, of course, if he was buried and, if so, where. The point was to try to fill in the terrible gap created by their having been absent and unable to give aid to the dying, the gap between wound and mortal agony, between agony and death, between death and burial – a gap of several hours or several days. It tormented the survivors and made their bereavement almost impossibly difficult.

The theme of the 'return of the dead', which was strikingly present in European art between the two world wars, is one proof among many of the difficulty of accepting loss in the societies so greatly affected by mass death. The rise of spiritualism, particularly in England, where so many bereaved parents, wives, brothers and sisters tried to communicate with the deceased, is another indication of the hardship of mourning. Both Sir Arthur Conan Doyle (who lost his son, his brother, a brother-in-law from his first marriage and three others from his second marriage) and Rudyard Kipling were convinced that they could still be in touch with relatives who had died on the battlefield. *Raymond*, written by Oliver Lodge in memory of his son, killed at twenty-six in September 1915, tells of the spiritualist seances that allowed the entire family to find out about the life of the deceased in 'Summerland'. This was republished twelve times between 1916 and 1919, translated into French in 1920, and issued in an abridged version (*Raymond revisited*) in 1922. [30]

The huge amount of commemorative activity that took place in the 1920s and 1930s can be seen as a way for contemporaries to alleviate their grief by experiencing bereavement collectively.[31] An unusual object in the museum at Verdun shows how commemoration can alleviate individual sorrow: a father whose son was killed, whose body had probably not been found, made a large model of the Arc de Triomphe in Paris; filling the entire space under the principal arch was a large portrait of his son; the bas-relief shows a helmeted child, gazing intently, leaning on the guard of a sword set in a bouquet of victory laurels; in the background are a Christian cross and sun rays.[32]

We must not forget that though it was sometimes endured collectively, mourning was first and foremost an individual ordeal experienced in dreadful solitude. Once the time of condolence letters and visits is past, the bereaved are *alone*; the war widow writing about her experiences stated this with a kind of anger in February 1915:

> War widow! They should hail in me He who gave his life for
> them. They should admire the greatness and beauty of his gesture
> and bow before me, living Grief that I am. But it is pity that I see
> in their eyes, and also, selfishness: 'She's the widow, not me,
> fortunately!' They approach mental suffering with a thousand
> precautions, like others approach a contagious disease with rubber
> gloves.[33]

Sometimes the solitude was unintentional, but at other times it was intentional. The bereaved often wanted to be alone and therefore declined to take part in the great commemorative events. Of course, plenty of people attended the celebrations of 11 November 1918 and 14 July 1919 in France. An even greater number attended the burials of the Unknown Soldiers on 11 November 1920 in Paris and in London, and collective emotion was intense during the two minutes of silence observed by the huge crowd assembled in front of the Whitehall cenotaph. But commemorative ceremonies in general, particularly the annual ones on 11 November, occupied only a small place in the lives of many of the bereaved.

When victory came on 11 November 1918, Jane Catulle-Mendès could only express despair: 'Tears ... tears ...' The following year, she refused to attend the victory parade: 'I will not see the Victory. I couldn't bear to see it without You.' She had already made her feelings clear on Bastille Day in 1917: 'I will not go. The very thought of those handsome soldiers, like him, who will be cheered in the daylight, makes me collapse in overwhelming despair.' And instead of attending the 14 July parade in 1919, she preferred to go to her son's grave on 10 July, his birthday. She laid down two silver palm leafs, 'the straight, white wings of Victory'. It was a characteristic reversal: 'For your birthday, France's most beautiful day is placed on You.' In a tragic inversion of the official rhetoric her words were unusually cold-blooded, though she may not have gauged their deep significance: 'I know, my little child. You're one of the blue uniformed soldiers who will surprise and delight the future. But you're dead ... You are eternal beauty. But You, you are dead. I know it. They all say that tomorrow under the Arc de Triomphe the Dead will be resurrected. For all of them, you will be resurrected, but not for me.'[34] Though a Parisian patriot, she made no mention in her diary of 11 November 1920, the day of the ceremony of the Unknown Soldier at the Arc de Triomphe; nor did she mention 11 November in the following years. The bereaved mother observed another, completely personal calendar, punctuated by her own pilgrimages: her son's birthday, the anniversary of her son's death. Nothing was more foreign to her than the collective aspect of mourning. Indeed, it is possible that the very idea that individual bereavement was by and large alleviated by intense commemorative activity may be largely informed by the reassuring logic of the outsider's view.

It is all the more legitimate to cast doubt on the 'effectiveness' of commemoration in helping the individual mourning process when we consider that in every country it always endowed the war dead with the stature of heroes animated by the spirit of self-sacrifice. Making the fallen soldiers into heroes went on within their families, of course, as attested by the prominently displayed portraits embedded in patriotic compositions,[35] the framed medals and the 'diplomas' with the words 'Died for his country' (issued in France from 1919). In the more religious families, it was not unusual for the dead relative to graduate from hero to saint; such was the case among the relatives of Maurice Gallé, whose grandmother wrote a prayer for him that ended: 'Because You granted him the most beautiful death and opened Your paradise to him, where I see him as a Saint. I thank you Lord. Amen.'[36] And in many instances the bereaved person capitalised the first letter of the personal pronoun when referring to the deceased. Françoise Vitry wrote: 'He is gone … so that I may keep a bright memory of Him, and my young god, so handsome, made even taller by his generous death, will now be my entire Religion.'[37] Vera Brittain did the same in her diary, writing 'Him' or 'He' when referring to her fiancé, Roland Leighton, who died in December 1915. Yet making a hero of the deceased seems to make 'the resolution of mourning'[38] even harder. 'The epilogue of mourning', a specialist points out, 'seems blocked and delayed by the idealisation of "the hero who died in the war" and by the veneration of his memory.'[39]

We can imagine the guilt that weighed on orphans from the idealised representations of their departed fathers. Geoffrey Gorer, who was ten when his father died in 1915, described it in 1963:

As a child I never saw my mother cry. But if my mother did not then consciously add to the burden of responsibility I felt and feared, my aunt Nance did so without scruple. She was my father's only sister ... When I came home for the holidays she came to the house and somehow got me alone; she enveloped me in an embrace of black material, burst into a flood of tears, and pleaded with me to grow up quickly, to be big and strong like my father, and to look after the widows and orphans in my charge. My father had helped her and her children, and she was putting this on me also. This scene was a traumatic one for me, still today a vivid, painful memory.[40]

In the same vein, here are some painful words written by a sister to her young brother, away at a religious boarding school, after their older brother's death on the front in 1915:

By now you must know about the dreadful bereavement that has struck us. I hadn't wanted to tell you about it, it would have been too hard, you know, since in spite of your indifference I'm certain the loss of our dear brother made you shed bitter tears. It is so hard, too, his not having left until the 2nd and being killed between the 23rd and 24th at 11 o'clock at night by shrapnel straight in the heart – he lived only 20 minutes without regaining consciousness. It would be a welcome consolation for our dear parents if you would try to be like him, my little Joseph; for you know that though you're his brother, you're the opposite of him. You will say I'm being very harsh and strict saying this to you, won't you; but for several days I've realised that our dear departed never made mother, or even me, shed a single tear. Can we say as much for ourselves? Have we always acted as we should have? [41]

This feeling, so simply expressed, of the exceptional character of those who had died, reached its height in Germany – where it was exploited by the extreme right, with the success we all know – but also in Great Britain, where the social elites had in truth paid a very high price in the war. In Britain, the myth of the lost generation lasted for a long time. On the ninetieth anniversary of the Battle of the Somme in 1996, Lord Denning, aged ninety-seven, described the unfinished mourning for his brother, who fell in September 1916, in these terms: 'He was the best of us, better even than our brother Reg, who became a general and finished as GOC [General Officer Commanding] Northern Ireland.'[42]

This exaggerated admiration for the dead of the Great War was rooted in a war culture which transformed the dead into volunteers who had sacrificed themselves in a great crusade, an interpretation of death in combat that we can assume deeply affected the mourning process of the survivors. As we know from Freud's 1915 essay, the completion of the mourning process involves a progressive detachment from the lost object. 'Mourning has a quite specific psychologic task to perform,' he explained in *Totem and Taboo*, 'its function is to detach the survivors' memories and hopes from the dead.'[43] But this 'resolution of mourning' requires the non-idealisation of the departed person.[44] Because the lost soldiers had died in a war that was overly invested with lofty significance, the cult of the dead probably made it much harder for the survivors to achieve the needed detachment from those whom they had loved and lost.

This difficulty was further aggravated by what can only be called a 'mourning taboo'. This taboo was first formulated by the combatants themselves in their 'last letters', written for their family 'in case of misfortune'. Marc Bloch's revealing letter, written on 1 June 1915 as a last will and testament, is quite typical:

> By the time you read this letter, I will no longer be alive. I will have died on enemy soil. I won't ask you to have courage, I know too well that you will. May you not let your tears be too bitter! I died voluntarily for a cause I loved; I sacrificed myself; this is the most beautiful death. I would be lying if I said I won't miss life; it would be unfair to you, who made mine so pleasurable; but you've taught me to value some things above life. Just think, I might have fallen in August 1914, like so many others, during the

retreat, and died in despair for France; these are the men to be pitied. I died sure of victory and happy – yes, truly happy – I say it in complete truthfulness, to shed my blood for it.[45]

Bloch forbade his parents to mourn, or at least he forbade an excessively long or deep mourning period. Another graduate of the École Normale, Robert Hertz, who was killed in April 1915, was even clearer in his letter to his wife: 'Death can be conquered when we understand that it is part of the plan of life. Promise me that if by chance I were to join the fate of so many others already departed, you would not mourn for me, you would keep your soul valiant, serene, lucid, even happy, as it is at present.'[46]

Paradoxically, it would seem, for a nation so massively in mourning as France, this kind of taboo was relayed to the home front by talk that was deeply guilt-inducing for the bereaved. Here is how Georges Lecomte, president of the Société des gens de lettres, chose (at a time when the war was not yet over) to preface the widow's diary mentioned earlier:

> Once their first sobs have subsided – and who would fail to understand that they need time for this? – these bereaved war victims will say themselves that the sacrifice of our dead requires us to equal the courage they have shown. If we are to be worthy of the valiant Frenchmen whose deaths cause so many tears to flow, grief must not remain sterile. Heartbroken mothers and widows will prove their loyal tenderness and console themselves by pursuing the patriotic effort of the men they weep over.[47]

To grieve for too long and too intensely was to betray the dead, betray the cause for which the heroes had died. This strange attempt at censuring grief was all the more powerful in that by and large the bereaved shared the same view of sacrifice as the soldiers had. The weight of the Catholic faith also made its presence felt particularly strongly. For example, several priests rather harshly pressed a taboo on mourning on Maurice Gallé's family, and Abbé Conen was blunt: 'We will not feel sorry for

him, for we would be wrong!'[48] Of course, Gallé himself had
said: 'One must not feel sorry for the fallen men, they are the
most fortunate,' and his parents posted this sentence on the door
to their son's room.[49] Even Maurice Genevoix concluded the
obituary notice of his friend Benoist with words that forbade
too much bitterness in mourning: 'May your tears be forever
gentle and calm, you who suffer being torn away, gentle and
calm from the serenity of this life and its ending – not arid and
withering tears that harm the dead over whom they are shed.'[50]
It was as if excessive grief about the dead heroes would betray
their memory by calling into question the very meaning of their
death. The desire to quell the mourning process before it was
over was another reason why the resolution of mourning was so
difficult in the societies where the emotional investment in the
war had been strongest.

In these circumstances, it is hardly surprising that mourning
from the Great War went on for so long. Often nearly ten years
were needed for the luckier ones to complete their mourning
process, ten years to detach themselves from the person, or
persons, they had lost. Vera Brittain could only marry ten years
after losing her first fiancé and then only because a set of circumstances allowed her to feel she wasn't betraying him: first, she
had to make a double pilgrimage, to the grave of her brother in
Italy and to the grave of her first fiancé in Picardy; second, her
future husband was a veteran who would have been at Oxford,
she realised, at the same time as her brother if it hadn't been for
the war; and finally, she had to make a trip to Germany and
Austria, to enemy territory, to realise the inanity of the assumptions to which her generation had been, she thought, needlessly
and cynically sacrificed.[51]

Specialists have many terms to characterise the different
kinds of grief that people who can't detach themselves from
their dead loved ones experience. After 1918, countless numbers
of Europeans never recovered from the pain of loss. Mourning,
for them, was endless, eternal.

Conclusion

'You didn't see anything in the 1920s and 1930s'

'You didn't see anything in Hiroshima.' That is what is said to the French woman in Alain Resnais' film *Hiroshima, mon amour*,[1] even though she has conscientiously visited the city museum, talked to survivors, and heard the cough of an elderly woman who was exposed to atomic radiation. But really she has 'seen' nothing. Similarly, from 1919 to the 1930s, many things were shown and said about the Great War and the post-war period, yet contemporaries did not really 'see' the profound consequences of the conflict in which they had been actively involved. As in Hiroshima, where the long-term physical, psychological and political after-effects of the bomb were infinitely more destructive than its immediate impact, the inter-war generations failed to see how irradiated the post-war world had been by the Great War's culture of violence. They were unable to see how deeply and irreversibly affected they were by its brutalisation, which was now lodged at the heart of Western society.

This blindness became reality at the Versailles Peace Conference. Since the victors chose to impose on the vanquished, who were absent from the negotiations, a very long treaty that included 400 articles, their diplomats, government leaders and experts put in a lot of serious, honest work. And this work shows both lucidity and blindness, as in Articles 231 and 232, which are concerned with reestablishing 'law' and 'justice' in a world forever altered by the violence of a 'legitimate' and 'just war'. These key articles are often mentioned but rarely quoted:

ARTICLE 231

The Allied and Associated Governments affirm and Germany accepts the responsibility of Germany and her allies for causing all the loss and damage to which the Allied and Associated Governments and their nationals have been subjected as a consequence of the war imposed upon them by the aggression of Germany and her allies ...

ARTICLE 232

... The Allied and Associated Governments ... require, and Germany undertakes, that she will make compensation for all damage done to the civilian population of the Allied and Associated Powers and to their property during the period of the belligerency of each as an Allied or Associated Power against Germany, by such aggression by land, by sea and from the air, and in general all damage as defined in Annex 1 ...

The Annex goes into detail about first the 'damage to injured persons and to surviving dependants by personal injury to or death of civilians caused by acts of war'; then 'civilian victims of acts of cruelty, violence or maltreatment (including injuries to life or health as a consequence of imprisonment, deportation, internment or evacuation, of exposure at sea or of being forced to labour)'; and finally 'damage caused by any kind of maltreatment of prisoners of war', providing in Point 5, 'as damage caused to the peoples of the Allied and Associated Powers, all pensions and compensation in the nature of pensions to naval and military victims of war (including members of the air force), whether mutilated, wounded, sick or invalided, and to the dependants of such victims'.[2] Five years after nearly 10 million men had faced war and died, the Allies had no doubt that the aggression of Germany explained everything; and the treaty, an act of revenge and punishment, sealed the validity of their way of seeing things. The pronouncements of Articles 231 and 232 seemed logical enough: a guilty Germany had to make reparations, and since it had targeted victims who were usually protected in times of war, these victims had to be compensated. Article 231, as the French diplomatic historian Pierre Renouvin pointed out more than forty years ago, set forth the reparations and responsibilities 'with regard to civil law'.[3] But neither side was under any illusion: Germany's responsibility for the war also had to be understood in the moral sense of the term.

Woodrow Wilson, the 'conscience of the Allies', was convinced of the correctness of this moral pressure: 'At present there is a passion for justice throughout the world,' he explained. 'Even some of the wrongdoings and crimes that were committed were done because of a wrong view of what is just ... This enthusiastic aspiration for just solutions would change into cynical scepticism if people thought we were remiss in following the rules of justice that we ourselves had set forth.'[4] Wilson was admitting, not quite explicitly, that while Germany was an enemy, one had to concede it had a kind of moral sense, albeit a perverted one. Prime Minister Georges Clemenceau, on the other hand, strongly disputed the validity of this viewpoint. 'Don't think that the principles of justice that satisfy us, satisfy the Germans ... I can tell you that their idea of justice is not ours.' He added, 'You seek to do justice to the Germans. Don't think they'll ever forgive us: all they will do is seek an opportunity to take revenge; nothing will destroy the rage of those who wanted to achieve domination over the world and who believed they were so close to succeeding.'[5] So while the French leader believed that the Germans should be denied any opportunity of revenge, the Anglo-Saxons (Wilson and Prime Minister Lloyd George) believed anything perceived as injustice would only lead to a recurrence of war.

It is hardly surprising that this kind of debate arose over the matter of the Saar, a disputed territory that Clemenceau wanted to see returned to France, a wish opposed by Wilson and Lloyd George. Though it would seem at first that the Saar issue was of secondary importance in structuring the new Europe, the contradiction between the historical arguments (that France should have its 1814 frontier restored), the desire for concrete payments of reparations (the Saar's coal mines in compensation for the destruction on French territory that Germany had occupied during the war), and the principle of self-determination for all peoples (the people of the Saar should choose to which nation they wished to belong) became obvious. Each side used its own war wounds as the only yardstick for understanding justice.*

Articles 231 and 232 are good examples of this central contradiction. In setting forth the requirement that reparations be paid for the most visible victims of the conflict (civilians, prisoners, relatives of the wounded and the dead), satisfaction was given to the French who had lived through war fought on their own land. A number of pressure groups saw to it that their demands were also considered. A 1919 poster declared: 'The few billion paid yearly by the enemy will hardly compensate for the disastrous consequences on [French] production, since we have no tools left ... It should be noted that the extraordinary losses suffered by France among the populations who lived under enemy rule in the invaded regions have not been taken into account ... where the most painful material hardships and moral torments were endured.'[6] Clemenceau himself was not outdone: 'The ordeals we endured have created in this country a strong sense of the reparations owed to us; and it is not just a question of material reparations: the need for moral reparations is just as great.'[7]

However, none of the conquerors thought about the *newness* of this particular type of victim, as the historian François Furet correctly notes in his very critical portrait of Clemenceau: 'The

---

*In 1935, a plebiscite in the Saar, conducted by the League of Nations in accord with the Versailles Treaty stipulations, resulted in 90 per cent of the electorate voting for reunion of the territory with Germany.

persistence of the wartime commander gave way to the blindness of a conqueror ... What did he make of the ruined and revolutionary landscape of Europe at the end of hostilities? Not
much ... He turned the diplomatic instrument with which he
hoped to found a new order into a verdict against a guilty
people.'[8] Clemenceau − and he was not alone − had doomed
himself to failure on two counts: France would not really obtain
reparations, and, more importantly, his policy did not prevent the
return of the barbarism he deplored. Yet the failure was not due
to the victors having neglected to place a denunciation of barbarism at the heart of their effort. The question was, was it still
appropriate to do so, now that the peace effort was on the
agenda? The treaty contradicted itself, using the arguments of
war while attempting to find guarantees that war would never
again be possible.

The heirs of Attila and the Huns being judged guilty, as
might be expected, of atrocities in Belgium and northern
France, specific reparations were demanded for the ill-treated
populations. Germany had to be made to pay in full for its guilt.
Its submarine attacks against merchant ships, its bombing of
cities by plane and long-range cannon (technical perversions of
scientific progress, for which Germany was severely reproached),
its infringements of the Geneva Convention in its internment
camps, its organised retaliatory measures (reprisals, in fact)
against captives, hospitals and ambulances − didn't all this justify,
in the eyes of the Allies, the infliction of very harsh treatment on
the conquered nation? No doubt. But there was no belligerent
party that could claim it had not slid into total war, into a brutality that was transmitted from the battlefield to all the men; and
they, once disarmed, should have been protected by the univer-
sally ratified conventions and should have been spared.

The Allies nonetheless persisted with the seemingly convincing argument about the atrocities committed against civilians,
since only the Central Powers had occupied alien territory in
Europe (and Russia, which had gone straight from the brutality
of the war to the brutality of revolution and civil war). The spe-

ciousness of this argument did not escape Count Ulrich von Brockdorff-Rantzau, chief of the German delegation at Versailles:

> Public opinion in all the countries of our adversaries is resounding with the crimes which Germany is said to have committed in the war. Here also we are ready to confess the wrong that may have been done ... But in the manner of making war, Germany is not the only guilty party ... Crimes in war may not be excusable, but they are committed in the struggle for victory, and in the defence of national existence, and passions are aroused which the conscience of peoples blunt.[9]

But the Germans were hardly in a position to make their erstwhile enemies reflect on the universal brutality of the war. None of the Allies questioned that the Germans were responsible for the initial aggression, and this conviction prevailed over all other considerations, so much so that it was included as a central clause in the 1919 Diktat.

In the end, it was their race, much more than their history or their authoritarian regime, that was given as the reason why the Germans had remained barbaric, the superficial polish of their technical efficiency and economic development notwithstanding. During the war many voices had loudly asserted that the Germans were biologically of a different, inferior race; the enemy was thus both hereditary and permanent. And since a people's racial and ethnic characteristics were not subject to amendment, the conditions for peace could not be dissociated from punishment of the 'Krauts'. Given the widespread conviction that they couldn't possible change, there was only one solution: to keep them from acting according to their innate disposition.

Among the negotiators, the desire to protect unarmed civilians was also linked to a desire to respect all minorities. But very soon, everyone realised the impossibility of these two goals. A lawyer for the American delegation explained it in the following terms:

The attempt made at Paris to assure to native races and to racial
and linguistic and religious minorities such protection that the
world may not be thrown into another holocaust to deliver them
from oppressors may prove only measurably successful. The limits
on effective legal action are nowhere more rigid than in dealing
with the imponderable elements which determine men's
willingness to admit to or exclude from their fellowship other
men of different shaped heads, or different styled clothes, or
different forms of worship, or different political views ... It will
not be surprising, therefore, if subterfuges are found, where Jew or
German or Magyar is disliked, for evading such provisions as
those in the minority treaties.[10]

The contradictions between the determination to re-establish
law and justice, the desire for punishment and the realities of the
post-war world were obvious.

Yet could reparations really make up for the personal and
collective tragedies experienced in 1914–18? The dominant impression one has is that neither the dead nor their families,
neither the prisoners nor the wounded, were really what was at
stake, although they were constantly invoked, and important
because they could be exploited. It is notable that during the
signing of the Treaty of Versailles, on 28 June 1919, the delegation
of 'gueules cassées' (disfigured men) and severely disabled veterans
behind the table was a prominent living reproach, but the men
were also nothing more than strange – and emblematic –
décor.[11] The mention of victims in the text of the treaty does not
mean that the negotiators had properly assessed their fate. Quite
the contrary. They – especially the mutilated soldiers – would
have to fight long and hard to obtain certain rights, not always
successfully, and soon they would be consigned to virtual oblivion, which only deepened as the years went by. Similarly, war
orphans – in 1917 generously adopted as wards of the nation,
'pupilles de la nation', because the French wanted to create a new
knighthood for them in recognition of their fathers' sacrifice –
by the early 1930s had been marginalised.[12] Many war victims

had lived through total war, but the memory of their painful experience could not be, and was not willing to be, a 'total' one.

Once the Versailles Treaty was ratified, civilians who had lived under enemy occupation and those who had been deported were excluded from the memory of the conflict, and so were prisoners of war. This was true also of the people who had helped them – the International Red Cross and the Vatican.[13] There was no recognition that a very large 'home front' might have included all such victims of the conflict. At best, these victims met with indifference at home, at worst contempt. Only the fallen heroes were assigned full posthumous glory. So the great principle of reparations had been nothing but empty talk. In the end, the treaty's clauses provided only a rather meagre judicial framework within which to care for the very people for whom Article 232 had been intended. Punishment and delegitimisation of the enemy's war was so important at Versailles that the features of the conflict which foreshadowed an even greater total war against unarmed populations vanished from memory. And once this dual goal was attained, the sections of the population that had been used as a pretext for this exemplary punishment were also forgotten. The paradox is striking: the accusatory, guilt-producing argument about Germany's treatment of defenceless enemies was used the better to punish Germany, after which the defenceless victims were quickly forgotten.

In a premonitory text written as early as October 1918, Captain Charles de Gaulle, then in a German internment camp, showed admirable insight into these issues. He believed that the peace had to be backed by a refusal on all sides ever to forget, but, in practice, it did the exact opposite:

> Will France quickly forget, if ever she forgets, 1,500,000 dead, a
> million mutilated men, and the complete destruction of Lille,
> Dunkerque, Cambrai, Douai, Arras, Saint-Quentin, Laon,
> Soissons, Rheims, Verdun? Will weeping mothers suddenly dry
> their tears? Will orphans cease being orphans and widows,
> widows? For generations, won't all the families in our country

inherit fearsome memories of the greatest of wars, and seeds be planted in the heart of children of that hatred of nations that nothing eradicates? ... Everyone knows and feels that this peace is merely an inadequate blanket thrown over unappeased ambitions, hatreds that are more indestructible than ever, and fierce, unextinguished national resentments.[14]

Georges Lecomte, who reported on the signing of the treaty several months later, also grasped that the emblematic victims of the war, disembodied and almost unreal, were present only in the background. But, for him, the silent presence of the civilian victims and the dead was transformed into vindictive anti-German rhetoric: 'Our thoughts go to our 1,600,000 dead, our 400,000 mutilated, our destroyed towns and villages, our devastated industry, our ten *départements* in ruins, our aged parents, our weeping wives and children.'[15] For the peace of Versailles to match its stated goal, the victims' symbolic presence would have had to become a real one. But the transubstantiation never took place.

In 1940, as war once again engulfed Europe, the exiled French writer and war veteran Georges Bernanos re-examined the 1919–39 period:

You can't be proud of parading in public on the arm of a beautiful woman who bears your name but refuses to sleep with you. Victory didn't love us ... Twenty years in such an arrangement is a long time. We had not been on speaking terms for years. She never actually admitted to being an impostor, but she no longer kept up appearances, she didn't even respond any more to the name Victory. On 3 September [1939], at five in the morning, we found our house empty. She left without saying a word and took the furniture ... The war of attrition had already frayed the peace, and so the war of attrition led to a frayed peace ... And now that it's worth no more than its weight in paper, you want to convince us you approved it. We signed it without reading it; we signed it with a cross.[16]

In this half-cynical, half-despairing way, Bernanos in 1940 had no trouble condemning the Versailles peace, which even the victors had known was stillborn. But what about the vanquished? The Versailles Treaty of 1919 sought to delegitimise Germany, considering it solely responsible for the war, and to delegitimise the war it had waged. But the end result was a re-legitimisation of war from the German point of view, since the nation felt justified in waging war again. And its bellicose intentions eventually prevailed, in a new war where violence and cruelty – particularly against civilians – reached new heights. Bernanos's extraordinarily lucid portrait of Hitler is an apt literary expression of this process:

> The master of Germany is really its slave: he is chained to the Germany of 1918, to his country's defeat and dishonour, so that even triumph would be wrapped in bitterness and equal to his hatreds … He holds [Marshal] Foch by the throat, flattens Mr Woodrow Wilson's ecclesiastic visage between two Bibles, and steps on Clemenceau's pug-nosed face with his corporal's boots still wet with the mud from Éparges.[17]

But Hitler was fuelled by more than just his memories of the Great War in 1940, and more than his experience as a 1914–18 soldier, as a gas victim and as a corporal who smarted from Germany's defeat and was shattered by the treaty signed by the 'November criminals'. Yet not everyone in Germany wallowed in endless imprecations against the 'stab in the back'. Though they believed they had been 'undefeated on the battlefield', many Germans had aspired to peace. But the forces of war – of a war unto death – came to power in the end. 'Since last September, I have been thinking of Mr Hitler as a dead man,' Bernanos added. 'I have no trouble honouring him as such. The Unknown German Soldier was he, why didn't we realise it sooner? I don't doubt for a moment that he will accomplish his destiny.'[18]

Bernanos affords us the opportunity to re-examine the

nature of the relationship between the violence of 1914–18, the political violence of the 1920s and 1930s, and the violence of the 1939–45 conflict. The question must be asked explicitly: was the experience of the Great War the matrix for the twentieth century's totalitarian regimes? The violence of the Great War was first harnessed in Russia, and indeed it is impossible to understand the atrocities of Russia's subsequent revolution and civil war without acknowledging this. The brutality of the conflict unleashed in 1914 was subsequently 'refracted', as one historian has put it, or better yet, heightened, into a radical experience of civil war and political oppression. Too often historians have linked the revolution of 1905 to that of 1917 without taking into account the legacy of the Great War years. Yet the accelerated break-up of a huge army of peasants who had been brutalised by three years of conflict and were deserting en masse from the front is a key to understanding the 1917 revolution and the nature of the Bolshevik state it produced.[19]

For the National Socialists in Germany, and to a lesser extent for the fascists in Italy, political violence was the precondition for a new, more systematic and more efficient violence in war. The nation first had to be purified of anything that might be an obstacle to the surge in warring energy. What part was played, in that dizzying escalation, by the biological arguments that had crystallised during the Great War? How was the transition made from an open violence, centred on the battlefields, to a hidden, 'administrative' violence, centred on files of people targeted for slaughter? In the trenches of the Great War, victims and heroes were interchangeable; any combatant might have been wounded, captured, killed, or survived. On the other hand, the treatment of civilians had changed the rules: those with military power could, with no risk to themselves, subject civilians to terroristic constraint.

In the Italy of the 1920s, in the Germany of the 1930s, in the young Soviet Union, are we to believe that the memory of this was beyond recall? In these three countries, it was as though the great messianic expectations of the Great War – among citizens disappointed that the better post-war world they had been promised had not come into being – were reclaimed by different forms of totalitarianism. This is not the place to assess the communist and fascist ideologies – so different and so deeply antagonistic – rather, we note the power of attraction that these dreadful enthusiasms had on the 'new men' born of the Great War, the 'new men' that the totalitarian regimes were out to promote. As we know, it wasn't long before these new men turned into assassins.

Notes

Introduction: **Understanding the Great War**

1 For more details, see Annette Becker, 'Réflexions sur le quatre-vingtième anniversaire de l'armistice en France, 1998', in *Forum Guerra e Pace*, Florence, 2000; Stéphane Audoin-Rouzeau, 'La Grande Guerre, le deuil interminable', *Le Débat*, March–April, 1999, no. 104, pp. 117–30, and Nicolas Offenstadt, *Fusillés pour l'exemple? Les Exécutions de la Grande guerre dans l'espace public 1914–1999*, Paris, Odile Jacob, 1999.

2 The phrase is borrowed from the speech of the Mayor of Craonne at the Chemin des Dames during the visit of Lionel Jospin, then prime minister, on 5 November 1998.

3 Jean-Michel Chaumont, *La Concurrence des victimes: génocides, identité et reconnaissance*, Paris, La Découverte, 1997.

4 Henry Rousso, *La Hantise du passé: entretien avec Philippe Petit*, Paris, Textuel, 1998, p. 89.

5 'Les personnalités et les événements marquants du XXe siècle', Enquête Ipsos Opinion, *Le Monde*/France 3/Festival du film d'histoire de Pessac, 9 November 1998. The poll was conducted by telephone on 1,015 people belonging to categories (gender, age, profession of the head of household, size of local population and region) constituting a representative sample of the French population over fifteen years of age.

6 See dossier no. 2 of the journal *14–18 Aujourd'hui, Today, Heute*, 'L'archéologie et la Grande Guerre', Paris, Noêsis, 1999.

7 Rousso, *La Hantise du passé*.

8 Especially the organising role played by the Centre de recherche de l'Historial de la Grande Guerre in Péronne, created in 1989 and directed by Jean-Jacques Becker. For a first synthetic approach to this renewal, see our 'Violence et consentement: la "culture de guerre" du Premier Conflit mondial', in Jean-Pierre Rioux and Jean-François Sirinelli, eds., *Pour une histoire culturelle*, Paris, Éditions du Seuil, 1997, pp. 251–71.

9 François Furet, *Penser la Révolution française*, Paris, Gallimard, 1978.

10 The book that most clearly typified this approach was Jean-Norton Cru's famous *Témoins: Essai d'analyse et de critique des souvenirs de combattants édités en français de 1915 à 1928*, Paris, Les Étincelles, 1929, reprinted in Nancy, Presses Universitaires de Nancy, 1993. See also Leonard Smith, 'Jean-Norton Cru, lecteur de livres de guerre', *Annales du Midi*, Oct–Dec. 2000, pp. 517–28.

11 However, there were some pioneer studies, notably Jay Winter, *Sites of Memory, Sites of Mourning: The Great War in European Cultural History*, Cambridge, Cambridge University Press, 1995.

12 We are deliberately using the title of the book by Alphonse Dupront, for whom the First World War's crusade-like feature did not go unnoticed: *Le Mythe de croisade*, Paris, Gallimard, 1997, 4 vols.

13 See Nathalie Zajde, *Enfants de survivants*, Paris, Éditions Odile Jacob, 1995.

14 See Roger Bruge, *Les Hommes de Diên Biên Phu*, Paris, Perrin, 1999.

15 The initial nucleus was created by Jean-Jacques Becker, then Professor at the University of Paris-X-Nanterre, and included Jay Winter, then of Cambridge University, Gerd Krumeich, then of the University of Freiburg, and the present authors. The board of directors is composed of this group; the scientific advisory committee is made up of

Didn't See Anything researchers from all over the world, including Australia, South Africa, the United States and Russia. The Historial is an international non-profit association, whose scientific coordination is administered by its secretary-general, Caroline Fontaine. We would like to take this opportunity to thank her for her constant assistance, in particular with this book.

16 See the judgement made by the historian Pierre Nora, who compared the historiographic fate of the Great War to the fate of the French Revolution under the impetus of François Furet, 'Grande Guerre et lieux de mémoire', *14–18 Aujourd'hui, Today, Heute*, no. 3, 2000, pp. 241–6.

I. VIOLENCE

1 Alain Corbin, *Time, Desire, and Horror: Towards a History of the Senses*, trans. Jean Birrell, Cambridge, UK, Polity Press; USA, Blackwell, 1995, p. 75.

1. Battle, combat, violence: a necessary history

1 See his article published in 1921 in the *Revue du synthèse*: 'Réflexions d'un historien sur les fausses nouvelles de la guerre', reprinted in Marc Bloch, *Écrits de guerre (1914–1918)*, Paris, A. Colin, 1997, pp. 169–84, and his posthumous work, *Apologie pour l'histoire ou le métier d'historien*, new edn, Paris, A. Colin, 1997. *The Historian's Craft*, introduction Joseph R. Strayer, trans. Peter Putnam, New York, Alfred A. Knopf, 1953.

2 John Keegan, *A History of Warfare*, New York, Alfred A. Knopf, 1993.

3 John Keegan, *The Face of Battle*, New York, The Viking Press, 1976.

4 Keegan, *A History of Warfare*, Chapter 3, 'Flesh'.

5 Victor Davis Hanson, *The Western Way of War*, New York, Alfred A. Knopf, 1989.

6 As a first approach, see the dossier 'L'archéologie et la Grande Guerre', *14–18 Aujourd'hui, Today, Heute*, no. 2, Paris, Noêsis, 1999.

7 Keegan, *A History of Warfare*, p. 90.

8 The attempt was made elsewhere, and it is neither the object of this book or of this chapter. For a brief overview, see Stéphane Audoin-Rouzeau, *Combattre (1914–18)*, Amiens, C.R.D.P., 1995.

9 See Vassily Grossman, *Life and Fate*, trans. Robert Chandler, London, The Harvill Press, 1995.

10 For more details on these numbers, see Stéphane Audoin-Rouzeau, 'La violence des champs de bataille pendant les deux conflits', contribution to the colloquium *La Violence de guerre: approche comparée des deux conflits mondiaux*, I.H.T.P. colloquium, Centre de recherche de l'Historial de la Grande Guerre, Cachan, 27–9 May, 1999, Paris, Éditions Complexe, 2002.

11 See Sophie Delaporte, 'Le Discours médical sur les blessures et les maladies pendant la Première Guerre mondiale', dissertation, Université de Picardie, 1998, 2 vols.

12 In particular through his book *The Great War and Modern Memory*, London and New York, Oxford University Press, 1975. The author's thesis is that the war brought a fundamental break in artistic and literary creation, especially in language, a thesis that is no longer accepted today, historians choosing to stress the cultural continuities linking the pre-war period, the war and the post-war period.

13 Paul Fussell, *Wartime: Understanding and Behavior in the Second World War*, New York and Oxford, Oxford University Press, 1989, p. 271. Cinematically, Steven Spielberg's *Saving Private Ryan* (1998) is an attempt that is somewhat comparable to Fussell's on the historiographical level.

14 See Delaporte, 'Le Discours médical', and *Les Gueules cassées*:

les blessés de la face de la Grande Guerre, Paris, Noêsis, 1996.

15 See the dossier on the traumatic shock of the war in *14–18 Aujourd'hui, Today, Heute*, no. 3.

16 François Lebigot *et al.*, *Le Traumatisme psychique: rencontre et devenir. Congrès de psychiatrie et de neurologie, Toulouse 1994*, Paris, Masson, 1994, and Louis Crocq, *Les Traumatismes psychiques de guerre*, Paris, Odile Jacob, 1999.

17 See *La Bataille de la Somme dans la Grande Guerre: Actes du colloque international, 1–4 July 1996*, Péronne, Centre de recherche de l'Historial de la Grande Guerre, 1999.

18 See Stig Forster and Jörg Nägler, eds., *On the Road to Total War: The American Civil War and the German Wars of Unification, 1861–1871*, Cambridge, Cambridge University Press, 1997.

19 As, for example, in Modris Eksteins, *Rites of Spring: The Great War and the Birth of the Modern Age*, New York, Anchor Books, 1990 (specifically Chapter 3 on the fraternisations of December 1914), and Roger Boutefeu, *Les Camarades: soldats français et allemands au combat, 1914–1918*, Paris, Fayard, 1966. The emblematic jacket design shows a photograph of fraternising soldiers taken in June 1915, with some of the persons identified. Similarly, in the Musée des Flandres in Ypres, fraternisation is the focus of the museography.

20 Alain Corbin, *Le Village des cannibales*, Paris, Aubier, 1990, p. 140. *Village of Cannibals: Rage and Murder in France, 1870*, trans. Arthur Goldhammer, Cambridge, Mass., Harvard University Press, 1992. The quoted sentence has been edited out of the English translation.

21 Norbert Elias, *The Civilizing Process*, trans. Edmund Jephcott, Oxford, UK and Cambridge, USA, Blackwell Publishers, 1994, p. 102.

22 *Ibid.*, p. 153.

23 *Ibid.*, p. 98.

24 Marc Bloch, *Memoirs of War, 1914–1915*, trans. Carole Fink, Ithaca, N.Y., Cornell University Press, 1980.

25 See Camille Maire, *1914–1918: des Alsaciens-Lorrains otages en France*, Strasbourg, Presses Universitaires de Strasbourg, 1988.

26 Norbert Elias, *The German Power Struggles, and Development of Habitus in the Nineteenth and Twentieth Century*, Michaël Schröter, ed., New York, Columbia University Press, 1998.

27 See George L. Mosse, *Fallen Soldiers: Reshaping the Memory of the World Wars*, Oxford, Oxford University Press, 1990.

28 See Nicolas Werth, 'Les déserteurs en Russie: violence de guerre, violence paysanne, violence révolutionnaire, 1916–1921', in Stéphane Audoin-Rouzeau, Annette Becker, Christian Ingrao, Henry Rousso, eds., *La violence de guerre: étude comparée sur les deux conflits mondiaux*, Paris, Éditions Complexe, 2002. Let us also note the role of former soldiers in the Irish civil war starting in 1919.

29 See 'L'archéologie et la Grande Guerre', *14–18 Aujourd'hui, Today, Heute*, no. 2.

30 See John G. Fuller, *Troop Morale and Popular Culture in the British and Dominion Armies, 1914–1918*, Oxford, Clarendon Press, 1990.

31 Stéphane Audoin-Rouzeau, *14–18: les combattants des tranchées*, Paris, A. Colin, 1986, and Annick Cochet, 'L'Opinion et le moral des soldats en 1916, d'après les archives du contrôle postal', dissertation, Université de Paris-X-Nanterre, 1986, 2 vols.

32 Louis Mairet in *Carnet d'un combattant*, Paris, G. Crès, 1919, p. 175.

33 Paul Tuffrau, *1914–1918: Quatre années sur le front: carnets d'un combattant*, Paris, Imago, 1998.

34 *Ibid.*, p. 14.

35 See the works of Laurent Veray, *Les Films d'actualité français de la Grande Guerre*, S.I.R.P.A./A.F.R.H.C., 1995, and 'La mise en scène du discours ancien combattant dans le cinéma français des années 1920 et 1930', *Les Cahiers de la Cinémathèque*, no. 69, November 1998, pp. 53–66.

36 Annette Wieviorka, *L'Ère du témoin*, Paris, Plon, 1998.

37 See Évelyne Desbois, 'Vivement la guerre qu'on se tue! Sur la ligne de feu en 14–18', *Terrain*, October 1992, no. 19, pp. 65–80. For an abrasive challenge of conventional accounts,

see also Joanna Bourke, *An Intimate History of Killing: Face-to-Face Killing in Twentieth-Century Warfare*, New York, Basic Books, 1999.

38 See the collections at the Historial de la Grande Guerre in Péronne. See also Stéphane Audoin-Rouzeau, 'Pratiques et objets de la cruauté sur le champ de bataille', *14–18 Aujourd'hui, Today, Heute*, no. 2, pp. 104–15, and, for a more detailed analysis, *Combattre*.

39 Blaise Cendrars, *J'ai tué*, Paris, G. Crès, 1919, pp. 147–52, p. 152.

40 Fernand Léger, *Une correspondance de guerre à Louis Poughon, 1914–1918*, Paris, Les Cahiers du musée d'Art moderne, Hors-série/Archives, p. 70.

41 Ernst Jünger, *Feuer und Blut*, Hamburg, Hanseatische Verlagsanstalt, 1925.

42 'Discours de notre camarade Brana, directeur d'école à Bayonne, à l'occasion de la remise de la rosette qui lui était faite', *Cahiers de l'Union fédérale*, 15 August 1936, cited by Antoine Prost, *Histoire sociale de la France au XXe siècle*, Paris, F.N.S.P., 1972–3, pp. 205–6.

43 Robert Graves, *Goodbye To All That*, New York, Doubleday Anchor Books, 1957, p. 287.

44 The complete collection of the series of lithographs *Der Krieg* by Otto Dix (1924) is on exhibition at the Historial de la Grande Guerre de Péronne in the Somme.

45 Philippe Dagen, *Le Silence des peintres: les artistes face à la Grande Guerre*, Paris, Fayard, 1996.

46 Fernand Léger, *Une correspondance de guerre*.

47 See Fussell, *Wartime*.

48 This is the subject of Roger Vercel's novel, *Capitaine Conan* (Paris, Albin Michel, 1934), largely inspired by the author's experience on the Eastern Front. (Bertrand Tavernier adapted the book to the screen in 1996.) The interest of fiction writers is inversely proportionate today: novels like Pat Barker's *Regeneration* or Sebastian Faulks's *Birdsong* focus entirely on this humiliation.

49 See Ludwig Renn, *Krieg*, Frankfurt am Main, Frankfurter Sociëtats-Druckerei, 1930.

2. Civilians: atrocities and occupation

1 Stéphane Audoin-Rouzeau, *L'Enfant de l'ennemi, 1914–1918: viol, avortement, infanticide pendant la Grande Guerre*, Paris, Aubier, 1995.

2 Michaël Pollack, 'Mémoire, oubli, silence', *Une identité blessée: études de sociologie et d'histoire*, Paris, Anne-Marie Métailié, 1993, p. 22.

3 *Rapports et procès-verbaux d'enquête de la commission instituée en vue de constater les actes commis par l'ennemi en violation du droit des gens*, Paris, Imprimerie Nationale, 1915. On the subject of the deportation and massacre of Armenians in the Ottoman Empire, see *The Treatment of Armenians in the Ottoman Empire, 1915–16: documents presented to the Secretary of State for Foreign Affairs by Viscount Bryce*, ed. Arnold Toynbee, Beirut, G. Doniguian, 1979 (previously issued by the Foreign Office of Great Britain as Miscellaneous Report no. 31, 1916, Parliament. Papers by command Cd. 8325, London, Sir Joseph Causton, 1916).

4 Dr. R.A. Reiss, *Report upon the atrocities committed by the Austro-Hungarian army during the first invasion of Serbia*, trans. F.S. Copeland, London, Simpkin, Marshall, Hamilton, Kent, c. 1916, pp. 70–71.

5 *Ibid.*, pp. 144, 184–5.

6 *Ibid.*, p. 185.

7 *Ibid.*, p. 37.

8 A 1914 illustrated poem attributed to Mayakovsky by the curator of the 'Russian Collection' of Rutgers University, New Jersey.

9 See John Horne, 'Les mains coupées, "atrocités allemandes" et opinion française en 1914', in Jean-Jacques Becker, Jay Winter, Gerd Krumeich, Annette Becker, Stéphane Audoin-

Rouzeau, eds., *Guerre et cultures, 1914–1918*, Paris, A. Colin, 1994, pp. 133–46.

10 Bloch, *The Historian's Craft*, pp. 51–2.

11 Bloch, 'Revue de synthèse historique', 1921, reprinted in *Écrits de guerre*.

12 *Ibid.*, p. 178.

13 *Ibid.*, p. 179.

14 *Ibid.*, pp. 181–2.

15 Léon Bloy, *Lettres à ses filleuls*, Paris, Stock, 1928. Letter to Pierre Van der Meer de Walcheren, 13 January 1915, pp. 199–200.

16 Annette Becker, *La Guerre et la foi, de la mort à la mémoire, 1914–1930*, Paris, A. Colin, 1994, and J. Horne, 'Les mains coupées'.

17 'Journal de David Hirsch', 27 April 1916, in Annette Becker, ed., *Journaux de combattants et civils de la France du Nord dans la Grande Guerre*, Lille, Septentrion, 1998.

18 Claude Debussy, *Noël des enfants qui n'ont plus de maison*, 1915. Debussy's commitment is also apparent in his pieces for two pianos, *En blanc et noir*.

19 See Annette Becker, 'La "Grosse Bertha" frappe Saint-Gervais', *14–18 la très Grande Guerre*, Paris, Le Monde Éditions, 1994, pp. 209–13.

20 Occupations during the Great War became a subject of study only at the end of the 1990s. See Annette Becker, *Oubliés de la Grande Guerre*, Paris, Noêsis, 1998, and Helen McPhail, *The Long Silence: Civilian Life under the German Occupation of Northern France, 1914–1918*, London, Tauris, 1999. The choice of the words '*oublié*' (forgotten) and 'silence' in the two titles shows how neglected the subject was.

21 Archives nationales, f/23/3, Réfugiés et rapatriés, 1914–1919. Circulaire no. 65 de L. Malvy, Ministre de l'Intérieur, 21 October 1916.

22 Archives départementales du Nord, 9R514. Quoted by Murielle Rigole, 'Les Brassards rouges: travailleurs forcés de la Grande Guerre', dissertation, Université Charles-de-Gaulle/Lille-III, 1995, p. 22.

23 Letter of Major Hoffman, 20 June 1915. Archives départe-
    mentales du Nord, 9R515.

24 See Jay Winter and Jean-Louis Robert, eds., *Capital Cities at
    War: Paris, London, Berlin, 1914–1918*, Cambridge, Cambridge
    University Press, 1997.

25 'Journal de David Hirsch', in *Journaux de combattants et civils*.

26 See Winter and Robert, eds., *Capital Cities at War*, and John
    Horne, introduction to 'Nouvelles pistes de l'histoire
    urbaine, 1914–1918', *Guerres mondiales et conflits contemporains*,
    no. 183, October 1996, pp. 3–10.

27 *The Treatment of Armenians in the Ottoman Empire*, p. 659.

28 *The Treatment of Armenians in the Ottoman Empire*, pp. 524–8.

29 Cited in Yves Ternon, *Les Arméniens: histoire d'un génocide*,
    Paris, Éditions du Seuil, 1996, p. 311.

30 Ernest Laut, 'Au pays des massacres', *Le Petit Journal*, 5 March
    1916.

31 *La Baïonnette*, 1916, drawings by Henriot.

32 See Vahakn Dadrian, *Histoire du génocide arménien*, Paris,
    Stock, 1996, p. 634.

33 'Errinern Sie sich an die Ausrottung Armeniens', quoted in
    Dadrian, *Histoire du génocide arménien*, p. 632.

34 *Ibid.*, p. 630.

35 See Dzovinar Kenovian, 'Réfugiés et diplomatie humani-
    taire: les acteurs européens et la scène proche-orientale
    pendant l'entre-deux-guerres', dissertation, Université de
    Paris-I-Panthéon-Sorbonne, 1999, 3 vols.

3. The camp phenomenon: the internment of civilians and military prisoners

1 See Elikia M'Bokolo, *Afrique noire: histoire et civilisation*, Paris,
   Hatier, vol. II, 1995.

2 See Michael Walzer, *Just and Unjust Wars: A Moral Argument*

with Historical Illustrations, New York, Basic Books, 2000.

3   See Annette Wieviorka, 'L'expression "camp de concentration"', *Vingtième Siècle*, no. 54, April–June 1997, pp. 4–12.

4   See also Jean-Claude Farcy, *Les Camps de concentration français de la Première Guerre mondiale (1914–1920)*, Paris, Anthropos-Economica, 1995.

5   Archivio Segreto Vaticano, 244K4b, volume 298–299, no. 38566. Letter sent from occupied Oise.

6   See Aline Faille, 'Warmeville 1914–1918: une communauté villageoise face à l'occupation allemande', dissertation, Université de Reims-Champagne-Ardennes, 1998.

7   The commander of the Étape de Lille, 10 XI 1916. Quoted in Rigole, 'Les Brassards rouges', p. 116.

8   28 March 1916. Quoted in Rigole, 'Les Brassards rouges', p. 130.

9   Archives départementales du Nord 9R698. Quoted in Rigole, 'Les Brassards rouges', p. 58.

10 Archives nationales, f23/14.

11 See Walzer, *Just and Unjust Wars*.

12 The phrase is Bernard Delpal's, in 'Prisonniers de guerre en France, 1914–1920', in André Gueslin et Dominique Kalifa, eds., *Les Exclus en Europe, 1830–1930*, Paris, Éditions de l'Atelier, 1999, pp. 145–59.

13 André Warnod, *Prisonnier de guerre: notes et croquis rapportés d'Allemagne*, Paris, Fasquelle, 1915, p. 34.

14 *De Gaulle soldat, 1914–1918*, Historial de la Grande Guerre/Institut Charles de Gaulle, Amiens, Martelle Éditions, 1999.

15 Captain de Gaulle, prisoner in Ingolstadt, letter to his parents dated December 1917, in Charles de Gaulle, *Lettres, notes et carnets, 1905–1918*, Paris, Plon, 1980, p. 411.

16 Niall Ferguson, *The Pity of War: Explaining World War I*, New York, Basic Books, 1999. See Jay Winter's and Andrew Latcham's critiques in *14–18, Aujourd'hui, Today, Heute*, no. 3, 1999.

17 Article signed X, from a newspaper clipping pasted inside

the *Bulletin international de la Croix-Rouge*, 18 March 1915 (Collections de la Bibliothèque du C.I.C.R., Geneva).

18 C.I.C.R., *Actes, 1914–1918*, Geneva, 1919, vol. XIV, pp. 39–41.

19 Archives of the International Committee of the Red Cross, 411/VII.

20 Article in the *Norddeutsche Allgemeine Zeitung*, 17 April 1915. Quoted in Delpal, 'Prisonniers de guerre en France, 1914–1920', p. 151.

II. CRUSADE

1 Pierre Chaunu, *La France: histoire de la sensibilité des Français à la France*, Paris, Laffont, 1982, p. 20.

2 Raoul Girardet, 'L'ombre de la guerre', in Pierre Nora, ed., *Essais d'ego-histoire*, Paris, Gallimard, 1987, p. 140.

3 François Furet, *The Passing of an Illusion: The Idea of Communism in the Twentieth Century*, trans. Deborah Furet, Chicago, The University of Chicago Press, 1999, p. 20.

4. The beginnings of war

1 See Jean-Jacques Becker, *1914: comment les Français sont entrés dans la guerre*, Paris, P.F.N.S.P., 1977, and 'Les entrées en guerre en 1914', *Guerres mondiales et conflits contemporains*, no. 179, July 1995. See also John Keiger, 'Britain's "Union Sacré" in 1914', in Jean-Jacques Becker and Stéphane Audoin-Rouzeau, eds., *Les Sociétés européennes et la guerre de 1914–1918*, Centre d'histoire de la France contemporaine, Université de Paris-X-Nanterre, 1990, pp. 39–52.

2 Becker, *1914: comment les Français sont entrés dans la guerre*; Jean Stenghers, 'La Belgique', in *Les Sociétés européennes et la guerre de 1914–18*, pp. 75–91. Gerd Krumeich, 'L'entrée en guerre en Allemagne', in *Les Sociétés européennes ...*, pp. 65–74.

3 Quoted in Modris Eksteins, *Le Sacre du printemps: La Grande*

Guerre et la naissance de la modernité, Paris, Plon, 1991, p. 114. *Rites of Spring: The Great War and the Birth of the Modern Age*, New York, Anchor Books, 1990.

4   Cited in Annie Kriegel and Jean-Jacques Becker, *La Guerre et le mouvement ouvrier français*, Paris, A. Colin, 1964, pp. 137–8.

5   Stenghers, 'La Belgique'.

6   See Giovanna Procacci, 'La neutralité italienne et l'entrée en guerre', in 'Les entrées en guerre en 1914', *Guerres mondiales et conflits contemporains*, pp. 83–98, and Brunello Vigezzi, 'L'Italie libérale – gouvernement, partis, vie sociale – et l'intervention dans la Première Guerre mondiale', in *Les Sociétés européennes et la guerre de 1914–1918*, pp. 93–115.

7   See John G. Fuller, *Troop Morale and Popular Culture in the British and Dominion Armies, 1914–1918*, Oxford, Clarendon Press, 1990.

8   Nicholas Hiley, 'La bataille de la Somme et les médias de Londres', in Jean-Jacques Becker *et al.*, eds., *Guerre et Cultures, 1914–1918*, Paris, A. Colin, 1994, pp. 193–206.

9   Philippe Boulanger, 'Géographie historique de la conscription et des conscrits en France de 1914 à 1922', dissertation, Université de Paris-IV, 1998, 2 vols.

10 See Margaret Randolph Higonnet, *Lines of Fire, Women Writers of World War 1*, New York and London, Plume, 1999.

11 Marc Ferro, *The Great War, 1914–1918*, trans. Nicole Stone, London and New York, Routledge, 2001.

12 See *Marginaux, marginalités, marginalisation en Grande Guerre*, Franco-German colloquium, 11–12 June 1999, Centre Marc-Bloch, Berlin, proceedings in *14–18 Aujourd'hui, Today, Heute*, no. 4, Paris, Noêsis, 2001.

13 *Rapports et procès-verbaux d'enquête de la commission instituée en vue de constater les actes commis par l'ennemi en violation du droit des gens (décret du 23 septembre 1914)*, Paris, Imprimerie Nationales, I–XII, 1915–19.

14 *Ibid.*, vol. I, 1915, p. 8.

15 Robert Graves, *Goodbye To All That*, p. 67.

16 Arthur Winnington-Ingram, Bishop of London, 1915.

Quoted in Jay Winter, *The Experience of World War One*, London, Macmillan, 1988, p. 169.

17 Dr Bérillon, *La Bromidrose fétide de la race allemande*, Paris, *Revue de psychothérapie*, 1915, pp. 5–6, 11. See also *La Polychésie de la race allemande*, Paris, Maloine et fils, 1915.

18 See John Horne, ed., *State, Society, and Mobilization in Europe during the First World War*, Cambridge, Cambridge University Press, 1997.

19 See Hiley, 'La bataille de la Somme et les médias de Londres'.

20 See Péter Hanák, quoted in Eric Hobsbawn, *Nations and Nationalisms since 1780: Programme, Myth, Reality*, Cambridge and New York, Cambridge University Press, 1992.

21 See Guy Pedroncini, *Les Mutineries de 1917*, Paris, Presses Universitaires de France, 1967.

22 Leonard V. Smith, *Between Mutiny and Obedience: The Case of the French Fifth Infantry Division during World War I*, Princeton, Princeton University Press, 1994.

23 See Horne, *State, Society, and Mobilization in Europe during the First World War*.

24 See Annette Becker, 'La "Grosse Bertha" frappe Saint-Gervais', *14–18 la très Grande Guerre*, Paris, Le Monde Editions, 1994.

25 See Laurent Veray, *Les Films d'actualité français de la Grande Guerre*, S.I.R.P.A./A.F.R.H.C., 1995.

26 See Olivier Forcade, 'La Censure politique en France pendant la Grande Guerre', dissertation, Université de Paris-X-Nanterre, 1999.

27 See Stéphane Audoin-Rouzeau, *La Guerre des enfants, 1914–1918*, Paris, A. Colin, 1993.

28 See Anaïs Nin, *The Early Diary of Anaïs Nin*, preface Joaquin Nin-Culmell, vol. I, New York, Harcourt, Brace Jovanovich, 1978–85. For a discussion, see Stéphane Audoin-Rouzeau, 'Une enfant catholique dans la Grande Guerre, le *Journal d'enfance* d'Anaïs Nin', in Nadine-Josette Chaline, ed., *Chrétiens dans la Première Guerre mondiale*, Paris, Édition du Cerf, 1993, pp. 35–46.

29 The child Yves Congar, *Journal de guerre, 1914–1918*, Paris, Édition du Cerf, 1997.

5. Civilisation, barbarism and war fervour

1 See Giovanna Procacci, 'Attese apocalittiche e millenarismo', *Ricerche storiche*, September 1997, pp. 657–72, and Antonio Gibelli, *L'officine della guerra: la grande guerra e le transformazioni del mondo mentale*, Turin, Bollati-Boringheri, 1991.

2 Alphonse Dupront, *Du Sacré*, Paris, Gallimard, 1987. For a detailed analysis of objects of religious fervour, see Annette Becker, *Croire*, Amiens, C.N.D.P., 1996.

3 See 'Pour une histoire religieuse de la guerre', *14–18 Aujourd'hui, Today, Heute*, no. 1, Paris, Noêsis, 1998, and Annette Becker, *La Guerre et la foi, de la mort à la mémoire, 1914–1930*, Paris, A. Colin, 1994; Annette Becker, *War and Faith, the Religious Imagination in France, 1914–1930*, Oxford, Berg. 1998.

4 Conor Cruise O'Brien, *God Land: Reflections on Religion and Nationalism*, Cambridge, Mass., Harvard University Press, 1988.

5 Alphonse Dupront, *Le Mythe de croisade*, Paris, Gallimard, vol. II, 'Croisade nom commun', pp. 1184–5, 1188, 1195.

6 See Laurent Gambarotto, *Foi et Patrie: la prédication du protestantisme français pendant la Première Guerre mondiale*, Geneva, Labor et Fides, 1996, and 'Guerre sainte et juste paix', *14–18 Aujourd'hui, Today, Heute*, no. 1.

7 See Roger Chickering, *Imperial Germany and the Great War, 1914–18*, Cambridge, Cambridge University Press, 1998.

8 Maurice Barrès, *Mes cahiers, 1896–1923*, Paris, Plon, 1916, 1993, p. 756.

9 Richard Millman, *La Question juive entre les deux guerres: ligues de droite et antisémitisme en France*, Paris, A. Colin, 1992, p. 34.

10   Edmond Fleg, *Le Mur des pleurs*, C. Block, 1919.

11   *L'Univers israélite*, 1 December 1916 and 6 September 1917.

12   Quoted by E. Poulain in *Réfutation décisive des 13 rumeurs infâmes*, 1916.

13   See Jacqueline Lalouette, *La Libre Pensée en France, 1848–1940*, Paris, Albin Michel, 1997, pp. 68–70.

14   Cited in Philippe Landau, 'Les Juifs de France et la Grande Guerre, un patriotisme républicain', dissertation, Université de Paris-VII, 1992, 3 vols. Vol. I, Paris, Éditions du C.N.R.S., 1999.

15   Maurice Barrès, *Les Diverses familles spirituelles de la France*, 1917, reprinted Paris, Imprimerie Nationale, 1996, p. 73.

16   Guillaume Apollinaire, 'Il y a', *Calligrammes*, 1915. *Oeuvres poétiques*, Paris, Gallimard, Bibliothèque de la Pléiade, 1956, pp. 280–81.

17   Roland Dorgelès, *Wooden Crosses*, New York and London, G.P. Putnam's Sons, 1921.

18   George L. Mosse, 'The Jews and the German war experience, 1914–1918', *The Leo Baeck Memorial Lecture*, no. 21, New York, 1977, p. 6.

19   The General and commander in chief of the S.H.A.T. 16N 1657 GQG, December 16, 1915

20   André Vervoort, *Les Juifs et la guerre*, Part I, 1915, p. 9.

21   The last will and testament of Abbé Ditte. Quoted in F. Gaquère, *Sous le feu, en ville et à l'institution Saint-Vaast de Béthune*, 1928, p. 64.

22   Letter to Abbé Bailleul. Quoted in A.M. Goichon, *Ernest Psichari d'après les documents inédits*, Paris, 1925, p. 343.

23   Alfred Cazalis to his parents, 7 April 1915, Société d'histoire du protestantisme.

24   Rabbi Samuel Korb at the Nantes synagogue, 20 September 1914. Quoted in Landau, *Les Juifs de France et la Grande Guerre*, vol. I, p. 271.

25   Ernest Psichari, *Le Voyage du Centurion*, Paris, Conard, 1916.

26   Henri Massis, *Le Sacrifice*, Paris, Plon, 1917, pp. 204–6.

27   Pierre Teilhard de Chardin, *Écrits du temps de la guerre*, Paris,

Grasset, 1961, pp. 229–39. A collection of Teilhard's wartime writings exists in English (but not with this extract): *Writings in Time of War*, trans. René Hague, New York, Harper & Row, 1968.

28 Henri Ghéon, *L'Homme né de la guerre: témoignage d'un converti (Yser Artois, 1915)*, Paris, N.R.F., 1919, p. 193.

29 *Ibid.*, p. 122.

30 See Frédéric Gugelot, *La Conversion des intellectuels au catholicisme en France, 1885–1935*, Paris, Éditions du C.N.R.S., 1998.

31 See Annette Becker, *La Guerre et la foi* (in English translation as *War and Faith*), and Frédéric Gugelot, 'Henri Ghéon ou l'histoire d'une âme en guerre', in Nadine-Josette Chaline, ed., *Chrétiens dans la Première Guerre mondiale*, Paris, Édition du Cerf, 1993, pp. 87–93.

32 Étienne Fouilloux, 'Première Guerre mondiale et changements religieux en Europe', in *Les Sociétés européennes et la guerre de 1914–1918*, p. 440.

33 Mireille Dupouey, *Cahiers 1915–1919*, Paris, Édition du Cerf, 1944, 4 September 1915, 31 December 1915, 20 March 1917, pp. 36, 96, 117.

34 Léon Bloy, *Méditations d'un solitaire en 1916*, XVI, 'Il est incontestable que Dieu n'existe plus', XVII, 'Les pauvres soldats qui agonisent', *Oeuvres*, Paris, Mercure de France, no date, vol IX, pp. 258–62.

35 Postcard of Joseph Foulquier's sister, 1915. Quoted in Rémy Cazals *et al.*, *Années cruelles: 1914–1918*, Villelongue-d'Aude, Atelier du Gué, 1983, p. 69.

36 Jacques Maritain, *Carnets de notes*, Paris, Desclée, 1965, p. 159. *Notebooks*, trans. Joseph W. Evans, Albany, N.Y., Magi Books, 1984.

37 *Pluies de Roses: interventions de Soeur Thérèse de l'Enfant-Jésus pendant la guerre*, Bayeux, Le Carmel de Lisieux, 1920.

38 Quoted by Bernard Gouley, Rémi Mauger, Emmanuelle Chevalier, *Thérèse de Lisieux*, Paris, Fayard, 1997, p. 83.

39 *L'Anthropologie*, 1916, p. 251.

40 Cited in Charles Calippe, 'Prières efficaces et porte-

bonheur', *Revue du clergé français*, vol. LXXXIX, 1917, pp. 241–53, citation on p. 246.

41 Maurice Ponsonby in *The Committee on the War and Religious Outlook: Religion among American Men*, New York, Association Press, 1920, p. 89. For more details in this area, see the chapter on spiritualism in Jay Winter, *Sites of Memory, Sites of Mourning: The Great War in European Cultural History*, Cambridge, Cambridge University Press, 1995.

42 Historians of wartime Britain, who once limited their studies to the actions of military chaplains and neglected the soldiers' spirituality, have started to fill the lacuna. See Rich Schweitzer, 'The Cross and the Trenches: Religious Faith and Doubt among some British Soldiers on the Western Front', *War and Society*, vol. 16, no. 2, October 1998.

43 Ernest Lavisse, *L'invasion dans le département de l'Aisne*, Laon, 1872, p. 10.

44 'Discours de M. Ernest Lavisse pour la remise des prix de vertu, 15 décembre 1916', *Institut de France*, 1916, pp. 85–109.

45 Dr Frédéric Ferrière, *Bulletin international*, no. 192, October 1917, p. 413. Dr Eugster, 16 March 1915, *Rapports sur les camps allemands*, pp. 32–3.

46 See Michael Ignatieff, *The Warrior's Honor: Ethnic War and the Modern Conscience*, London and New York, Vintage, 1999.

47 Cited in *L'École des Chartes et la Guerre (1914–1918), Livre d'or*, Paris, 1921, p. 96.

48 Charles de Gaulle, letter to his mother, 17 September 1916, *Letters, notes et carnets, 1905–1918*, Paris, Plon, 1980, p. 320.

49 *L'École des Chartes et la Guerre*, p. 153.

50 Sigmund Freud, *Thoughts for the Times on War and Death*, The Standard Edition of the Complete Psychological Works, vol. 14, London, The Hogarth Press, 1964, p. 275.

51 *Anthologie des écrivains morts à la guerre*, Amiens, 1924–6, 5 vols., pp. 745, 786, 820, 783, 817.

52 See Annette Becker, 'Les chartistes dans la Grande Guerre', in Yves-Marie Bercé, ed., *Histoire de l'École nationale des chartes depuis 1821*, 1997, Thionville, Gérard Kloop, 1997, and

Olivier Chaline, 'Les normaliens dans la Grande Guerre', *Guerres mondiales et conflits contemporains*, no. 183, July 1996, pp. 99–110.

53 See Christophe Prochasson and Anne Rasmussen, *Au nom de la patrie, les intellectuels et la Première Guerre mondiale (1910–1919)*, Paris, La Découverte, 1996, p. 10.

54 Claude Cochin, *Dernières pages: notes du front et de l'arrière*, Paris, Hachette, 1920, pp. 124–5. 'Les archives et la guerre', *La Revue hebdomadaire*, 7 July 1917.

55 Frédéric Duval, in *Histoire de l'École nationale des chartes*, p. 116.

56 *Le Capitaine Augustin Cochin, quelques lettres de guerre*, Bloud et Gay, Collection Pages actuelles, 1917, preface Paul Bourget. Letters of 6 and 7 July 1916, sent from the front on the Somme, where he died on 8 July.

57 Henri Bergson, speech given on 8 August 1914 before the Académie des sciences morales et politiques. Quoted by Prochasson and Rasmussen, *Au nom de la patrie*, p. 131.

58 Édouard Herriot, preface to Gaston Riou, *Journal d'un simple soldat: guerre-captivité, 1914–15*, Paris, Hachette, 1916, p. xv.

59 Gabriel Petit and Maurice Leudet, eds., *Les Allemands et la science*, Paris, Félix Alscan, 1916, pp. vii, xviii.

60 Georges Blondel, *La Doctrine pangermaniste*, Paris, Chapelot, 1915, quoted by Michel Korinman, *Deutschland über alles, le pangermanisme, 1890–1945*, Paris, Fayard, 1999, p. 13.

61 *Appeal to the Civilised World (Aufruf an die Kulturwelt)*, quoted in Louis Dimier, *L'Appel des intellectuels allemands*, official texts and translation and commentary, Paris, Nouvelle Librairie Nationale, 1914.

62 *Ibid.*

63 Pierre-André Taguieff, *La Force du préjugé*, Paris, Gallimard, 1990, p. 144.

64 Freud, 'The Taboo of Virginity' (1917), *The Standard Edition*, vol. 11, p. 199.

65 Freud, 'Group Psychology and the Analysis of the Ego' (1921), *The Standard Edition*, vol. 18, p. 101.

66 As Michael Ignatieff does, using Freud to analyse the nationalisms in ex-Yugoslavia in his remarkable book, *The Warrior's Honor*.

67 Annie Deperchin-Gouillard, 'Responsabilité et violation du droit des gens pendant la Première Guerre mondiale: volonté politique et impuissance juridique', in Annette Wieviorka, ed., *Les Procès de Nuremberg et de Tokyo*, Brussels, Éditions Complexe, 1996, pp. 25–50.

68 *Appeal to the Civilised World*, point no. 5.

69 Cited in the *International Bulletin* of the International Committee of the Red Cross, January 1916, pp. 85–7.

70 See Marc Michel, 'Intoxication ou "brutalisation"? Les représailles de la Grande Guerre' in *Aujourd-hui, Heute, Today*, no. 4, 2001, pp. 175–97.

71 '1915: la violation du droit des gens de la part de l'Angleterre et de la France par l'emploi des troupes de couleur sur le théâtre de la guerre en Europe', cited in Michel, 'Intoxication ou "brutalisation"?'

72 See *Die Kriegsgefangenen in Deutschland*, Berlin, 1915, 250 photos, plate no. 112.

73 See *Album de la Grande Guerre*, Berlin, Deutscher Ubersedienst, 1915, vol. II, p. 28. The captions in these photographic albums are in six languages – German, English, Spanish, French, Italian and Portuguese, which shows the intention to send the pictures to the neutral countries and occupied zones.

74 *Die Kriegsgefangenen*, pp. 106, 110, 111.

75 Collections of the Historial de la Grande Guerre.

76 The expression is from Leopold von Vietinghoff-Scheel in 1915, quoted in Korinman, *Deutschland über alles: le pangermanisme*, p. 242.

77 Dr Edgar Bérillon, 'La psychologie de la race allemande d'après ses caractéristiques objectives et spécifiques', lecture of 4 February 1917, *Association française pour l'avancement des sciences*, Paris, Masson, 1917, pp. 77–139, pp. 118, 121.

78 Lucien Roure, 'Superstitions du front de guerre', *Les Études*, vol. 153, 1917, pp. 708–32.

79 Bérillon, 'La psychologie de la race allemande...', p. 139. For the superstitious and fetishist aspects of the Franco-German struggle, see Becker, *La Guerre et la foi*, pp. 87–94.

80 *L'École des chartes et la guerre*, p. 135.

81 Quoted by Olivier Lepick, *La Grande Guerre chimique 1914–1918*, Paris, Presses Universitaires de France, 1998, p. 72.

82 Gustave Le Bon, *Enseignements psychologiques de la guerre européenne*, Paris, Flammarion, 1916, p. 295.

83 Gustave Le Bon, *Premières conséquences de la guerre*, Paris, Flammarion, 1917, pp. 157 and 185.

84 See Jean-Marc Bernardini, *Le Darwinisme social en France (1859–1918): fascination et rejet d'une idéologie*, Paris, C.N.R.S. Histoire, 1997.

85 See Michael Jeismann, *La Patrie de l'ennemi: la notion d'ennemi national et la représentation de la nation en Allemagne et en France de 1792 à 1918*, Paris, Éditions du C.N.R.S., 1997, p. 311.

86 Dr André Gilles, 'Commotionnés et hystériques chez nos ennemis et quelques observations sur la psychologie allemande', *Annales médico-psychologiques*, 10th series, no. 11, 1919, pp. 356–66, pp. 489–500, pp. 357–8.

87 *Ibid.*, pp. 359–61.

88 Prof Chauffard, 'La guerre et la santé de la race', lecture given 6 January 1915 at the Alliance d'hygiène sociale, *Revue scientifique*, 16–23 January, 1915, pp. 18–25. Quoted in Bernardini, *Le Darwinisme social en France*, p. 641.

6. **Great expectations, eschatology, demobilisation**

1 Jacques Copeau, *Journal*, vol. I, Paris, Seghers, 13 November 1914, p. 624.

2 Gustave Hervé, 'Le maître d'école à la jambe de bois', *La Guerre sociale*, 21 October 1914, reprinted in *La Patrie en danger*, Bibliothèque des Ouvrages documentaires, 1915, pp. 320–22.

3 See Avner Ben Amos, 'The Marseillaise as Myth and Metaphor: The Transfer of Rouget de l'Isle to the Invalides during the Great War', *France at War in the Twentieth Century: Propaganda, Myth and Metaphor*, New York and Oxford, Berghahn Books, 2000.

4 Henri Barbusse, *Under Fire: The Story of a Squad*, trans. Fitzwater Wray, New York, E.P. Dutton, 1917, pp. 342–6.

5 *Ibid.*, p. 346.

6 Apollinaire, 'La petite auto', *Oeuvres poétiques*, p. 208.

7 In 1915 Raoul Dufy painted a tricoloured rooster that he entitled *The End of the Great War*.

8 Apollinaire, 'Zone', *Oeuvres poétiques*, p. 39.

9 Thus did Albert Roussel offer a justification for his plotless symphonic poem *Pour une fête de printemps*. Letter of 26 April 1916, quoted by Robert Bernard, *Albert Roussel*, Paris, 1948, p. 17.

10 Texts dated 2 and 4 March 1916, quoted by Gerd Krumeich, '"Saigner la France"? Mythes et réalité de la stratégie allemande de la bataille de Verdun', *Guerres mondiales et conflits contemporains*, no. 182, April 1996, pp. 17–29.

11 The contribution made by Pierre Renouvin as early as the 1920s is well known (*Les Origines immédiates de la guerre, 28 juin–4 août 1914*, Paris, 1925). Among the best syntheses are Jacques Droz, *Les Causes de la Première Guerre mondiale: essai d'historiographie*, Paris, Éditions du Seuil, 1973, and James Joll, *The Origins of the First World War*, London and New York, Longman, 1984.

12 Furet, *The Passing of an Illusion*, p. 34.

13 See Panagiotis Grigoriu, 'Vie et représentations du soldat grec pendant la guerre gréco-turque en Asie Mineure, 1919–1922', dissertation, Université de Picardie, 1999.

14 See the dossier on traumatic war shock in *14–18 Aujourd'hui, Today, Heute*, no. 3.

15 See Sophie Delaporte, *Les Gueules cassées: les blessés de la face de la Grande Guerre*, Paris, Noêsis, 1996.

16 See David De Sousa, 'La Reconstruction et sa mémoire dans

les villages de la Somme', dissertation, Université de Picardie, October 1997. On the region of the Pas-de-Calais, see P. Marcilloux *et al.*, *1914–1918, le Pas-de-Calais en guerre: les gammes de l'extrême*, Archives départementales du Pas-de-Calais, 1998.

17 Cited in Gerd Krumeich, 'Le soldat allemand sur la Somme', in *Les Sociétés européennes et la guerre de* 1914–1918, pp. 367–74 (Hindenburg quoted on p. 372).

18 See Pierre Jardin, 'La légende du "coup de poignard" dans les manuels scolaires allemands des années 1920', in Jean-Jacques Becker *et al.*, eds., *Guerre et cultures, 1914–1918*, Paris, A. Colin, pp. 266–77.

19 Quoted by George L. Mosse, in *Fallen Soldiers: Reshaping the Memory of the World Wars*, Oxford, Oxford University Press, 1990.

20 Ernst Jünger, *Storm of Steel: From the Diary of a German Stormtroop Officer on the Western Front*, trans. Basil Creighton, New York, Doubleday, Doran, 1929, and *Copse 125: A Chronicle from the Trench Warfare of 1918*, London, Chatto & Windus, 1932.

21 Christopher Browning, *Ordinary Men: Reserve Police Battalion 101 and the Final Solution in Poland*, New York, HarperCollins, 1992.

22 Although not in the sense understood by Daniel Jonah Goldhagen in his *Hitler's Willing Executioners: Ordinary Germans and the Holocaust*, New York, Alfred A. Knopf, 1996.

23 Serge Berstein, Jean-Jacques Becker, *Victoire et frustrations: 1914–1919*, Paris, Éditions du Seuil, 1990, and *Histoire de l'anticommunisme en France*, vol. I: *1917–1940*, Paris, Orban, 1987.

24 Gabriel Chevallier, *La Peur*, Paris, Stock, 1930; Louis Ferdinand Céline, *Journey to the End of the Night*, trans. Ralph Manheim, New York, New Directions, 1980 (published in France in 1932); Jean Giono, *To the Slaughterhouse*, trans. Norman Glass, London, Owen, 1969 (published in France in 1931).

25 Ladislas Mysyrowicz, *Autopsie d'une défaite: La France, 1939–1940*, Paris, L'Âge d'homme, 1973.

26 See Antoine Prost, *Les Anciens Combattants et la société française, 1914-1939*, Paris, P.F.N.S.P., 1977, 3 vols.

27 Maurice Genevoix, *Ceux de Verdun, Les Éparges*, 1st edition, 1923, Paris, Omnibus, 1998, p. 690. These are the last sentences of the fourth volume of the series *Ceux de Verdun*.

28 See Henry Rousso, *Le Syndrome de Vichy, 1944–198...*, Paris, Éditions du Seuil, 1987 (English translation available as *The Vichy Syndrome*, London, Harvard University Press, 1991).

III. MOURNING

1 But see 'Pour une histoire de la douleur, pour une histoire de la souffrance', collective article, *14–18 Aujourd'hui, Today, Heute*, Paris, Noêsis, February 1998, no. 1, pp. 100–105.

7. Historicising grief

1 See I. Levav, I. Krasnoff, B.S. Dohrenwend, 'Israeli peri-life event scale: ratings of events by a community sample', *Israel Journal of Medical Science*, February–March 1981, vol. 17, no. 2–3, pp. 176–83; I. Levav *et al.* 'An epidemiologic study of mortality among bereaved parents', *The New England Journal of Medicine*, vol. 319, 25 August 1988, no. 8, pp. 457–61; C.D. Spielberger and I.G. Saranson, eds., *Stress and Anxiety*, vol. 8, Washington, New York, London, Hemisphere Publishing, 1982, XXIV.

2 See Fanny Cosandey, *La Reine de France: symbole et pouvoir, XVe–XVIIIe siècle*, Paris, Gallimard, 2000.

3 Jay Winter, 'Communities in Mourning', in Franz Coetzee and Marylin Shevin-Coetzee, eds., *Authority, Identity, and the Social History of the Great War*, Oxford and New York, Berghahn Books, 1995, p. 325.

4 Collection of the Historial de la Grande Guerre. Reproduced in Annette Becker, *Croire*, C.N.D.P., Amiens, 1996, p. 91.

5 *Ibid.*, p. 93. See also Stéphane Audoin-Rouzeau and Annette Becker, *La Grande Guerre, 1914–1918,* Paris, Gallimard, collection 'Découvertes', 1998, p. 129.

6 Philippe Ariès, *Essais sur l'histoire de la mort en Occident du Moyen Âge à nos jours*, Paris, Éditions du Seuil, 1975 (also in English as *Western attitudes toward death: from the Middle Ages to the present*, London, Marion Boyars, 1976), p. 17, and Geoffrey Gorer, *Death, Grief and Mourning in Contemporary Britain*, New York, Doubleday, 1965.

7 *Ibid.*, p. xx.

8 Lou Taylor, *Mourning Dress: A Costume and Social History*, London, G. Allen & Unwin, 1983, p. 266. The author based her research on fashion magazines and on data derived from the sales records at the clothing store Courtauld's; sales of black crêpe were stable from 1913 to 1918, rose slightly in 1919, and began to drop in 1920 (p. 271).

9 Michel Vovelle's preface to the French edition of Gorer's *Death, Grief and Mourning in Contemporary Britain*. See also David Cannadine, 'War and Death: Grief and Mourning in Modern Britain', in J. Whaley, ed., *Mirrors of Mortality*, London, Europe Publications, 1981, and Jennifer Lorna Hockey, *Experiences of Death: An Anthropological Account*, Edinburgh, Edinburgh University Press, 1990.

10 See Cannadine, 'War and Death'.

11 See, for example, those conducted by Olivier Faron, *Les enfants du deuil: orphelins de guerre et pupilles de la nation de la Première Guerre mondiale (1914–1941)*, Paris, Éditions de la Découverte, 2001.

12 The documentary was *À fleur de terre*, made by Jean-Pierre Helas and Alain Ries and produced by Expression Meuse.

13 Madame Marinette P—'s letter of 8 November 1997, in response to an inquiry made in *La Faute à Rousseau*, no. 16, p. 34. The authors are grateful to her for this contribution.

14 Letter to the authors following the series of articles 'La Très Grande Guerre', *Le Monde*, July–August 1994, published as a book of the same title, Paris: Le Monde-Éditions, 1994.

8. Collective mourning

1 Sigmund Freud, *Thoughts for the Times on War and Death*, *The Standard Edition of the Complete Psychological Works*, vol. 14, London, The Hogarth Press, 1964, pp. 299–300.

2 *Letters of Marcel Proust*, trans. Mina Curtiss, New York, Random House, 1949. Letter to Madame Strauss, pp. 313–14.

3 Freud, *Thoughts for the Times*, p. 290.

4 See Richard Goodkin, *Around Proust*, Princeton, Princeton University Press, 1991, p. 145.

5 Maurice Halbwachs, *La Mémoire collective*, ed. Gérard Namer, Paris, Albin Michel, 1997, p. 99. In English, *On Collective Memory*, ed., trans. and with an introduction by Lewis Coser, Chicago, University of Chicago Press, 1992. See also his *Les Cadres sociaux de la mémoire*, ed. Gérard Namer, Paris, Albin Michel, 1994. This second book, written in the 1930s and early 1940s, was first published posthumously as 'Mémoire et société', *L'Année sociologique*, 3rd series, 1940–48, vol. 1, 1949, pp. 11–177. In English, *The Collective Memory*, introduction by Mary Douglas, trans. F. and Y. Ditter, New York, Harper and Row, 1980. (The English versions of these two books differ slightly from the definitive French versions of the 1990s.) See also Annette Becker, *Maurice Halbwachs, entre mémoire et oubli, 1914–1945*, forthcoming, 2003.

6 See Annette Becker, 'Les deux rives de l'Atlantique, mémoire américaine de la Grande Guerre', *Annales de l'Université de Savoie*, no. 18, January 1995, pp. 23–36.

7 George L. Mosse, *Fallen Soldiers: Reshaping the Memory of the World Wars*, Oxford and New York, Oxford University Press, 1990.

8 Maurice Agulhon, *Histoire vagabonde*, Paris, Gallimard, 1988, 2 vols.; *Marianne au combat*, Paris, Flammarion, 1979; and *Marianne au pouvoir*, Paris, Flammarion, 1989. See also Pierre Nora, ed., *Realms of Memory: Rethinking the French Past*, 3 vols., trans. Arthur Goldhammer, New York, Columbia University Press, 1996–8, especially the two contributions by

Antoine Prost: 'The Monuments to the Dead', vol. II, pp. 307–30, and 'Verdun', vol. III, pp. 377–401.

9 See Adrian Gregory, *The Silence of Memory, Armistice Day, 1919–1946*, Exeter, Berg, 1994.

10 See Robert Bellah, 'Civil Religion in America', *Daedalus*, no. 96, 1967.

11 Freddy Raphaël, 'Le travail de la mémoire et les limites de l'histoire orale', *Annales E.S.C.*, 1980, pp. 127–45. The phrase is from p. 130.

12 See Ken Inglis, *Sacred Places, War Memorials in the Australian Landscape*, Melbourne, Melbourne University Press, 1998. This remarkable book is the most complete study of commemorative forms in any country.

13 Reinhart Kosseleck, 'Les monuments aux morts, lieux de fondation de l'identité des survivants', *L'Expérience de l'histoire*, Paris, Gallimard/Seuil, 1997, pp. 135–60. See p. 138: 'The dead are supposed to have defended the cause that the survivors who are founding the monument intend to defend.'

14 Ken Inglis, 'War Memorials: Ten Questions for Historians', *Guerres mondiales et conflits contemporains*, 'Les monuments aux morts de la Première Guerre mondiale', no. 167, July 1992, pp. 5–21.

15 Kosseleck, 'Les monuments aux morts', p. 56.

16 See Annette Becker, 'Les monuments aux morts, un legs de la guerre nationale? Monuments de la guerre de Sécession et de la guerre de 1870–1871', *Guerres mondiales et conflits contemporains*, no. 167, July 1992, pp. 22–40.

17 The Peace Treaty of Versailles, 28 June 1919, The World War I Document Archive online, Part VI, 'Prisoners of war and burial'.

18 *Heldenhaine* for the Germans. See George L. Mosse, 'National Cemeteries and National Revival: The Cult of the Fallen Soldiers in Germany', *Journal of Contemporary History*, vol. 14 (1979), pp. 1–20.

19 Winston Churchill as President of the War Graves Commission, to the House of Commons, 4 May 1920. *Complete*

Speeches, 1897–1963, New York and London, Chelsea House in association with R.R. Bowker, 1974, vol. III (1914–1922), pp. 2993–4.

20 *L'Humanité*, 31 July 1919, p. 1.

21 See Ken Inglis, 'Entombing Unknown Soldiers: From London and Paris to Baghdad', *History and Memory*, vol. V, no. 2, Autumn–Winter 1993, pp. 7–31.

22 See Catherine Brice, *Monumentalité publique et politique à Rome: Le Vittoriano*, Rome, École française de Rome, 1998.

23 See Volker Ackermann, 'La vision allemande du soldat inconnu', in Jean-Jacques Becker *et al.*, eds., *Guerre et cultures, 1914–1918*, Paris, A. Colin, 1994, pp. 385–96.

24 See Jean-François Chanet, '"Les Invalides de la Liberté": les débats sur le Panthéon et le choix des grands hommes de la IIIe à la Ve République', in *La France démocratique, mélanges offerts à Maurice Agulhon*, Paris, Publications de la Sorbonne, 1998, pp. 267–76.

25 Pastor Wilfred Monod, 'Le prix du sang', in *Pendant la guerre*, 11 July 1915, Paris, Fischbacher, 1916, p. 47.

26 Honel Meiss, 'Au soldat inconnu du 11 novembre', *L'univers israélite*, 26 November 1929, p. 271.

27 Gabriel Reuillard, *L'Humanité*, 12 November 1920, p. 2.

28 Maurice Agulhon, *La République: 1880 à nos jours*, Paris, Hachette, 1990, p. 224.

29 Patrick Cabanel, *La Question nationale au XIXe siècle*, Paris, La Découverte, 1997, p. 40.

9. **Personal bereavement**

1 *Annuaire de l'Assocation amicale de secours des anciens élèves de l'E.N.S.*, 1916, p. 136. See also Olivier Chaline, 'Les normaliens dans la Grande Guerre', *Guerres mondiales et conflits contemporains*, no. 183, July 1996.

2 On French war orphans, see Faron, *Les Enfants du deuil*.

3 See Jean-Charles Jauffret, 'La question du transfert des corps,

1915–1934', *Les Oubliés de la Grande Guerre. Supplément d'âmes*, hors-série no. 3, pp. 67–89.

4   Letter of Auguste P—, 168th Infantry Regiment, 27 November 1915. Fonds 'Bretagne 14–18'. The English translation can only hint at the actual orthography and syntax of the original document. We are grateful to the association 'Bretagne 14–18' for their help in sending us documents on war bereavement.

5   Maurice Genevoix, *Trente mille jours*, Paris, Éditions du Seuil, 1980, p. 186.

6   Françoise Dolto, *Correspondance*, I, 1913–1938, Paris, Hatier, 1991.

7   Cited in Jean Guirbal, *La Grande Guerre en compositions françaises*, Paris, Nathan, 1915, pp. 72–3.

8   On those points, see Eva Lelièvre, Catherine Bonvalet, Xavier Bry, 'Analyse biographique des groupes', *Population*, July–August 1997, pp. 803–30, and Catherine Bonvalet, Dominique Maison, Lionel Charles, Hervé Le Bras, 'Proches et parents', *Population*, January–February 1993, pp. 83–110. We are grateful to Jean-Marie Poursin for pointing out these studies to us and for his help in this area.

9   *Annuaire de l'Association amicale de secours des anciens élèves de l'E.N.S.*, 1916, pp. 144–7.

10 For the German figures, see Winter, 'Communities in mourning', in *Authority, Identity and the Social History of the Great War*, pp. 345 ff. For the French figures, see Antoine Prost's excellent analysis, *Les Anciens Combattants et la société française, 1914–1939*, Paris, P.F.N.S.P., 1977, 3 vols., pp. 11 ff.

11 As estimated by Michel Huber and approved by Alfred Sauvy. Other sources estimate 1.2 million war orphans. Olivier Faron favours an estimate of 1.1 million, not all of whom were actual orphans, however, since the children of disabled veterans were entitled to that appellation.

12 See, on this point, Karin Hausen, 'The German Nation's obligations to the heroes' widows of World War I', in Margaret-Randolph Higonnet, Jane Jenson, Sonya Michel, Margaret

Collins Weitz, eds., *Behind the Lines: Gender and the Two World Wars*, New Haven and London, Yale University Press, 1987.

13 See Prost, *Les Anciens Combattants et la société française*, p. 11 ff.

14 Lelièvre, Bonvalet, Bry, 'Analyse biographique des groupes', pp. 822–3. This figure is confirmed by INSEE which shows that kinship, on the average, creates a social environment of 24 people, and 27 for persons aged 15 to 39 (*Le Monde*, July 1998).

15 See Stéphane Audoin-Rouzeau and Nathalie Garreau, *Maurice Gallé: vie d'un soldat, deuil d'une famille (1914–1929)*, Creil, Les Amis du Musée Gallé-Juillet, 1998.

16 Jean-Claude Chesnais, *Les Morts violentes en France depuis 1826: Comparaisons internationales*, Paris, P.U.F., 1976, table no. 58, p. 183.

17 Letter of Madame Veuve Colmant to Colonel Détrie, commander of the 2nd B.O.P., 8 July 1916. Document kindly provided by Paul-Henri Détrie.

18 Maurice Barrès, *L'Écho de Paris*, 11 December 1914.

19 See Éric Thiers, *Intellectuels et culture de guerre 1914–1918: l'exemple du Comité d'études et de documents sur la guerre*, D.E.A., E.H.E.S.S., Jacques Julliard, ed., 1996. See also Émile Durkheim, *Letters to Marcel Mauss*, Philippe Bernard and Marcel Fournier, eds., Paris, P.U.F., 1998.

20 See Winter and Robert, *Capital Cities at War: Paris, London, Berlin, 1914–1918*, Cambridge, Cambridge University Press, 1997, esp. Chapter XVI.

21 Marc-L. Bourgeois, *Le Deuil: clinique et pathologie*, Paris, P.U.F., 1996, p. 79. See also Ginette Raimbault, *Lorsque l'enfant disparaît*, Paris, Odile Jacob, 1996, who recounts several bereavement cases of well-known personalities; among them, Freud confronted with the shock of his daughter's and granddaughter's deaths in 1920, directly linked to what was for him the ordeal of the war. The systematic observations in Israeli society made after the Six-Day War in 1967, the Yom Kippur War in 1973, and the War in Lebanon in 1982, amply confirm this judgement.

22   In the DSM-III-R (1987) classification, quoted by Bour-
     geois, *Le Deuil*, pp. 75–6. In Israeli society, according to a poll
     study made in the early 1980s, the 'loss of a son at war' is the
     'life event' that obtains the highest ranking in terms of mag-
     nitude, well before the loss of a child in peacetime. Levav,
     Krasnoff, Dohrenwend, 'Israeli peri life event scale: ratings of
     events by community sample', pp. 176–83.

23   See Jauffret, 'La question du transfert des corps'.

24   Jane Catulle-Mendès, *La Prière sur l'enfant mort*, Paris, Lemerre,
     1921. See Stéphane Audoin-Rouzeau, 'Stabat Mater', *Le fait de
     l'analyse*, no. 7, 'Les morts', October 1999, pp. 57–88.

25   Quoted by Yves Pourcher, *Les Jours de guerre: la vie des
     Français au jour le jour entre 1914 et 1918*, Paris, Plon, 1994, pp.
     469–70.

26   Vera Brittain, *War Diary, 1913–1917: Chronicle of Youth*, Alan
     Bishop and Terry Smart, eds., London, Victor Gollancz, 1981;
     *Testament of Youth: An Autobiographical Study of the Years
     1900–1925*, London, Virago Press. 1978. See also Paul Berry
     and Mark Bostridge, *Vera Brittain: A Life*, London, Pimlico,
     1995.

27   Cited by Claire Trévisan, 'Le Corps disparu ou le "cadavre
     noir" de l'Histoire: à propos de *L'Acacia* de Claude Simon',
     unpublished article kindly submitted to the authors.

28   Marie-Frédérique Bacqué, *Le Deuil à vivre*, Paris, Odile
     Jacob, p. 108. For an anthropological point of view that sup-
     ports this interpretation, see Louis-Vincent Thomas, *Le
     cadavre: de la biologie à l'anthropologie*, Brussels, Editions Com-
     plexe, 1980.

29   Françoise Vitry, *Journal d'une veuve de guerre*, Paris, La maison
     française d'art et d'édition, 1919, pp. 56–7.

30   Cited in Winter, *Sites of Memory, Sites of Mourning*.

31   Here again, a study of Israelis who lost relatives in Israel's
     wars shows that their grief was relieved by commemorative
     activity (I. Levav *et al.*, 'An epidemiologic study of mortality
     among bereaved parents', *New England Journal of Medicine*,
     vol. 319, 25 August 1988, no. 8, pp. 457–61).

32 Catalogue of the exhibit *14–18. Imaginaires et réalités: Messages d'hier pour la paix*, Collection Meuse, 1998, p. 63.

33 Vitry, *Journal d'une veuve de guerre*, p. 91.

34 Catulle-Mendès, *La Prière sur l'enfant mort*, pp. 290, 209, 391, 392, 393–4.

35 See Becker, *Croire*, Amiens, C.N.D.P., p. 91

36 See Audoin-Rouzeau and Garreau, *Maurice Gallé*, p. 104.

37 Françoise Vitry, *Journal d'une veuve de guerre*, p. 88.

38 The phrase is from Anita Morawetz, 'The impact on adolescents of the death in war of an older sibling', in Speilberger and Sarason, eds., *Stress and Anxiety*, pp. 267–74.

39 Bourgeois, *Le Deuil*, p. 79. See also Emmanuel Sivan, 'To remember is to forget: Israel's 1948 War', *Journal of Contemporary History*, 28 March 1993.

40 Gorer, *Death, Grief and Mourning*, p. xx.

41 Letter from M. to J.G., 8 October 1915, 'Extraits de correspondance de la famille G. de P.-J. (Côtes d'Armor), de la mort de son fils aîné E. en octobre 1915 à 1917', Archives Bretagne 14–18.

42 *The Times*, 29 June 1996, p. 9.

43 Freud, *Totem and Taboo*, in *The Standard Edition*, vol. 13, p. 65. Freud's model has been both contested and refined. See for example, Simon Rubin, 'A two track model of bereavement: Theory and application in research', *American Journal of Orthopsychiatry*, vol. 51, no. 1, January 1981, pp. 101–9.

44 See Simon Rubin, 'Mourning distinct from melancholia: the resolution of bereavement', *British Journal of Medical Psychology*, 1984, 57, Part IV, December 1984, pp. 339–45.

45 Bloch, *Écrits de guerre, (1914–1918)*, Paris, A. Colin, 1997, p. 106.

46 Cited in *Annuaire de l'Association amicale de secours des anciens élèves de l'E.N.S.*, 1916, p. 119. Hertz's obituary notice was written by Émile Durkheim, a friend and former teacher. Several months later Durkheim lost his son.

47 Georges Lecomte, preface to Vitry, *Journal d'une veuve de guerre*, pp. 5–7.

48 Cited in Institution Saint-Vincent, *Livre d'or, 1914–1919*, p. 144.

49 Audoin-Rouzeau and Garreau, *Maurice Gallé.*

50 *Annuaire de l'Association amicale de secours des anciens élèves de l'E.N.S.,* 1916, p. 147.

51 Brittain, *Testament of Youth,* and Berry and Bostridge, *Vera Brittain: A Life.*

Conclusion: 'You didn't see anything in the 1920s and 1930s'

1   *Hiroshima, mon amour,* film by Alain Resnais, 1959, based on a screenplay by Marguerite Duras (Paris, Gallimard, 1960).

2   The Peace Treaty of Versailles, 28 June 1919, The World War I Document Archive online.

3   Pierre Renouvin, *Histoire des relations internationales,* vol. III (1871–1945), Paris, Hachette, 1958, 2nd edn, 1994, p. 446.

4   Woodrow Wilson on 28 March 1919, cited in Paul Mantoux, *Les Délibérations du Conseil des Quatre,* Paris, Éditions du C.N.R.S., 1955, ('Jusqu'à la remise à la délégation allemande des conditions de la paix',), p. 71.

5   Georges Clemenceau on 27 March 1919, cited in *ibid.,* pp. 44, 70.

6   Poster entitled *Le Désastre* and signed Cléanthe, Archives nationales, fonds Albert Thomas, 94AP229, 30 March 1919.

7   Clemenceau, 28 March 1919, in Mantoux, *Les Délibération du Conseil des Quatre,* p. 69.

8   François Furet, *The Passing of an Illusion: The Idea of Communism in the Twentieth Century,* trans. Deborah Furet, The University of Chicago Press, 1999, p. 59.

9   Cited in Karl Friedrich Nowak, *Versailles,* New York, Paysan and Clark, 1929, pp. 221–2.

10 Edward Mandell House and Charles Seymour, eds., *What Really Happened at Paris: The Story of the Peace Conference, 1918–1919 by American Delegates,* New York, Charles Scribner's Sons, 1921, pp. 228–9, esp. Manley Ottmer Hudson, Chapter IX, 'The Protection of Minorities and Natives in the Transferred Territories'.

11 See Stéphane Audoin-Rouzeau, 'La délégation des gueules cassées à la signature du traité de Versailles', *Versailles quatre-vingts ans après*, published in German as 'Die Trauer des Papstes' in *Versailles 1919, Ziele – Wirkun – Wahrnehmung*, Gerd Krumeich, ed., Die Deutsche Bibliotek, 2001.

12 See Olivier Faron, *Les Enfants du deuil: Orphelins de guerre et pupilles de la nation*, Paris, Éditions de la Découverte, 2001.

13 On the mutual incomprehension of the papacy and the negotiators at Versailles, see Annette Becker, 'La tristesse du pape', *Versailles quatre-vingts ans après*, published in German as 'Die Trauer des Papstes' in *Versailles 1919, Ziele – Wirkun – Wahrnehmung*, Gerd Krumeich, ed., Die Deutsche Bibliotek, 2001.

14 Charles de Gaulle, lecture, 'La limitation des armements', October 1918, *Lettres, notes et carnets, 1905–1918*, Paris, Plon, 1980, p. 536.

15 *L'Illustration*, 5 July 1919.

16 Georges Bernanos, *Les Enfants humiliés*, Paris, Gallimard, 1949, in *Essais et écrits de combats*, Paris, Gallimard, Bibliothèque de la Pléiade, vol. I, pp. 777–905; see pp. 776 and 779, 792.

17 *Ibid.*, p. 852.

18 *Ibid.*, p. 857.

19 See Nicolas Werth, 'Les déserteurs en Russie: violence de guerre, violence paysanne ..., 1916–1921', in Stéphane Audoin-Rouzeau *et al.*, eds., *La violence de guerre: étude comparée sur les deux conflits mondiaux*, Paris, Éditions Complexe, 2002.

Index